ENTREPRENEURIAL
JOURNALISM

ENTREPRENEURIAL JOURNALISM

How to Build
What's Next for News

by *MARK BRIGGS*

Los Angeles | London | New Delhi
Singapore | Washington DC

Los Angeles | London | New Delhi
Singapore | Washington DC

FOR INFORMATION

CQ Press
An Imprint of SAGE Publications, Inc.
2455 Teller Road
Thousand Oaks, California 91320
E-mail: order@sagepub.com

SAGE Publications Ltd.
1 Oliver's Yard
55 City Road
London, EC1Y 1SP
United Kingdom

SAGE Publications India Pvt. Ltd.
B 1/I 1 Mohan Cooperative Industrial Area
Mathura Road, New Delhi 110 044
India

SAGE Publications Asia-Pacific Pte. Ltd.
33 Pekin Street #02–01
Far East Square
Singapore 048763

Acquisitions Editor: Charisse Kiino
Production Editor: Catherine Forrest Getzie
Copy Editor: Anna Socrates
Typesetter: Hurix Systems Private Ltd.
Proofreader: Tara L. Masih
Indexer: Julia Petrakis
Cover Designer: El Jefe Design
Marketing Manager: Chris O'Brien

Printed in the United States of America.

Library of Congress Cataloging-in-Publication Data

Briggs, Mark, 1969–
Entrepreneurial journalism: how to build what's
next for news / Mark Briggs.

p. cm.
Includes bibliographical references and index.

ISBN 978-1-60871-420-9 (pbk. : alk. paper)

1. Electronic newspapers. 2. News Web sites.
3. Online journalism. I. Title.

PN4833.B74 2011

070.4—dc23

2011038372

This book is printed on acid-free paper.

11 12 13 14 15   10 9 8 7 6 5 4 3 2 1

For my mother, whose creative energy and enterprising spirit inspired me. And my father, whose strength and work ethic grounded me. I'm so lucky to have you both in my life.

Table of Contents

BUSINESS APPENDIX

About the Author

 Mark Briggs is the author of *Journalism 2.0: How to survive and thrive in the digital age*, which was published by J-Lab and the Knight Citizen News Network in 2007 and downloaded as a PDF more than 200,000 times in English, Spanish and Portuguese. An updated version of the book, *Journalism Next*, was published by CQ Press in December 2009.

He is also a Ford Fellow for Entrepreneurial Journalism at the Poynter Institute in St. Petersburg, Florida, where he teaches and writes about the emerging forms of news and helps guide startup companies. Previously, he co-founded Serra Media, a Seattle-based startup technology company, and spent nine years running newspaper websites in Everett and Tacoma, Washington.

As part of his mission to help journalists transform in the digital age, Mark has served as a speaker, trainer and consultant for various projects around the United States, Europe and the Middle East.

A generation ago, this book's mission—as well as my current vocation to train journalists to become entrepreneurs—would have been heresy. When I came up through journalism, I was taught that commerce was corrupting. I was told to keep my distance—safely on my side of the temple wall—from the moneychangers who brought in the revenue to support our work. I was led to believe that we didn't need a business strategy; we already had one.

This willful ignorance of the business of news is precisely what made us journalists such awful and irresponsible stewards of journalism. It is a key reason why the industry is in a dire plight today. Too many journalists believed they were exempted from changing, even as the world around them exploded. They did not understand the business dynamics that would lead to the downfall of their old models and monopolies. Many were only belatedly curious about the opportunities technology presented for new ways of practicing journalism. We journalists let the people on the business side of the wall determine the industry's strategy, and we did little to help them.

No more.

Journalists must now take on the urgent responsibility of building the future of news. That work is more likely to happen in new, entrepreneurial ventures than through continuing to try to right the unwieldy old ships of media. In these new enterprises, our task is not only to serve society but to find sustainable ways to do so—efficient, economical and profitable ventures that fully leverage new technologies. We journalists must create new business models. We will try, fail and learn before we can succeed. Along the way, we should rethink the very nature of news and its value to the public. We should also reimagine our relationship with our public, collaborating with them because now we can.

Journalists need help to embrace this mission. They have to be taught the skills of business, even as part of journalism school. At the City University of

New York's Graduate School of Journalism, where I direct the Tow-Knight Center for Entrepreneurial Journalism, we hope to bring to journalism what Stanford and MIT bring to technology: We want to help produce the innovation and innovators that our industry urgently needs. We will do that with education and research and also by incubating and even investing in news startups.

This book is an indispensable resource for that work: for every student and every new business. It offers a clear and complete roadmap to each step in creating a new venture. More important, the book recasts the discussion of the future of the news business in practical, realistic and economic terms rather than as emotional matters. Too often, I hear newspaper folk lament that people "should" pay for their news. I have never seen a successful business model built on the verb "should," nor on tradition, entitlement, virtue or what a journalist most wants to do. Successful, sustainable businesses are built on the public's needs, and our success will be measured on how well we satisfy those needs in a competitive marketplace.

The economic trends hammering the legacy newspaper business are incontrovertible: Circulation for subscription media will continue to decline. Advertising revenue will fall with the declining circulation numbers. Balancing budgets with cutbacks will hurt quality, which will in turn lower circulation and continue to erode advertising—a vicious cycle, becoming a death spiral. Meanwhile, the local retail sector will continue to shrink, and other advertising categories—real estate, auto sales and classified merchandise—will more and more frequently deal directly with their customers until they completely bypass their former media gatekeepers. And the competition—most of it available for free in this age of abundance—will only multiply, which will in turn put pressure on both readership and advertising pricing.

But don't despair. Really, don't. Depression, anger and surrender—a few of the Kübler-Ross stages of grief—have been the reflexive responses of the industry. Not so for the entrepreneurs who will be the salvation of the news business. Entrepreneurial opportunities are many. Our news entrepreneurs today—our Hearsts, Pulitzers, Luces, Sarnoffs and Paleys—can launch media ventures at incredibly low cost and low risk, thanks to open and inexpensive platforms that reduce the cost of development and distribution. Entrepreneurs can operate in networks and ecosystems that allow them to specialize—to do what they do best and link to the rest—and find new efficiencies. They can also find efficiencies through collaboration with many constituencies and, of course, through new technologies.

With few lucky exceptions, these new businesses will not operate like the giant media monopolies of the past. They will be much smaller. But their costs will be low, so they can become profitable sooner. In our research at CUNY on the emerging ecosystem for local news (available at newsinnovation.com), we found hyperlocal blogs covering towns of 50,000-plus that today bring in more than $200,000 in advertising revenue. By expanding to other revenue sources (event organizing is proving to be very successful for some local sites); improving the advertising services they sell to local merchants (why not help customers with their Google ads?); joining in networks that can sell to larger advertisers (shouldn't newspapers form these networks?); and finding new sales solutions (you've heard of citizen journalists—why not a citizen salesforce?), we projected that these businesses could grow revenue by at least 50 percent and bring in more people to create more content—creating a virtuous cycle. Many of these Ideas are covered in detail in this book.

Though entrepreneurs will be starting their own, independent enterprises, they may also act as models to show the rest of the news industry how to solve some critical problems. For example, there's the issue of audience engagement. News sites that we studied get roughly a dozen page views per user per month, while Facebook gets that much usage every day. The Huffington Post also beats news sites on engagement because it understands the value of the conversation. What can startups do to teach news organizations how to be truly a part of their communities and engage their members?

Can startups find new ways to scale local sales before Google, Facebook, Groupon and AOL beat the news industry to the punch? Can they explore new revenue sources? Can entrepreneurs find new ways to create investigative journalism by working together with the crowd? Can new concerns—like Texas Tribune—demonstrate the value of data as news? Can innovators make sense of and add value to the live news that now flows from witnesses to events (see what National Public Radio's Andy Carvin—@acarvin—is doing with revolutions and natural disasters on Twitter)? Can niche organizations serve underserved communities efficiently?

The opportunities are indeed endless. That is why I am a cockeyed optimist about the future of news. There is more demand for and interest in news than ever. We have more ways to gather, analyze, and distribute news than we ever could have imagined before the Internet. We have new ways to listen to the public, so we can serve them better. We have new efficiencies to exploit.

But most important, we have entrepreneurs and journalists who have the courage to try to build the future of news. And now, thanks to this book, they have a plan.

—Jeff Jarvis, author of *Public Parts* and *What Would Google Do?*, director of the Tow-Knight Center for Entrepreneurial Journalism at the City University of New York's Graduate School for Journalism.

Preface

Each morning, my son begins his day with a banana and the sports section of the morning newspaper. He started this habit five years ago, when he was six years old, about the same age I was when I started poring over the scoreboard page of my own hometown newspaper.

The similarities end there. Sam also checks scores and weather with apps on his iPod Touch and gets the latest headlines from the ESPN app on the Xbox. He researches homework on Google and browses news apps on my iPad.

Still, like millions of other—mostly older—readers, my son will miss printed newspapers if they go away. How much longer will he have the pleasure of reading a printed newspaper? And what are the chances that *his* son will have his journalism delivered on newsprint to enjoy each morning?

> Figure 0.1 Sam's morning ritual <

Industry executives and people from all walks of life have spent almost two decades debating the fate of the printed newspaper, but here's the secret: It doesn't matter. Whether or not news continues to be printed on newsprint, the business of news and the practice of journalism will continue. People need news to understand their world, and these days news consumers are enjoying more choice than ever before. The news can come to them when they want it and where they want it. And they are no longer passive consumers but active participants, armed with cameras and insights and motivated to join in the process.

Newspaper readers are a romantic lot, but sentimental attachments won't turn around an industry that has been disrupted by digital technology. The newspaper industry isn't alone: Books, magazines, music, movies, video games, television and radio are also reeling from digital disruption and fretting over their fates. If you care about news, about what people know and how they learn it, it's time to stop worrying and start inventing the future.

"There are threats and disruption all over the place," says Debbie Galant, who co-founded Baristanet in 2004, one of the first independent local news websites to build a sustainable business. "We had sort of a monopoly on the online news for a while and we don't anymore. We constantly have disruption in the marketplace."

"You have to keep nimble, have to keep aware," she added.

This book is about looking forward. Contrary to popular belief, the news industry is not broken and does not need "fixing." In the second decade of this century, we're living in a new ecosystem for news. It's a land of opportunity for enterprising journalists, such as former *New York Times* columnist Galant, who want to find better ways to report and publish news and engage with a community—while making money.

Yes, this book is about making money, for that is the lifeblood of any business and the true measure of market acceptance for any product. As more than one newspaper publisher said during the last century: "We don't publish the newspaper to make money; we make money so we can publish the newspaper." So it is with news entrepreneurs in the digital age.

Though the news business is by no means a get-rich-quick scheme, plenty of journalism entrepreneurs have already built successful businesses by harnessing the power of the Internet to serve a new audience. If you hope to emulate them, finding sustainable sources of income will be a critical part of your startup mission. Fortunately, some of the traits that propel success in journalism are also useful in business. Journalists know how to ask good questions and find good sources of information, how to look for holes and maneuver to fill them, how to navigate around obstacles and find a new path, how not to be taken in by hype. Above all, journalists know how to collect information and produce good content to meet people's needs.

The entrepreneurs profiled in these pages have varying levels of journalism experience, from decades' worth to almost none. But having some journalism knowledge will make the lessons and messages of this book easier to grasp. If that's not you, consider supplementing this book with more direct journalism training, so you can start developing an understanding of the skills that produce the news—reporting, editing, writing, photography, video—as well as issues like ethics, balance and fairness that journalists encounter every day.

Credible, compelling content is the crux of any news business. Because this book focuses on getting your business started, how to report and present that content is beyond our scope here. If you don't have journalism experience, you might need to recruit people who do.

Journalism has long been considered a public service, more of a calling than a profession. Now it is also a business opportunity. Whenever a lucrative industry goes through disruption, space opens for newcomers to get in on a piece of the action. Investors know this and actively look for markets that have been disrupted, which is why there has been so much outside investment in the news businesses since the mid-2000s.

For many journalists, the public service mission of news has meant an aversion to dealing with money—unless they encounter it while exposing government fraud for a story. If you don't feel comfortable working with or talking about money—well, that can change. You'll learn that money does not equal greed, and getting rich is almost never the goal for launching a news startup. Sure, a few entrepreneurs have caught lightning in a bottle. For the rest of us, money is simply the air that allows a business to continue to breathe. Without it, you—and your business—die.

I wrote this book to provide aspiring news entrepreneurs with a crash course in starting their own news business. As the co-founder of a Seattle-based startup called Serra Media, I have first-hand experience taking an idea and turning it into a business. We launched Serra Media in 2007 to provide publishers with a new kind of online mapping tool that would allow them to organize their content—and content submitted by users—geographically. By 2009 our tool was live on more than a dozen websites, but the model proved too demanding on the publishers' staffs (which had been thinned out through massive layoffs) and the concept never really "took off." The company continues, though, providing custom software development for publishers, while we evaluate options for our next product.

As an author and blogger writing about the news industry, I have witnessed and analyzed the evolution of entrepreneurial journalism since the early 2000s. I wanted to merge the lessons that I learned from starting my own company with best practices from other successful ventures to give you an actionable game plan for launching your own news enterprise.

This book is intended for anyone with an idea for a better news product, be it a website, mobile app, email newsletter or some new form we have yet to experience. You'll need more than an idea, however. You need the passion to drive the idea forward, because ideas don't magically become businesses without hard work and long hours. This book is for people who love working on their ideas, who see that "work" as something they *get* to do, not something they *have* to do.

*   *   *

To establish context, we'll start with a look backward. It's instructive to know how technology has disrupted the news industry if you're going to take advantage of that disruption to create something new. Then you'll be inspired by examples of successful startups and the many different paths they've taken in creating a new-era news business. These first chapters aim to spark some new ideas for you, or some new thinking about a startup idea you already have.

Next we turn to innovation and the challenging task of turning your idea into a business. Once you've defined your audience and what you want to do for them, you can move on to the business essentials of starting a company, getting the work done, leveraging the latest technology and taking your company or product to market. In each chapter you'll go behind the scenes with a different news startup to see how its founders got off the ground and how they are faring now.

You will also be challenged to "Build Your Business" with a set of questions at the end of each chapter. Upon completion of all eight assignments, you'll have the foundation for a full-blown business plan. A "business appendix" shows you one company's actual business plan and provides a quick glossary of business terms, with resources for learning more about business development.

I compiled the information for this book through interviews with dozens of entrepreneurs, news executives and news industry analysts who follow news startups. I also relied heavily on my personal experience in testing ideas and researching topics while launching my own company. Taking full advantage of the social media age, I drew upon a wealth of information discovered through the hundreds of people I follow on Twitter and the hundreds of RSS feeds that overflow my Google Reader. And finally, I drew from dozens of the top business books influencing today's entrepreneurs and have summarized their most important findings for you.

The most difficult part of writing this book was trying to account for all of the new websites and initiatives that are constantly popping up all around us. There are simply too many to fit into one book, so I've done my best to choose examples that offer the most varied and practical lessons for would-be entrepreneurs.

Change is hard. Many journalists and news executives have struggled with the changing dynamics of the news business. But remember: Change and disruption mean opportunity. This book will help you seize that opportunity with your own ideas about building a better future for news.

ACKNOWLEDGMENTS

This project would not have been possible without the generous support and assistance of a great many people.

I would like to thank Charisse Kiino for believing in the project and making it happen at CQ Press. Her guidance and support throughout the past three years (over two books) has been invaluable. As has the editing expertise of Jane Harrigan, who takes a big lump of clay and helps me mold it into something worthy of being called a book. This project wouldn't have been possible without either one of them. I would also like to thank the rest of the team at CQ Press, as well, for providing support, expertise and life to this endeavor.

I would also like to thank my colleagues at The Poynter Institute who have pushed me to explore many of the topics that appear in this book—and assisted me with their knowledge:

Ellyn Angelotti

Jeremy Caplan

Rick Edmonds

Howard Finberg

Kelly McBride

Bill Mitchell

Wendy Wallace

Of course, I leveraged the entrepreneurial experience and expertise of dozens of smart, enterprising individuals who gave their own time to help me develop the lessons and the examples found in this book. These individuals are incredibly busy people and I am forever in debt to them for taking the time to share their knowledge with me—and you.

Rafat Ali	Rich Gordon
David Ardia	Monica Guzman
Paul Bass	Rita Hibbard
Greg Beato	Adrian Holovaty
Cory Bergman	Ben Ilfeld
Scott Berkun	Mark Josephson
David Boraks	Scott Karp
Mark Britton	Jerimiah Kastner
Merrill Brown	Marshall Kirkpatrick
Justin Carder	Scott Lewis
Jennifer Carroll	Om Malik
David Cohn	Mike Masnick
John Cook	Michele McLellan
Mike Davidson	Doug McLennan
Ken Doctor	Susan Mernit
Tom Ferrick	Pierre Omidyar
Laura Frank	Sharon Prill
Brad Flora	Scott Porad
Debbie Galant	Vikki Porter
Anne Galloway	Mark Potts

Tracy Record	Tom Stites
Steve Safran	Matt Waite
Clark Scott	Lisa Williams
Julia Scott	Shawn Williams
Chris Seper	

A few people deserve special thanks: Mike Orren for providing one of the original business plans found in the appendix, complete with Mike's annotations and insight (his knowledge is found in several places throughout the book as well); Jeff Jarvis for crafting a compelling foreword to set the table for the lessons that follow; and Laura Cochran, whose design touch at the 11th hour completed the book's cover in time for business cards to be printed before I spoke at the SXSW Interactive conference in 2011.

I owe Jan Schaffer a great deal, for providing information for this book, but also for helping to launch my career as an author. It was her idea in 2006 that I put together the lessons that became *Journalism 2.0,* my first book, which she published through J-Lab with a grant from the Knight Foundation.

And I would be remiss if I didn't mention my business partner and mentor, Glenn Thomas. While his name may not appear in the pages that follow, his knowledge and influence are present throughout. I first worked with Glenn in 2000, when he was running Smashing Ideas, the company he co-founded. I was running the website for a newspaper in Everett, Wash., and we wanted to do an interactive, Flash-based mapping project. We didn't have those skills at the newspaper, so I hired Glenn's company, using a grant the newspaper had won from the Pew Center for Civic Journalism, whose executive director at the time was Jan Schaffer.

Serendipity, for sure. I went on to write a book for Jan and start a company, Serra Media, with Glenn. The experience that you gain today, and connections that you make, may not be "the thing" that takes off as your long-term career. But they just might open the door to a big opportunity or teach you how to get there.

You'll never know until you get started.

CHAPTER 1

Understand the News Ecosystem

Mike Orren, the former publisher of *Texas Lawyer* magazine, considers himself to be a newspaper junkie. In 2004, frustrated with only one choice of morning paper, he brainstormed about a new kind of publication for the Dallas area. "If you relaunched the *Dallas Times-Herald* as a website, what would it look like?" he asked others in town who shared his view that the *Times-Herald*'s closing had left a big gap in the local media scene.

Orren wanted to fill that gap. Enthusiastic about the growing online news movement, he thought creatively about the best model for a new publishing venture in Dallas. The scheme would have to be easy and fairly inexpensive to launch, with the potential to become a sustainable business relatively quickly. He envisioned a website that would publish local interest stories that emphasized events and entertainment. He imagined reader interactivity, databases with deep local information, and content and advertising customized to individual users.

Launching a successful startup requires an innovative idea, hard work, good timing and a bit of luck. And Orren had the luck: one night he won $2,000—the incorporation fees for his enterprise—in a poker game. Orren's winning hand beat that of James McManus, the author of *Positively Fifth Street* and a recent competitor in the World Series of Poker—and Orren played his victorious hand "in the wine cellar of Dallas' finest strip club."

Of course, Orren also pursued more conventional financing—through his extensive network of local media contacts—to assemble a solid business plan for the new digital publication. He envisioned building a loyal local audience for an innovative website that would be irresistible to area residents seeking customized local news and indispensable to local businesses seeking a viable advertising alternative.

Figure 1.1 Pegasus News

Orren quickly raised $70,000 in seed money from his media contacts. He warned his wife that he would be foregoing a salary for six months and he notified his employer of his departure. The new venture was risky, for sure. But Orren believed that he could invent a new kind of local publishing that would not just serve local residents and advertisers but be the most fulfilling career that he'd ever had.

As it turned out, he went 22 months without a salary, and then his take-home pay was about one quarter of his previous income. Pegasus News began to grow its audience, though, and within a year, Orren's venture employed more than a dozen, including a few interns.

"We were the pirate ship," Orren says of his overachieving staff, whose belief in Orren's vision kept them going. "It was a cause, it wasn't a job. I discovered you get a lot more out of people when it's a cause, than when it's a job."

Pegasus traffic grew quickly, heavily driven by its databases of local bands, events, and restaurants and its witty, conversational news writing. The audience played along too, tagging content and adding feedback, and after three months, the site drew 200,000 unique monthly visitors.

When Orren launched Pegasus News in 2006, he never expected his grass-roots local media site to be acquired; he was just building a local information source that he would find useful, since the local newspaper didn't satisfy his needs. Like many other entrepreneurs, he solved his own problem.

Soon, other investors—including *The Dallas Morning News*—wanted a piece of this new enterprise. Pegasus News had developed a model that delivered each user a customized homepage with targeted news, information, and advertising. Media companies from other cities called Orren about importing his new online local journalism model to their town. Pegasus News, with its groundbreaking content, was waiting for the business side to catch up. Rather than opting for a big buyout, Orren sought strategic investments to keep the site going.

"Traffic growth was great," Orren says about growing his business. "Advertising sales were slow because we couldn't afford to pay salespeople. And the hardest thing was getting brand recognition in the ad community." Local companies understood about buying magazine or TV ads, but at first, they were skeptical about online advertising, especially on a new independent website. Gradually, word of mouth created brand awareness for Pegasus News in the local ad community, allowing Orren and his team to push ad sales forward.

In 2008 Fisher Broadcasting acquired Pegasus News. Fisher then sold it to another media company later that year. The sale meant a happy ending for Orren as well as for the investors who had initially bankrolled the venture. Orren left the company at the end of 2010, just as the second buyer, Archstream, launched his local news and entertainment website model in cities across the United States, where Archstream operated radio stations. Orren recalled his first creation with pride as he hunted for the next big idea to pursue.

Every day, the new information ecosystem lures entrepreneurs like Orren with a mission—seize the opportunity. Whether you're working for a company or you're out on your own, the rapidly changing media landscape means you have a chance to create the future you envision. This time of change is unprecedented in the history of media. And if you know a little something about the news business and have a good idea on how to do things differently, you already have what you need to get started.

To define the news business of tomorrow, you must first look at where things stand today. The field is wide open, an opportunity that is invigorating or intimidating, depending on your point of view. The more you learn about the current news ecosystem, the more likely you'll be to create your own news species. And the more you know about some organizations' missteps, the better prepared you'll be to blaze the trail.

For established media companies, the disruption of the Internet looks like a problem. For entrepreneurs, disruption means an opening to attack the established marketplace. Vinod Khosla, the co-founder of Sun Microsystems, famously said, "The bigger the problem, the bigger the opportunity." This chapter will outline the problem. The rest of the book will focus on the opportunity.

To set you on your future course, this chapter will help you understand:

> ▶ The forces that shaped today's news business.

> ▶ The lessons from yesterday's media world.

> ▶ The advantage of news startups over traditional media companies.

HOW DID WE GET HERE?

We'll begin this exploration of what's new in the news business by looking at what's old.

Second-guessing legacy media companies and dissecting their missteps in the information age is not our aim here. Instead, let's look at what once worked for traditional media and why it no longer works. This knowledge will be the foundation for your own news startup plan, and may also help you to identify undiscovered opportunities.

A "digital Darwinism" touches nearly every industry, but its impact has been especially heavy on mainstream news companies. Newspapers, magazines and broadcasters—finally having been forced to acknowledge the new digital reality—now must immediately innovate to survive and thrive in a digital age, where the rules are still being written.

This new digital reality means opportunity for news entrepreneurs, as long as they don't try to replicate unsuccessful past models.

▶ Digital rewind: The disruption begins

It has been said that Pulitzer Prizes didn't make great newspapers; distribution monopolies did. Today, however, those monopolies are dying or are already dead. In fact, long-respected journalistic values are as responsible for undoing the newspaper business model as the upstart Internet that is usually blamed.

In their best year (2005), newspaper companies combined to bring in $48 billion in annual revenue. In 2010, revenues plummeted to $23 billion, a 53 percent decrease in five years. We've all heard the rest of the bad news about the news business. About a third of the newsroom jobs that existed at U.S. newspapers in 2001 were gone by 2010, according to the *State of the News Media* report. Newspaper circulation declined more than 25 percent in the same period.[1]

Whenever monopolies are disrupted, investors and entrepreneurs see opportunity. New technology may cause some income streams to disappear (think of the decline in music CD sales), but usually it opens new doors at the same time (think of the increase in digital downloads).

The stranglehold of local newspapers and local broadcasters on local audiences during the age of mass media powered soaring profit margins in most U.S. markets. Through daily newspaper deliveries, advertisers could go through your front door every day. Through television commercial broadcasts, advertisers joined you in your living room. Through the morning and afternoon radio programs, advertisers rode with you to and from work.

Before the Internet, advertisers had few alternatives to mass media advertising, and none were as powerful or as cost-effective. Thus, media companies controlled the advertising market. A culture of greed and power developed in many media companies; media advertising rates customarily rose each year well into the 2000s, even as audiences shrank.

Yes, that's right: A business based on delivering audience to advertisers actually demanded more money for less audience. And advertisers paid up, because most had been trained that they had no choice. Each year, media executives would comfort themselves with increased revenue numbers, even though most knew this model was not sustainable in the long run.

"Digital disrupts the aggregation model that was so profitable for so long," states the comprehensive 2011 Columbia University report on the business of digital journalism. "Almost no one used to read the entire newspaper every morning, and audiences frequently tuned in and out of the network news at night. Yet, news organizations sold their advertising as if every page was turned and every moment was viewed."[2]

The emergence of digital technology, the Internet and mobile communication disrupted the business model and opened the gates to competition. These new platforms offered many advantages over print and broadcast media to advertisers. New media was cheap, fast, measurable, interactive and direct. Car dealers could now list cars on their own websites instead of in the Sunday newspaper. Realtors could now feature homes for sale on regional networks with dozens of photos and virtual tours. Retailers quickly discovered email newsletters as a cost-effective (and practically free) solution for building loyalty and promoting sales and special events.

Figure 1.2 craigslist

Then came craigslist and eBay and Monster.com and Google, plus hundreds—if not thousands—of other online options for anyone wanting to place an ad or communicate a commercial message to an audience. The traditional news company, fresh from years of Wall Street profits and glory, was now under siege.

The rate at which the old-style media empire crumbled occurred is still a source of debate. Some executives say they saw the iceberg in the distance but couldn't steer their particular media Titanic to a new course fast enough. Most experts talk about a 10-year period—from 1995 to 2005—as the opportunity window for news companies to have invested their bloated profit margins into research and development to combat this digital disruption.

"I think we all underestimate how much of a catastrophe it has been over the last decade," says Rick Edmonds, a media analyst with the Poynter Institute. "There was an assumption that there would be an orderly transition from the old world to the new—that, as people go there, the ads will too."

As revenues begin to decline, newspapers cut back on expensive, time-consuming reporting. Audiences had begun to decline, however, even before these cuts, probably because of the proliferation of media choice (cable TV, the Internet), rather than the decrease in journalism with a capital "J."

"The idea that newspapers lost audience because they stopped doing the hard news is simply not true," says Greg Beato, a media reporter who wrote extensively about the evolution of media for more than 15 years for *Reason* magazine. "As self-important as journalists are, that's a stretch even for them."

Revenues declined because traditional media companies jealously guarded their cash cows instead of pushing new lines of business. Audiences still wanted news, and they migrated to news websites, but most media companies failed to fully capture that shift with ad revenues. Businesses spent more on new media advertising and less on traditional ads. As less money came in the door, media companies downsized, and laid off staff. Job cuts protected profit margins but did nothing to improve the quality of the product, and thus the vicious downsizing cycle continued.

Today it doesn't matter how we got here, only that we recognize that there is no way back. Or is there? If you look back at the evolution of newspapers a century ago, you'll find striking similarities to today's emerging news media landscape.

▶ Flashback: Change has happened before

The late 20th and early 21st century marked a golden era for publishers: News organizations grew large and consolidated, pushing profit margins up and supporting publicly traded companies. But describing the media business as a *stable* industry looks shortsighted when you view the history of newspapers through a longer lens.

Before 1970, many more organizations of differing sizes practiced journalism (as is the case in many other countries). Further back— more than 100 years ago—the newspaper industry was dealing with technological change on a scale comparable to today. In the 1890s, telephone service and improved transportation revolutionized reporting, while the Linotype machines dramatically increased the speed of printing, allowing a single machine operator to do the work of five men. These changes led to an explosion of newspapers—and newspaper readers— that is comparable to what we're seeing today with digital journalism startups.

Look at the media landscape during the Progressive Era, described in the *Encyclopedia of American Journalism* entry:[3]

- The number of English-language daily newspapers grew from 850 in 1880, to 1,967 in 1900, to 2,200 in 1910.

- Daily circulation totals grew from 3.1 million in 1880, to 15.1 million in 1900, to 22.1 million in 1910.

- Chicago and Boston each had eight newspapers in 1900. New York had nine.

The technology that allowed the number of newspapers to grow 123 percent in 20 years resembles what we saw in the last decade with the Internet. The *rate* of change, however, has increased exponentially. It took *The New York Times* half a century, from 1850 to 1900, to reach 30,000 subscribers. Internet upstarts like Politico, Gawker, TechCrunch and a slew of others have grown much faster in a shorter time period. The Huffington Post, for example, was launched in 2006, but took just four years to draw more than 13 million unique monthly visitors—more than the websites of the *Washington Post* or the *Wall Street Journal.*[4]

Free publishing platforms like Blogger and Wordpress have given thousands of new blogger voices their own virtual printing presses. Facebook and Twitter have allowed millions of people to share news and information with newly founded communities of interest. Knowing that all this happened in just the last 10 years, what do you think will happen in the next decade? While it's impossible to predict the future, reviewing the way traditional media have dealt with disruptive technology can help you identify opportunities and leverage the new technology to pursue them.

▶ How traditional media evolved

Most people assume that technologies like the Internet and cable television caused the decline in newspaper readership, but the percentage of Americans reading newspapers actually began to drop in the late 1940s. Still, newspaper circulation continued to rise simply because the U.S. population was growing so fast.

Newspaper reading in the United States peaked in 1970, when 62 million newspapers were sold in the country every day, and these sales stayed relatively stable for 20 years. However, a smaller *percentage* of Americans were reading a newspaper every day, especially after the evolution of TV news in the 1960s. The stable circulation numbers were fueled by a nearly 50 percent increase in the number of U.S. households between 1970 and 1990.[5]

Audience, of course, drives revenue for newspapers. Newspapers began charging customers a penny per issue in 1833. It wasn't until the 1880s that advertising slowly began to replace sales and subscriptions as the chief source of newspaper revenue. By 1911, some newspaper critics feared the influence of advertising on journalism. One proposed, but unsuccessful, solution, was to create an "ad-free" newspaper supported by paid subscriptions. Another solution was to create a non-partisan, ad-free newspaper funded by the city government.

These models have seen a comeback, at least in theory. Many news companies have explored charging for content on the Web. And some public officials and journalists have called for public funding of newspapers, for the same reason citizens pay taxes to support local libraries. While a small percentage of news companies will continue to experiment with charging for online content, neither of these revenues appears to be a panacea for what is essentially a business problem. This narrative describes the same business problem that newspapers faced in 1911.

By 1914, 66 percent of newspapers' revenue came from advertising, and business was good. Throughout the 1970s, 1980s and 1990s, that figure was about 80 percent, and business—not to mention profits—was even better.

The business model for a printed newspaper is simple: The more copies a newspaper can sell and distribute, the more the paper can charge for advertising. As advertising revenues grew, so did the number of pages in the newspaper. The costs of printing and delivering more copies are substantial. When newspapers had a monopoly on news dissemination, those costs were part of the deal, but once the monopolies were gone, printing and delivery costs became a significant drag on the overall health and profitability of the newspaper business.

Remarkably, newspaper companies were able to increase revenues even during a period of circulation decline. The tipping point occurred in 2005, when revenues hit their peak. After that year, decreasing circulation and digital competition, combined with a recession in 2008, forced overall revenue figures to sink like a rock in the ocean.

Local TV news has a shorter history but many of the same problems as newspapers. As local TV stations began making more money from newscasts in the 1970s and 1980s, the news divisions were expected to bring in even more profit. From the mid- to late 1980s and early 1990s, advertising revenue flooded into local stations as more businesses wanted to use video to promote their products and services.

"These places just printed money," says Steve Safran, a longtime industry analyst. "There was no real competition for the ads for people who wanted to hit the video market. The ratings were terrific because there was less competition; we're talking 40 to 50 percent margins at the peak."

Figure 1.3   NEWSPAPER REVENUE 1985–2009

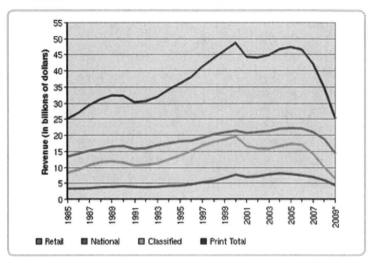

Local TV stations saw journalism as a good deed, a civic duty. But each year brought more and more pressure on news divisions to increase revenue. Stations added newscasts as a low-cost option to bring in more ad dollars. For example, with staff already in place to do a newscast at 6:00 P.M., the cost to add a 5:00 P.M. newscast was relatively small.

When the Internet became mainstream in the mid- to late 1990s, slow connection speeds and the lack of a standardized player limited the amount of video that could be shown online. Thus, the Internet didn't affect TV news as immediately as newspapers; audiences still had to turn on the TV if they wanted compelling video footage.

Now, of course, that's no longer the case. The video news audience has fragmented, since viewers can watch any one of seemingly hundreds of news options on cable, stream movies on Netflix or view video clips online. Safran notes that the top-rated shows these days draw 12 million to 14 million viewers. "In the '70s, that would have got you canceled," Safran says. "It's a significant audience problem."

Because stations could not maintain high advertising revenues at decreased viewership levels, local TV operations have had to make significant cuts. Estimates show that stations have cut their network news staffs by roughly half from their staffing peak in the 1980s.[6]

> Figure 1.4 NPR

Local news radio has experienced the most consolidation. Most markets have fewer commercial news stations than in previous decades. The stations that focus on news continue to fare well. NPR, for example, has used an aggressive digital strategy to significantly grow the audience for its audio journalism. Some "news radio" stations survive by tapping the power of the crowd, using a talk radio format as a form of news. Talk radio is cheaper to produce than straight news programs, and, in many cases, is more attractive to audiences, especially if the topics are regularly controversial.

Compared to newspaper and local TV audiences, audio audiences are more stable. In 2011, more than nine in 10 Americans listened to at least some AM or FM radio in an average week. The audience specifically for news on the radio continues to grow. NPR saw its audience increase 3 percent in 2010, to 27.2 million weekly listeners.

Traditional radio is not immune to digital technology, however. More than four in 10 Americans now say they listen to less terrestrial radio because of iPod/MP3 use, and nearly one in three now say they listen to online radio with services like Pandora.[7]

▶ Now you invent the Web

In the first decade of the 21st century, news companies learned the hard way what doesn't work: taking traditional journalism that worked in newspapers or on television broadcasts—and simply shoveling it online.

Today, a mix of upstarts, startups and other new projects are "inventing the Web" for news in the digital age. As Clayton Christensen observed in *The Innovator's Dilemma,* small-and-scrappy trumps big-and-bloated when it comes to innovation. Big news companies now learn from neighborhood bloggers, nonprofit news websites, and other previously unheard of digital news creations how to connect with an audience and serve advertisers.

"The passion in these new enterprises versus the old enterprises is striking," says Ken Doctor, author of *Newsonomics* and a former executive with Knight Ridder. "These people might be getting paid half as much, and that's hard to compete with."

Nationally, we've experienced an explosion of news outlets that thrive by covering a specific topic or niche, including politics, technology, sports, health, entertainment, and finance/business. Meanwhile, as we will explore later, in several U.S. cities—most notably New York, Washington, D.C., Chicago, Seattle and San Diego—emerging new media enterprises are changing the local news ecosystem.

Have we seen this before? A century ago, cities and towns had multiple newspapers competing for readers, scoops and advertising dollars. That glimpse of the past could be a view into the digital future.

Looking forward, the state of the news media of the early 21st century will probably look a lot more like the way it did at the turn of the 20th century, when far more news organizations competed for an audience. Each outfit was tiny compared to the behemoths of the 1990s and 2000s, but there were many more of them. In the near future, instead of a daily newspaper with 150 journalists, a small city might have 20 digital news operations, each with a handful of journalists and each working in a clearly defined content and audience niche.

The news may be delivered through a website, a mobile app, or a social networking platform like Facebook or Twitter. The business model may rely on a new form of digital marketing format or on traditional advertising done in nontraditional ways. As we will explore throughout this book, the innovation and experimentation now happening all around us are the seeds of even more future innovation.

While traditionalists focus on the impact of new media on journalism, the early success of many of these enterprises—both as journalism and business organizations—must be recognized as a view into the future. It's the business side of these news startups that is under the closest scrutiny. The big media companies that have failed to find new forms of digital revenue are watching their innovative competitors, hoping to learn some new tricks. Startups and aspiring entrepreneurs, meanwhile, should not just explore these new models, but analyze where big media companies went wrong, if they want to avoid the same plight.

WEST SEATTLE BLOG

www.westseattleblog.com

STARTUP SNAPSHOT

STARTED: 2005.

FOUNDER: Tracy Record, previously a TV and radio news manager.

MISSION: Provide real-time news and an online community for West Seattle.

STAFF: 2 fulltime (the co-owners), about a dozen freelance photographers, writers, Web developers.

STARTUP CASH: None.

WROTE A BUSINESS PLAN?: No.

MEASURE OF SUCCESS: 11 million page views, more than $100,000 in revenue in 2011.

TOP BUSINESS TIP: Don't do what you think you want to do unless you know there's a need for it and someone will be helped by it. That's the sort of thing you can do as a hobby; it won't be a business. If you don't have any idea what there's a need for, are you sure you want to do this?

TOP CONTENT TIP: Be a human presence on Facebook and Twitter. Don't just attach your RSS feed to them and walk away. Answer questions, post fragments, let people post to your wall/page. Be present.

(For more on West Seattle Blog, see Chapter 2.)

YESTERDAY'S MISSTEPS, TODAY'S OPPORTUNITIES

In case you missed it, newspapers aren't dead yet. In fact, more people read a newspaper in print or online on a weekly basis (165 million readers) than watched the Super Bowl in 2011 (111 million watchers). How can this be? If these figures are true, why have thousands of journalists lost their jobs? It's not a readership problem; it's a revenue problem, especially on the digital side of the business.

The percentage of Americans who read a newspaper every day has been declining since the 1970s—well *before* the Internet age. While many people blame the Web for "killing" newspapers, the Web has actually saved newspapers to some degree, adding millions of readers through websites and other digital products. Newspaper companies can brag that they are reaching a larger combined audience than even before.

Unfortunately, revenues at newspaper companies have not kept pace with the growth in an online audience. The same holds true for local broadcasters. Evening news viewership has dropped significantly during the last decade, but like newspapers, local TV stations now attract sizable online audiences. And like newspapers, broadcasters have not been able to cash in on this new audience—or "monetize" it, in the parlance of the Internet—fast enough to fill the hole created by a fading legacy business model.

 **ADVERTISING REVENUE**

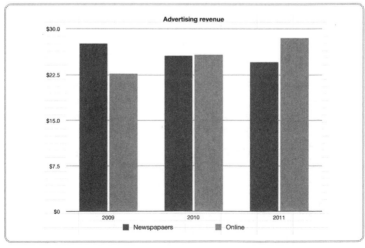

Local media companies showed growth by summarily raising ad rates each year, meaning overall revenues increased each year even if the company didn't sell any more ads. This paper profitability made corporate consolidation inevitable. Steady, predictable growth is too attractive to Wall Street, thus a market for media companies—and the ensuing merger and acquisitions spree—naturally ensued. Corporate control and quarterly profit pressures have certainly taken their toll on the way news companies operate.

Those pressures are not likely to change in the near future, and neither are some other fundamental economic truths that news entrepreneurs must embrace up front.

▶ New world, new models

The most damaging misconception that still pervades the newspaper industry today is the belief that consumers used to pay for their news. In fact, U.S. readers, whether those who spent a quarter at the newsstand for a single copy or $15 to $25 per month for home delivery, barely subsidized the cost of the ink and paper. That revenue didn't come close to paying for the news reporting, photography, design or syndicated material that filled the pages.

The typical U.S. newspaper company collected about 20 percent of its annual revenue from its customers through the 1980s and 1990s. The rest of its revenue came from advertising. (In Europe and Asia, where newspaper readers spend two or three times more to purchase each copy, companies enjoyed a more healthy revenue split of 60/40, or even 50/50.)

Yet the creation and publication of newspaper websites in the 1990s came with the assumption that consumers should pay for the online news. This misguided approach created opportunities for new competitors as newspapers either withheld some news from their websites or experimented with different forms of "pay walls," where users had to pay for access.

Newspaper executives feared that customers would stop buying the printed product if it were available for free online. While this argument makes sense on its face, its logic is flawed because of two incorrect assumptions: that the product would, should or could be the same online as it was in print; and that customers would continue buying the print product if the publisher refused to provide a free alternative online.

Each of these assumptions was dangerous on its own. Together, they compounded the strategic misdirection of local newspaper companies. Similar assumptions also misguided local TV news companies. Let's look at these assumptions to see what can be learned in hindsight.

▶ ▶ *The product: immediate, interactive or irrelevant*

In the 1990s, publishing companies saw the Internet as a new, low-cost distribution platform, a chance to take their previously created news and content, and deliver it electronically to a bigger audience. Publishers didn't recognize, at least not right away, that the Internet's unique capabilities would make their content look like black-and-white TV in the age of color.

Online audiences expect immediacy, interactivity, customization, personalization and, more recently, social connection. Traditional news stories, reprinted online as they appeared in the morning newspaper, looked generic and lifeless in comparison.

Publishers missed a huge opportunity to leverage what makes the Internet unique. Instead, the online attribute that most appealed to news companies was "low-cost." The siren's song of low-cost investment lured publishers to the rocky shoals with visions of new audiences and new advertising dollars for as little additional expense as possible.

Most traditional media companies hired as few people as possible to manage their digital products, and at first, most of the new hires spent their time reformatting print journalism for online audiences. Other websites and blogs, meanwhile, took advantage of the Internet's unique attributes to invent a new form of collaborative, timely and multidimensional journalism. Bloggers and other new media content creators were not burdened by the once-a-day publishing cycle or the one-way lecture that mainstream news had been delivering for decades. Free from these antiquated constraints, these new online publishers quickly built their own audiences from scratch. You will meet some of these publishers in Chapter 2.

Traditional newspaper stories and TV news broadcasts are the product of the age of scarcity; limited space in print and time on air shaped this scarcity model for news reporting. But as Chris Anderson observed in *The Long Tail,* the Internet obliterated the concept of scarcity and introduced us to the era of abundance.

The advantage of professionally trained reporters, editors and photographers that newspaper and TV news companies enjoyed was mostly wasted as content moved online. The old-style journalists were comfortable with their native format and resisted change. The publishers and general managers hesitated to make more than a minimum investment in new technical staff. When legacy news publishers forced the same content product into a new Web-based market, they were offering the equivalent of VHS cassettes on Netflix.

Entrepreneurs who try to reproduce a newspaper in digital form are doomed to the same obsolescence. Journalists who have connected with a community of interest know the difference between the static Web and the live Web. The next generation of news enterprises will be guided by the users as much as—if not more than—the publishers. Embracing this uncertainty and feeling comfortable without absolute control is something old-guard publishers have struggled with. If you're building a news startup, you cannot make the same mistake.

▶▶ *The customers: new needs, many options*

Before the Internet, the audience and the advertisers—both were the "customers" in this case—had few options for local news and information outlets. In many cases, they had *no* options other than the local newspaper or TV station. That's a monopoly. When a news provider controls a monopoly, that owner sets the terms and makes the rules. The Internet changed the rules by disrupting that monopoly.

Suddenly, news consumers could get their national, foreign, sports, business, weather and entertainment news from a multitude of sources online. Pretty soon, advertisers could fill jobs and sell cars on craigslist. Shoppers could find a new house online and arcane collectibles or the latest technological gadget on eBay.

The traditional construct that bundled all that information into one package—the daily newspaper or TV news broadcast—used to make sense in a situation of scarcity. When the Internet arrived, however, the breadth of coverage by traditional news sources was suddenly no match for the depth of online offerings that could cover a single niche comprehensively.

In the first part of the 20th century, advertising became the primary business model for newspapers, and everyone assumed advertising would always be the revenue driver. When the customer had no choice but to take the general, one-size-fits-all news product, advertisers had no choice but to pay news publishers for the ability to reach their audiences. Today, in contrast, advertisers are overwhelmed with options and news companies are struggling to remain a viable choice.

▶ Opportunity knocks as ad dollars shift

Advertising is growing online and on mobile devices and declining in print and on TV and radio. Deliver a product that meets the needs of today's news consumer, and you will build an audience and reap the rewards.

Figure 1.6 MSNBC

It's true: lots of websites are making a fortune by selling advertising online. For example, although 2009 was a terrible year for most businesses, MSNBC.com had record revenues and missed profit projections by only 1 percent. "We're making plenty of money," MSNBC.com president Charlie Tillinghast told an audience in Bellevue, Wash., in November 2009, at the height of the recession. In 2010, the growth continued as MSNBC.com grew another 7 percent, according to *The State of the Media* report.

MSNBC.com is a joint venture of Microsoft and NBC News, but it has been free to operate like a startup since it was founded in the 1990s. Its innovative presentation of digital news and significant distribution through the MSN websites has helped MSNBC.com become one of the most visited news sites on the Web. Unlike some legacy news companies, MSNBC.com has found a way to turn traffic into dollars.

For startups that can build an audience, the advertising money is there. Online advertising revenues grew 13.9 percent to $25.8 billion in 2010, the year online advertising spending eclipsed advertising spending in newspapers for the first time. Ad spending on newspapers is expected to continue declining, according to industry publication *eMarketer,* which estimates that print newspaper spending has already been cut in half since 2006, and online revenues at newspapers have done relatively little to make up the difference.

Figure 1.7 AUDIENCE CHART

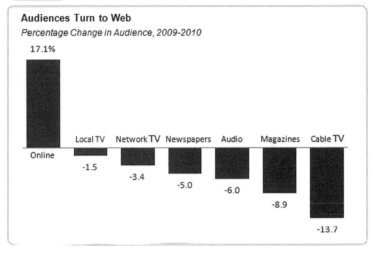

Audiences Turn to Web
Percentage Change in Audience, 2009-2010

By contrast, total U.S. online ad spending will continue double-digit growth through 2014, when it is expected to surpass $40 billion.[8]

Compared to traditional news companies, the titans of the Internet are playing on a different scale—all powered by online advertising. Facebook reportedly brought in upwards of $2 billion in 2010, up from $500 million in 2009, while Google continued to dominate the online revenue industry with more than $25 billion in revenue in 2010.[9]

Not everyone is growing, however. Revenue at Yahoo!, for example, fell approximately 10 percent in 2009 and 2010.[10] That figure represented a 10 percent drop from 2008. At AOL, advertising revenues dropped 29 percent between 2009 and 2010, the year the company invested $50 million to hire hundreds of journalists for its network of hyperlocal news sites called Patch. AOL hopes its investment in original content, as well as its acquisitions of popular news startups TechCrunch and the Huffington Post, will help spur faster ad revenue growth.

Newspaper companies, meanwhile, continue to cut staff and operations. In years past, 20 percent of newspaper revenues came from circulation (customers paying for the newspaper) and 80 percent came from advertising. Now almost 10 percent comes from online advertising. Unfortunately, that figure isn't growing fast enough—if at all—to replace the deficit from traditional print advertising. At local TV stations, online advertising accounts for a smaller percentage of total revenue—closer to 5 percent.

The audience has shifted online, but the ad dollars haven't followed as fast for news companies. The question is why. The simple answer is a lack of innovation on the part of traditional news companies. The way the traditional companies build and manage their sites, and the way they sell advertising space, is too similar to the way they've always done business in an offline world, but the model just doesn't work as well online.

This standoff has opened the door for you—the entrepreneur. In Chapter 2, you will meet news entrepreneurs who have launched successful—and profitable—enterprises to fill the gaps left by traditional news publishers. Some of the businesses were even launched from one person's bedroom. In Chapter 3 you'll examine different ways to bring in revenue to sustain a news enterprise. After that, you'll learn how to craft your idea into a business plan and launch your own startup into this new world of digital information and opportunity.

▶▶ *Jump into the innovation gap*

Large established companies rarely lead their industries with innovation. This is the primary principle behind *The Innovator's Dilemma,* one of the most influential business books of the last 20 years. Companies that enjoy significant market share spend their time and energy protecting their position instead of expanding into new markets or attempting to innovate with new products.

Traditional news companies certainly fall into that category, but the news industry hasn't always feared change. James Gordon Bennett, Horace Greeley, E.W. Scripps and Joseph Pulitzer were not just prominent editors and publishers, says former newspaper executive turned entrepreneur Howard Owens. "They were entrepreneurs, visionaries and risk takers who experimented and explored the capabilities of new technologies with a goal of meeting readers' needs and growing audience."

By embracing risk—an entrepreneurial must—and forming a business model that is native to the new digital information ecosystem, startups and other new enterprises can more quickly find business innovation where traditional news companies did not.

Though media companies struggled to seize the large-scale opportunity that arrived with the Internet, innovation did happen in the nooks and crannies, driven by trailblazers who refused to wait to be anointed or invited. Even without a Bennett, Greely, Scripps or Pulitzer to lead the change, a few individuals in some news organizations found a way to drive change, if only for their own small piece of the overall operation.

▶ ▶ *Going above and beyond a culture of resistance*

It's no easy task to reorient the business of news from the inside. Time and again, studies have found that newsrooms are among the most defensive cultures in any industry. People working in newsrooms have long enjoyed the luxury of thinking their business was different from other businesses. Journalism is critical to a functioning democracy, after all, and the press enjoys constitutional protection. Still, a few innovators understood early in the Internet age that, even if they're part of a public trust, news companies have to compete for attention—and business—like everyone else.

Strategic planning sessions at news companies outlined myriad ways to compete for audience and revenue in the Internet age. Most of these initiatives failed to gain traction because the existing culture immediately swallowed new strategies. Promising ideas weren't funded because news companies, like other successful big enterprises, had no appetite for risk and remained too protective of profits.

As the editor of two different newspaper websites in the 2000s, I can attest to the challenge of implementing new practices in a traditional newsroom. People resisted for reasons ranging from a fear of new tools and technologies to a denial of their impact.

Even against these odds, a few enterprising journalists in some newsrooms saw the potential of the new medium. Those who embraced the changing dynamics were mostly mavericks. With hindsight, it's obvious that editors and managers should have followed the example of these outliers.

People leveraged new tools to produce collaborative, transparent and authentic journalism. Here's how they did it:

- **Engaging with the audience:** Delivering news "from a castle," separated from the audience by a virtual moat, perpetuated the one-way direction of communication. New media sees news as a conversation, not a lecture, and early-adopting journalists understood the importance of **collaboration**.

- **Building trust:** When readers and viewers had few choices for their news, the lone provider could easily build trust. Once audiences could get their news from anywhere, that relationship changed and audience trust had to be earned every day. This made **transparency** critical, but interactive technology has made transparency easier to achieve.

- **Embracing diversity of voice:** The generic and evenly neutral tone of traditional news writing struggled to measure up to the quick, punchy writing published with personality at the leading new media sites. Writing with **authenticity** became important; journalists who used their voice with their own blogs, live chats and other new media flourished.

A defensive, low-risk mindset stymied media companies on the business side as well as the content side. Because they focused heavily on the same revenue streams for decades, traditional news companies paid little attention to new business development. The Internet meant lower-priced advertising, and more of it, something most media companies were ill equipped to sell. Highly paid account executives were very good at returning once a year to a big department store chain or auto dealer and signing a 12-month contract for six or seven figures. Prospecting for new clients to sell an Internet ad for a few hundred dollars a month was not in their DNA or job description.

In recent years, financial struggles, bankruptcy filings and cascading layoffs have set off enough alarm bells to startle even defensive-minded companies into thinking more about playing offense. Some, like Reed Business Information, have started new digital operations and are now letting the new divisions compete directly with the traditional parts of their business. The culture has softened somewhat, and attitudes continue to change.

As they say in Silicon Valley: "The bigger the problem, the bigger the opportunity." The news industry has a problem, but you can help solve it. Now that we understand more about the challenges, let's focus on the opportunities.

BUILD YOUR BUSINESS **Stage 1**

Now that you've reviewed the current state of the news ecosystem, focusing mostly on the disruption to traditional news companies, what is your biggest takeaway? Let that question sink in, and see how your thinking about the future shifts. Whether you have an idea for a new business or just some general thoughts, it's time to apply the lessons from this chapter to your understanding of the new digital landscape for news and information.

?? THINK: Everyone working in media in the 21st century should attempt to "invent the Web." The current wisdom about how best to do that changes almost daily.

✓ ACT: Interview someone at a local media company about that organization's response to the changing media landscape and what are the lessons learned. What's working for the company right now, and why? What hasn't worked in the past? If the company were starting over, what would it do differently?

?? THINK: The defensive culture of news organizations, often combined with the inertia of a big established company, kept traditional media from innovating quickly enough as the new Internet age dawned. At the same time, companies that embrace the Internet, and its disruptions, have thrived. Every industry experiences this situation. What non-media company can you think of that strikes you as truly innovative?

✓ ACT: Research that company and write a one-page summary (or better yet, a post on your blog) about its methods. How did the company ignore the status quo to find success? How does the company promote an appetite for risk and an excitement for trying new things? If you can wrangle an interview with someone who works at the company, so much the better.

?? THINK: Studying the news ecosystem is the first step in hatching a news startup idea. In your own experience, think about an opportunity that a news company failed to seize. Whether it was your local newspaper's failure to build a compelling website, the big-city TV station ignoring the smaller towns, or your favorite columnist's lack of audience engagement, what could have been done differently?

✓ ACT: List three examples of how a news company missed an opportunity to grow its audience or find new revenue through digital media. If possible, find another example that shows how a different approach could have worked and why that approach was feasible.

?? THINK: Analyze the news landscape in a geographical or subject area that interests you as an entrepreneur. It could be news in your hometown or coverage of your favorite sport, music or food. Do you see gaps or interesting areas left uncovered, such as what Mike Orren saw in Dallas? How would you define those gaps and pursue one or more as an area of opportunity?

 ACT: List the coverage gaps you see. What type of content is needed to fill the gaps? What audience would that content appeal to, and what companies might want to advertise? If there are no obvious gaps, identify the organizations that are already covering the area or subject you're interested in. List what they're doing well and not so well. Talk to others who visit these sites and ask them the same question. Compare your analysis to others and see which areas match up. What openings does that leave for you, the aspiring entrepreneur?

Notes

1. *The State of the News Media 2010: An Annual Report on American Journalism,* Pew Project for Excellence in Journalism, March 15, 2010. http://www.stateofthemedia.org/2010/

2. Bill Grueskin, Ava Seave, and Lucas Graves, "The Business of Digital Journalism," Columbia Journalism Review, May 10, 2011. http://cjr.org/the_business_of_digital_journalism/

3. Stephen L. Vaughn, *Encyclopedia of American Journalism* (New York: Rutledge, 2007).

4. Compete.com report generated in Dec. 2010.

5. *The State of the News Media* 2004.

6. *The State of the News Media* 2010.

7. *The State of the News Media* 2010.

8. eMarketer study, "Online Ad Spending Surpasses Newspapers," Dec. 21, 2010. http://www.emarketer.com/Article.aspx?R=1008126

9. "Facebook Revenues Up to $700 Million in 2009, On Track Towards $1.1 Billion in 2010," *Inside Facebook,* March 2, 2010. http://www.insidefacebook.com/2010/03/02/facebook-made-up-to-700-million-in-2009-on-track-towards-1-1-billion-in-2010/

For information from Google investor relations site, see http://investor.google.com/financial/tables.html

10. Yahoo! Reports Fourth Quarter 2009 Results, Company website, Jan. 26, 2010. http://yhoo.client.shareholder.com/releases.cfm

CHAPTER 2

Get Inspired by Success

I n 2002, Rafat Ali started a blog for a simple reason: "It was either that, or I didn't have any food to eat." After several freelancing and temporary stints, Ali was frustrated trying to find a new job in journalism. Publishing his own site, he hoped, would serve as an interactive resume that would set him apart from the job-seeking hordes.

As it turned out, he was lucky that nobody hired him.

Ali's blog, paidContent, became a company called ContentNext. In 2008 ContentNext was acquired by Britain's Guardian Media Group in a multimillion-dollar deal.[1] A look at how Ali made the leap from hungry job seeker to established online entrepreneur shows how finding a niche and working tirelessly can sow success in online news. Ali adeptly expanded his blog, making money through display advertising, job classifieds and event listings, while pushing an aggressive editorial mission to cover the business of digital media.

In the beginning, Ali just hoped to earn enough to survive. His work schedule entailed blogging from "the first thing in the morning, until you drop dead at night." He wrote about media companies struggling to build new business models in the digital age. At the time, people thought the Internet audience would have to pay to access online content because the ad market had crashed. But then the ad market began to rebound. As all sorts of new online businesses sprang up, paidContent's focus evolved into covering all of the different ways that online content gets paid for.

Ali recognized that he had discovered an untapped market. He'd found his niche with a topic that many industry insiders were obsessed with, but that hadn't been thoroughly covered on a regular basis. He kept blogging relentlessly, to the point where his family worried about his health. At least

Figure 2.1 Rafat Ali

twice, his bank account dropped to zero. For the first four months, he also continued his job hunt. But he stopped when he began receiving emails from businesses interested in advertising on his blog.

For the first ad he sold, Ali charged $400 a month, for no reason except that "it sounded better than $500 a month." He made some side money speaking at conferences, mostly held in Europe. As advertising revenue started coming in, he opened a business bank account. With that, he was on his way, starting to believe that his obsession might actually work as a business.

In June 2003, Wired News, the online site for *Wired* magazine, featured a story on Ali, with the headline "Blogging for Bucks." He calls this story his first big break. Soon after, paidContent won a European journalism award for best news blog, which led to a mention on the BBC website. Ali leveraged the media attention by networking constantly; he loved meeting new people, if only via email and phone calls. This network of contacts fueled the site. Once paidContent had established its credibility in the industry, the news tips and scoops started pouring in.

Figure 2.2 paidContent

Two years after his first blog post, Ali had enough income to live on. His family "ultimately came around" when they saw how much he loved his 24/7 work. He moved from London to Los Angeles to be with his future wife, and he started getting interest from investors. In addition to paidContent, he had launched mocoNews to focus on mobile content and had plans for a new site in India that eventually launched under the name of contentSutra. He started two other spinoffs, one on digital music and one on broadband, but shut them down after six months because he couldn't manage so many sites.

In 2006, after bootstrapping the business for four years, he took a round of investment from famed media investor Alan Patricof to expand company operations. Ali says he could have gone without Patricof's investment, but he wanted to grow the company. So Ali gave away a portion of the equity in exchange for "a few hundred thousand dollars." The money helped the company expand by adding more staff to write new content, break more news, sell more ads, and organize more events. He would later remark that the investment "validated us in the market."

During this time, Ali had also received interest from media companies who wanted to acquire his small network of sites. But he didn't like the way they were valuing the company—as a group of journalists instead of as a growing business. By the time the Guardian group had acquired paidContent, the company had nearly 30 employees and several million dollars in annual revenue, which had been doubling every year. Thus, "our value was based on our audience, our journalistic integrity and our potential for growth," Ali says.

Ali's story is rare, but not unique. To turn a blog into a news startup, and then grow that into a big business, takes talent, hard work and a community built around strong content. What's important about his story and the others in this chapter isn't the probability that a journalist—or any other entrepreneur—can start his or her own thing and hit a home run. It's the *possibility*.

Just about every journalism major who graduated from college before 1995 had to work for someone else to be able to publish journalistic writing. The Internet changed that, allowing anyone to publish what *they* thought was journalism. More important, it allowed journalists to publish themselves. On any topic, to any audience, at any time.

That freedom planted the seeds for the entrepreneurial journalism that is blossoming today. Both seasoned entrepreneurs and determined first-timers are finding success with online media enterprises that range from blogs to local news sites to "new news creatures" that no one could have imagined even a few years ago. The most successful—or most promising—share several characteristics that we explore in this chapter.

Understanding what's worked for those who came before you should help you to find confidence and build on these triumphs. Use this chapter to:

- ▶ Analyze the common traits that successful startups share.

- ▶ Learn how some blogs have grown into big businesses.

- ▶ Get inspired by entrepreneurs who beat the odds and succeeded in their own way.

WHAT MAKES A SUCCESSFUL NEWS STARTUP?

The news startups that you meet in this chapter would all be considered successful by most outside measurements. From the inside, though, each founder could tell you about missed opportunities, scarce resources and all the other hurdles that face every young business. Yet even amid those challenges, these startups stand out—and in this crowded online era, that's no small accomplishment.

"There are so many startup ideas, it's difficult to sort through them to get to the one that will work for a particular entrepreneur," says Lisa Williams, whose

Placeblogger site has become the largest searchable index of local blogs. In her view, a news startup can define success in several different ways, not all of which relate to money. "It can produce good work, it can be financially successful; [or] it can produce knowledge and career advancement for the people engaged in it, even if the actual startup doesn't end up taking off."

The ability to attract and serve a valuable audience with quality content is the first characteristic generally used in evaluating the success of a news startup. The next trick—which some would say is more difficult—is to make enough money to sustain the operation so that the audience continues to have access to that great content.

▶ Set your own goals

Audience and revenue are the primary measurements of success for online media. But how much audience and revenue is sufficient? The answer varies with the size and scope of the operation. In other words, the formula for success depends greatly on the goals and expectations set by a founding team.

Setting those goals for your business is a crucial first step. Obviously you can't know what the future will bring, but it's important to envision how big or small you'd like your company to be, if everything goes well, and then set benchmarks for how you'll measure success. These benchmarks will likely change as the project progresses. As you're getting started, the experiences of others can help you decide where you're aiming.

How you learn from other entrepreneurs depends on what you're aiming for. Maybe it's an idea that will convert good journalism into a solid business and consistent revenue. And just what is your particular definition of "solid business"? To CNN or the startup news site Global Post, it's worldwide penetration. To *USA Today* or the Daily Beast, it's national. To the West Seattle Blog or the New Haven Independent, it's local. You've got plenty of options; but what matters is finding your focus.

As an average member of the online audience, you can jump from site to site just enjoying what each has to offer. As an aspiring entrepreneur, your mission is to ask *why* and *how*. When a site makes you stick around and explore, what's the reason? What grabbed you, and how can you apply that to your own startup idea? Practice thinking analytically. For example, here's how paidContent founder Ali evaluated the online media landscape in 2010:

"One of the sites I like is Mashable, which is the biggest tech blog out there. It is trying to bridge the B2B (business-to-business) versus consumer gap,

Figure 2.3 Mashable

and make its service mainstream, which it has to a large extent. It has taken that zeitgeist interest in social media, and turned it into a how-to on the consumer side, and added classifieds and events to it. I think it could also easily expand into business services as well. Or even how-to educational classes. I think that is a very smart way to build a company, and they are a good template for the future of online publishing."

Like many of the companies discussed in this chapter, Mashable started as a blog with a handful of writers working around the clock, seven days a week, with no promise of "making it big." Timing was on the company's side, as it began covering social media just as Facebook and Twitter really took off. Now it is a formidable media company with dozens of journalists, strict editorial standards and innovative technology on its website.

Marshall Kirkpatrick, senior writer for ReadWriteWeb and one of the original writers for TechCrunch, has been analyzing startups for almost a decade. He says a startup's ability to differentiate itself the way Mashable did is the key to success. "My favorite news startups add substantial value to an already crowded news ecosystem. They offer compelling user experiences that I'm drawn to, that I don't have to struggle to train myself to return to," Kirkpatrick says.

Audience loyalty is a critical component of success in a news startup. Simply having audience "eyeballs" on your content, however, is rarely enough to guarantee success. The audience must be loyal and fully engaged if you want to produce dynamic, vibrant content and help your news site grow. "The really successful ones are the ones that have focused on building a loyal community," says Techdirt founder Mike Masnick. "Once you have that community in place, it enables so much more."

For the rest of this chapter we address who or what defines success in online news, including elements that you haven't even thought of. We'll look at what successful journalism startups have in common, so you can start thinking how you might incorporate those common themes into your own startup idea.

▶ The influence model: Quality content pays

For decades, this rule of the journalism business—influence makes markets—helped newspapers grow into hugely profitable enterprises. From the 1970s to the 1990s, newspapers' revenues steadily grew based on the audience they could attract with their journalism—and the relative lack of competition for that audience. Advertisers paid top dollar to have their messages appear alongside quality content. They didn't have much choice.

In his 2004 book *The Vanishing Newspaper,* Philip Meyer argued that newspapers were not in the news or information business but rather in the influence business, an idea proposed even earlier by former Knight Ridder vice president Hal Jurgensmeyer. "A newspaper, in the Jurgensmeyer model, produces two kinds of influence: societal influence, which is not for sale, and commercial influence, or influence on the consumer's decision to buy, which is for sale," Meyer wrote. "The beauty of this model is that it provides economic justification for excellence in journalism."[2]

Before the late 1990s, Meyer said, newspapers were able to leverage their influence and credibility through consistently publishing quality content. But then newspapers fell behind the digital competition. Still, the model that commercially supported newspapers for decades is essentially the same model that technology and political bloggers have used to build their "empires": When a publication builds a loyal audience based on the quality of its news coverage, advertisers pay to be seen in the same space. Digital innovations have created new ways to implement this model, but the essence remains the same.

"There are some fascinating sprouts popping up all over," says Ken Doctor, author of *Newsonomics*. "Reporting is timeless: People find out what's going on and tell other people about it. Storytelling is obviously hugely expanded and is no longer constrained by job duty. The blogger voice really added something to journalism: a direct connection to the audience. I'm very optimistic about what we should be able to create with [the] tools of [the] digital age."[3]

The user community is eventually what attracts advertisers, too. For example, TechDirt founder Mike Masnick built a highly engaged community around his technology news site, and then found innovative ways to leverage it for new revenue (which we explore in Chapter 3).

"I think quality content is always important in both creating influence and driving audience," Masnick says. "There is some correlation with revenue, but it's a mistake to think that quality content alone results in revenue (unless you're damn lucky). There are also successful business models *without* quality content, but I have trouble believing those are sustainable long term."

Most news entrepreneurs agree that publishing (or aggregating) great content is the best way to build an audience and then turn that audience into a community that adds value through sharing and engagement. Entrepreneurs, investors, foundations, pundits and even the end users define success differently. But the one thread that runs through all of the examples is the importance of great content.

Defining quality content means figuring out what will inspire your audience to join in. In some cases that might be as simple—and as complex—as delivering more local news than the established media are providing.

The New Haven Independent, a nonprofit local news site started by Paul Bass in 2005, features good work produced by "surviving reporters" from other local media, but the site has built its audience around original reporting beats—government, crime, business, arts and culture. "What's proving viable is creating value through reporting," Paul Bass says. "You gotta do good reporting. It's an old-fashioned idea, but you have to go out and interview people, look at records, and present it in a good way. Good reporting and analysis is the key to success."

Back when newspapers were the only publishers in town, it was relatively easy for a journalist to become an influential voice. Today, it's much more challenging to be heard amid the burgeoning online din.

Using the influence model now, Kirkpatrick suggests, requires complex relationships and calibrations. When you don't have a distribution monopoly as newspapers once did, there are more factors involved in establishing your influence. It works best if your content is "produced regularly, placed strongly in the news cycle, strategically linked to off-site resources and published in conjunction with an effective social media strategy"—which, according to Kirkpatrick, means using social media "to add value to the lives of others in order to re-enforce that influence." In its most basic form, re-enforcing means getting your content seen and making sure it's shared.

Venture capitalists understand the influence model and have increasingly placed their bets on content they believe is strong enough to create financial success. Investors love disruption. As traditional media have struggled to adapt to the digital age, opportunities for new business models have multiplied. While foundations and other philanthropists financially support news startups because they believe it's important to preserve quality journalism, venture capitalists and angel investors see quality journalism as a way to make money. With more and more funders valuing journalistic quality, why not try using the influence model to build your business? Other companies are already doing it.

For example, Xconomy is an online news startup covering the high tech and biotech industries in a handful of U.S. cities. The site launched in 2007 in Boston with several million dollars in funding and the goal of targeting a valuable demographic—the leaders of cutting-edge companies in "the exponential economy"—that were interested in one another's dealings *and* a group highly desirable to sponsors. Xconomy hired top-shelf writers and paid them handsome salaries to keep a traditional journalistic objectivity from these hot companies as the writers explore trends and personalities. Simultaneously, the site forged a unique news identity by recruiting a group of "Xconomists"—high-tech economy insiders for each city it covers, who share their views and insights in specially labeled posts. The audience weighs in with their own opinions, and this creates an engaged community that sponsors want to reach.

The influence model, which comes in many sizes and forms, can work for big companies or neighborhood blogs. Quality content combined with authentic community engagement make the model work in the digital age, just as it did before bits and bytes overtook ink and paper.

▶ Do business while being a journalist

"MONEY!" Say it to the mirror. Say it to your friends. Practice saying it over and over. If you've worked in journalism you probably think of *money* as a dirty word. You're accustomed to a solid wall between editorial and advertising. If you're a student, you might be comfortable talking about money only when you ask your parents for more of it.

Time to face facts: If you want to be an entrepreneur, you're going to have to make friends with money.

The comforting wall separating editorial and advertising at most media companies allowed journalists to operate unencumbered by the complexities of finding customers and getting them to pay. Once you create your own business, however, that wall is gone. Luckily, that doesn't mean you'll have to compromise journalistic values for the sake of profits. Your goal is entrepreneurial journalism. And if your background emphasizes more journalism than entrepreneurship, you've got some adjusting to do.

Douglas McLennan was a newspaper arts writer when he came up with the idea for ArtsJournal in 1999. A digest of the best arts writing from around the world sounded like what he and his artist friends would want to read. He wasn't thinking about making money. In fact, "[w]hen the first ad went up on the site, I kind of felt like a piece of me died," he recalled. "I had been doing this completely for myself. And now I've got this obligation that for the next two weeks [while the ad was scheduled to run]; I've got a *responsibility* to do this. It was a good lesson in knowing why you're doing it and who you're doing it for."

Entrepreneurial journalists recognize the potential pitfalls and conflicts of interest in running a news-based business. Most find that the slope is not as slippery as they'd feared. Smart, ethical professionals with good values, who practice serious journalism, can build trust with an audience, just as corporate news companies once did. It's not the wall that matters. It's the quality of the work.

Placeblogger founder Williams—who is not a journalist—thinks that the supposed conflict between journalism and business is largely a red herring. Just because an individual journalist in business for herself can't preserve the "set it and forget it" separation from business decisions, "doesn't mean that the moral compass of that individual journalist is gone," she affirms. "All that happens is that the journalist in question now makes those moral decisions for herself, a state of affairs I don't find particularly problematic or threatening."

For example, most of the early advertisers on paidContent were software companies. Ali strictly separated the editorial side from advertising, even though he was handling both aspects of the business in the beginning. Only once does he remember an advertiser who had already signed a contract pulling out when Ali published a negative story about that company.

Ali says advertisers eventually realized that they would have to coexist in the same industry as paidContent. He aimed to be aggressive but fair. If he wrote something negative about a company when it did something wrong, he also made sure to write positively about the company when it did something right.

For some, the precedent is a little more elusive. Justin Carder started a hyperlocal blog in a Seattle neighborhood to showcase the local publishing platform his startup company had created. Then came an advertising network and a platform. Through it all, the former Microsoft employee and college journalism major has kept one eye on journalism and the other on business. His site, Capitol Hill Seattle, aims to foster community conversation, but also to connect advertisers within that community.

"I'm healthily skeptical that there has ever been a balance," Carder says. Thinking about all of the missteps that have sullied the reputation of the mainstream media "reduces my guilt," he adds. "I'm glad I don't cover banks or major league sports. But I do prefer reporters who are abrasive—the 'comfort the afflicted and afflict the comfortable' crowd. They're the best reporters. That mean streak goes a long way toward 'balance.'"

Without the protection of that traditional wall, the balance now rests on trust: News entrepreneurs must make the decisions necessary to create and sustain trust with their audience. What it specifically takes to build that trust will vary from site to site, but here are some general guidelines that will help you get started:

- Never offer news coverage in exchange for money, either through paid advertising or other financial support. Do not allow someone to buy an ad or make a donation in the expectation of influencing your editorial decisions.

- Do not shy away from covering a story because it might upset a current or potential advertiser or financial supporter.

- Be transparent and fully disclose conflicts of interest. When writing about an advertiser, tell your readers that the company is one of your sponsors. If you don't, the appearance of impropriety may be worse than any actual impropriety.

If you or someone on your team is engaged in both editorial and advertising functions, transparency is crucial. Be open and upfront with your advertisers or other financial supporters. Explain how your journalistic ethics guide your decisions about what topics or issues you cover. Transparency will build your credibility—and influence—which, in turn, will help your business succeed faster than if you made a quick buck.

"If you can come up with a certain set of principles—this is what I will do and this is what I won't do—and draw that line in big, red neon, it really helps a lot," McLennan explains.

Xconomy, for example, proudly displays its code of ethics on its "About" page. "Our editorial principles are old-fashioned and simple. We believe that our content is only of value to our audience if we ensure that it is trustworthy."[4]

Ideally, a news startup will develop content that builds its credibility and its business prospects—and then that reputation will, in turn, lead to greater credibility and more business prospects. The nonprofit news site Voice of San Diego (VOSD), for example, started The Fact Check to hold people accountable for what they say. "We wanted to check the statements of education leaders, sports figures, even a Chinese restaurant," explains CEO Scott Lewis. "We were inspired by Politifact but didn't want to limit it to politics." Lewis's goal was to centralize The Fact Check, brand it, and include a determination.

Taking a stand on issues in the local community helped the site bolster its business opportunities. Voice of San Diego's local television partner NBC San Diego liked the idea and created a segment for it. The TV spot helped the news site secure a sponsor to support the whole endeavor. VOSD receives revenue from the sponsor and from the NBC station for The Fact Check, which became the most popular blog on the VOSD site.

The credibility that VOSD had established before launching The Fact Check laid the groundwork for The Fact Check's success. Startup news sites have a difficult challenge establishing trust in a particular community, but trust is essential to growing audience and revenue. VOSD originally launched in 2005, so it had a five-year track record to rely on by the time The Fact Check started. VOSD's credibility helped The Fact Check win the partnership and sponsorship.

Even solo bloggers have used credibility to build their business, growing from one-person sites into million-dollar companies. From the beginning, even when he was writing posts all day from his bedroom, Ali set a high standard for paidContent that eventually paid off. "Our standards are we don't publish rumors," Ali said in a 2008 interview while he was still running paidContent. "When we break a story, we know it's true. There's absolutely no doubt—when we write a story, it just won't be wrong. We've held ourselves to that standard, and that's helped us define our position in the industry."[5]

If you do publish rumors, Ali warns, you might get away with it a few times, but in the long term it will likely harm you—both in your editorial reputation and in your business. "I do think being a gossip rag is tough to monetize," Ali concludes. "You might get a lot of page views, but if you want to scale into a multimedia business with multiple revenue streams, you always run into some kind of wall."

Paul Steiger, ProPublica's editor-in-chief, echoed that sentiment during a 2010 lecture at the University of Georgia. Business models that are largely dependent on page views (as advertising inventory) will drive publishers to favor content with a better chance of "going viral," he noted, rather than content that is "primarily thought-provoking, or challenging, or discomfiting, or even educational." Those adjectives, of course, describe the goals of ProPublica, a nonprofit that does some of the best investigative journalism in the United States.

Steiger also spoke in favor of transparency, both editorially and with business operations. "I think we have an obligation to be as transparent as possible," Steiger confirmed. "It's hard to explain these days, I think, why we should decline to disclose information about our own operations that we want those we cover to disclose about theirs."[6]

Journalists—the skeptics that they are—might be surprised to learn that strong values and ethics help build businesses. Those that have never been privy to the business side of an operation might have expected the opposite to be true. Fortunately, as many startups have already proved, good journalism is good business.

▶ Test, try, play, fail, try again

The examples in this chapter and the rest of the book highlight certain paths to success. You can always benefit from learning about what's worked before. But in the volatile, evolving online world, it's entirely possible that your startup can be successful in ways no one has yet imagined.

Every day, entrepreneurs and journalists are inventing the future, creating new models, discovering new tactics and embracing innovation and

> Figure 2.4 Spot.Us <

experimentation—all an essential parts of any startup's strategy. The ability to adapt to a changing environment will separate success from failure.

Innovation comes in all sizes and takes many forms. It may be a new way to cover a particular news story, engage an audience or sell advertising. (Chapter 4 explores innovation in greater detail.) Often, an experiment leads to innovation, so it's important to try new ideas. "Throwing spaghetti on the wall to see what sticks" may be a cliché, but it is also an apt description of the experimentation and innovation needed in a startup.

David Cohn created Spot.Us, one of the most experimental and innovative journalism models, in 2009. The goal of the enterprise is to support freelance reporting through crowdfunding. Journalists pitch story ideas on the Spot.Us website and specify the minimum cost to do the story— say $250, for example. The audience pledges varying amounts of money, from as little as $10 or $20, to support a particular story. If the minimum is met, the journalist receives the money from the funders and pursues the story. Then Spot.Us helps the journalist to publish the story in a mix of mainstream and independent news organizations.

Sustaining the operation financially is a challenge. Cohn received a Knight News Challenge grant to launch this new concept and has been exploring different revenue streams ever since. To meet his goal of making it easy for people to fund the journalism pitched on the site, he needed to expand the revenue pool beyond individuals. Advertisers make an attractive funding target, but Cohn didn't have a large enough audience on Spot.Us site for a traditional ad model. So he created a new one— "community-focused sponsorships," which allow the Spot.Us audience to earn credits by answering questions. The credits, which are provided as dollars by advertisers, can be applied to funding stories. The advertisers get users engaging with their message, and the users get to support the journalism of their choice without spending their own money.

"We already let people vote [with their dollars] towards the story they want to see," Cohn explained. "With sponsorship, all we did was make it so that the dollars aren't the individuals'—but somebody else's."

Cohn happened upon the idea because an organization wanted to give Spot.Us money, and he needed to create a firewall that stayed true to the site's mission. To do so, he decided to use the community to "filter" the funds. The sponsor has no say in where the funds go; in fact, not even Spot.Us has a say. The user community is who controls where funds are applied on a per-story basis.

A big part of experimentation, of course, is failure. Every entrepreneur must be ready to deal with that reality. Ali, who found plenty of success with his paidContent blog, always searched for the next niche audience to serve. In 2003 he launched a site about digital music that might have taken off— had he been able to properly support it. With paidContent and mocoNews demanding so much of his time, and no money to pay someone else to run the music site, he shut it down within six months to protect his other two sites. A couple of years later, he started a weekly email newsletter about broadband Internet service. He closed the newsletter six months later. "One of the lessons that I learned was that this is how the online media business works," Ali emphasizes. "It's low-cost and if it works, it works. And if it doesn't, you quickly adapt."

Of course, Ali had several ideas that worked really well, such as turning a section on the paidContent site into a direct revenue stream. He had been blogging about new digital media jobs as a market intelligence tool, to help him figure out which companies were hiring and what new services and products they were working on. The blog's jobs report caught on, and soon people started asking if Ali could feature jobs. He created a premium jobs listings feature to generate revenues. The premium listings led to a jobs classifieds section, which turned out to be his most profitable service.

In 2005 Ali started publishing research reports as downloadable PDFs. Not knowing whether there was a market or what the market would bear, he priced first report at $30 and sold 200 copies. Premium research soon became another important revenue stream for the company.

Joshua Micah Marshall, the founder of Talking Points Memo, originally thought that several spinoffs would fuel the popular political blog's future growth. Instead, he ended up consolidating, launching three new ideas not separately but as sections of the main site: TPM Café, which is devoted to policy and culture debates; TPM Muckraker, a collection of posts with the potential for political scandal; and TPMLivewire, a linkblog that curates news from other sources of interest to the TPM audience. The sections let the company connect with additional audiences, without diluting the political reporting that won TPM a 2008 George Polk award.

When asked what he wished he'd known in 2000 when he started his blog, Marshall replied, "I'm glad I didn't know any of it. The pleasure for me has been exploring, learning, coming up with ideas or more often finding half-formed ideas and wrestling with them until I find some way to use them to improve what we do. I wouldn't want to rob myself of that."[7]

Journalist Mark Potts left the *Washington Post* to launch one of the first attempts at a hyperlocal network, named Backfence, in 2005. The company lasted only two years, but Potts learned a great deal about local news sites and later launched a consulting company called GrowthSpur to use that knowledge to help other publishers. Potts likes the model attempted by TBD.com, the local news site launched in Washington, D.C., by Albritton Communications in 2010. TBD's original goal was to create a significant metro news site with minimum expense by tapping into the huge number of local bloggers already covering the Washington, D.C., metropolitan area. Supplementing the work of those bloggers with a small, focused local reporting team would reduce costs immensely.

Potts and GrowthSpur helped TBD engineer a local ad network that would allow local bloggers and TBD to share advertising revenue. The project lasted less than two months before being shelved, to be retooling before an attempted relaunch. Though the TBD model hadn't worked yet, Potts didn't consider it a failure. "This is a radical experiment, but I think it's the future of local coverage on a budget," he said.

NEWSVINE

www.newsvine.com

STARTED: 2005.

FOUNDER: Mike Davidson, previously an art director and creative director at ESPN.com and Walt Disney Internet Group.

MISSION: To create a big news site that did what the big news sites weren't doing at the time: hosting an interactive news community.

STAFF: 8.

STARTUP CASH: $1 million from Second Avenue Partners

WROTE A BUSINESS PLAN?: Yes

MEASURE OF SUCCESS: 5 million monthly unique visitors in 2010. Acquired by MSNBC.com in 2009.

TOP BUSINESS TIP: Concentrate less on saving endangered values and business models and focus more on creating entirely new value chains.

TOP CONTENT TIP: Social media lets you leverage the brains of thousands of individuals willing to create content for millions of other individuals.

We will see more radical experiments in the near future. In this age of rapid technological evolution and business disruption, the more radical an idea, the better.

GROW A BLOG INTO BIG BUSINESS

The Internet's disruption to *what* news got covered opened the door for Rafat Ali and paidContent. The Internet's disruption in *how* news got

Figure 2.5 Talking Points Memo

covered opened the door for Josh Marshall and Michael Arrington. They and others have blazed one possible that trail a news entrepreneur can follow—starting with a blog and growing it into a full-blown business.

In November 2000, Marshall started Talking Points Memo to blog about the presidential election recount in Florida. After five years of blogging about national politics, TPM had built a large following and Marshall decided to grow it beyond a blog into a business. He planned to develop a multi-person news organization on his already established Talking Points Memo brand and to support the operation with paid advertising.

As the site turned 10, Marshall was leading one of the most acclaimed models for online journalism in the world, winning prestigious awards and growing to a staff of almost 20.

Five years after TPM began, Arrington started TechCrunch as a blog covering the venture capital scene in Silicon Valley. Even though the Valley had suffered the dot-com bust in 2000, technology startups had rebounded; by 2005, entrepreneurial activity was hotter than ever.

Entrepreneurs and investors worked day and night to become the next Google, eBay or Amazon.

Arrington, a lawyer, started TechCrunch when he was in his early 30s; he had some entrepreneurial experience but no journalism training. After bouncing among several jobs, he'd taken time off and decided he needed to get up to speed on new business models. The Internet was disrupting business models everywhere, he reasoned, so he tried to learn as much and as quickly as he could. The blog became the outlet for his research and quickly found a following in Silicon Valley. Recognizing he had tapped into something new, Arrington threw himself into it, working 16 hours a day, seven days a week to launch and grow TechCrunch.[8]

Arrington saw a value in the timely publishing of information around this industry. At the time, the *San Jose Mercury News, San Francisco Chronicle, New York Times* and *Wall St. Journal* served as the primary sources for this beat. But publishing just one or two stories a day—mostly in the mornings on their traditional print-based news cycle—prevented them from covering the field with the intensity and speed for which the target audience was hungry.

Arrington battled these big, established brands with hustle and a prolific publishing schedule. News editors have long talked about "flooding the

Figure 2.6 TechCrunch

zone" during a big breaking news event, which means pulling out all the stops and using every resource to get all angles of the story. Arrington treated the technology startup beat as if it were a big breaking news event—all day, every day.

The Internet is the only medium that could support the ambitious agendas of Arrington and Marshall. Broadcast would be too costly, print too slow. Plus, the interactive nature of blogging meant that Arrington's and Marshall's readers could contribute, too, sharing insider insight in the comments—which then led to more story ideas—and spreading links to the blog posts through emails to friends and colleagues.

A publishing model that broke news stories many times a day got both Arrington and Marshall noticed. Being first still matters, especially in high-profile niches like national politics and technology startup news, but being frequent counted as well. This formula allowed the blogs to grow fast, attracting a critical mass of readers that also proved to be target-rich audiences for advertisers.

As more revenue came in, both Arrington and Marshall hired additional writers to increase the rate and amount of news published on the site. They added sales reps to handle the growing number of requests by companies wanting to spend money to advertise. Eventually they hired business managers to point the company in the right direction so the entrepreneurial journalists could continue to pump out scoop after scoop on their websites.

"VCs and entrepreneurs read Arrington for the same reason they pay attention to any top journalist or columnist: He's smart, sourced up, and ahead of the curve," *Wired* magazine wrote in 2007.[9] The same could be said for Marshall.

▶ Use digital media for a new kind of journalism

Blogs covering technology, politics and celebrities were the first topical sites to illustrate financial sustainability. The model seems simple on paper: low overhead plus a big audience equals a viable business. With just a handful of writers (or even fewer), often no office space, some web server costs and some commission-based advertising sales reps, it doesn't take much revenue to turn a profit.

The blog format changed the game of publishing news because of its immediacy and interactivity. Blogs are so simple that anyone can set one up and publish as many posts each day as they can write. RSS feeds make it easy for the audience to follow many blogs. And readers can quickly and easily react to the posts. By questioning, analyzing and supporting a blogger's posts, audience comments make the content better and improve the overall experience.

The users who read, comment and share the news from a blog also fuel that blog's growth. The most difficult challenge to overcome as a new blogger or publisher is the lack of brand awareness. Even on blogs, credibility defines success. The blog format allows the community to contribute to the credibility of that site. First-time visitors who judge a site by the quality of the content in a given post are also swayed by the quality—and quantity—of discussion around the post. Five years ago, that discussion was limited to the comment section at the bottom of the post, but now the conversation extends to Twitter and Facebook and other social media platforms.

Growing by word of mouth— or "word of link"—enabled many blogs and blog networks to launch and get big relatively fast without having to employ one of the most expensive items in startup business: marketing. Even without big brand campaigns or expensive public relations efforts, many blogs have been able to draw thousands—or even millions—of monthly visitors organically.

This natural growth, built on quality content that is narrowly targeted to a specific niche, creates a stronger base for a business. The prolific publishing schedule—the "flooding the zone"—that TechCrunch and other successful blog sites use so well fuels growth. That level of coverage creates a more stable and loyal audience than a flashy marketing campaign would draw, which helps increase the attractiveness to advertisers, as well as the rates.

▶ Blog networks: Strength in numbers

As the first decade of the 21st century wore on, more and more topical blogs were finding business success. Blogs were becoming big media. Sometimes with individual titles, and sometimes grouped together under umbrellas like Gawker and Weblogs, the blog grew out of its infancy as an online diary and became a respected publishing model.

Maybe the startup seed sprouting in your brain does not, even in your wildest daydreams, look like the next TechCrunch. It might, however, make a great component of a larger group. Partnerships are much more probable and powerful with online media, as blog networks have demonstrated.

Five years before AOL acquired TechCrunch, the company purchased Weblogs, a group of blogs founded by Jason Calacanis and Brian Alvey and originally funded by Mark Cuban. Weblogs has encompassed as many as 90 blogs at one time and includes the popular technology blog Engadget. Nick Denton's Gawker network has featured a dozen or so blogs at any given time, highlighted by the tech blog Gizmodo and the personal productivity blog Lifehacker. Denton has sold a few blogs, such as Wonkette and Consumerist, that were popular but not profitable. In 2009, one estimate suggested the Gawker network drew 23 million unique visitors each month and served 250 million page views, bringing in $60 million in advertising revenue each year.[10]

Andrew Breitbart, meanwhile, started a group of conservative political blogs and related websites, including the flagship Breitbart.com, BigHollywood, BigGovernment and Breitbart.tv. More than 3 million unique visitors and 18 million page views helped the network pull in $2.5 million in advertising revenue in 2010.[11]

In a way, this aggregation activity is a modern version of the old newspaper business model: bundling together many different types of content (local news, sports, business, lifestyle) to make it more interesting for advertisers and build a business on a larger scale. The blog network takes it one step further, however. Think of it like a newspaper having separate websites for its beat reporters and columnists. Each by itself might not be able to bring in enough revenue to support sales staff, technology development and business management. Grouped together, however, that scale makes good business sense.

▶ One formula, many successes

The term "blog" is not a business model, but a style of Web publishing with the lowest barrier to entry. A blog is simply the easiest way to get started in publishing, allowing entrepreneurs a way to test a concept with very little investment or risk. Remember how Ali and Arrington started as individual bloggers and were able to grow their Web enterprises as the audience and market grew. The original launch of the blogs required just a few dollars a month for hosting.

The formula is similar across all of the popular and profitable blog sites, whether operating in a network or independently: low operating costs (meaning a small paid staff and publishing costs) plus an almost maniacal devotion to covering a niche topic develops a targeted audience that advertisers love.

In many cases, the successful blogs today used a first-mover advantage to secure their niche before their competitors arrived. Yet in some topic areas—technology, politics and entertainment, for example—many competing sites are operating, all with sizable audiences and profit margins. Examples of some blog sites that may not be in the game to win journalism awards, but have earned large followings without a network include the following:

- The Drudge Report has about 9 million unique visitors each month and annual revenue of $8 million. With very little staff, the profit margin is estimated to be significant.

- Perez Hilton, an entertainment and gossip site with 7 million monthly unique visitors, brings in more than $6 million per year.

- Boing Boing, which highlights the Web's most sensational content, has been one of the most popular blogs for almost a decade, drawing some 3 million visitors and recording revenues of $4 million per year.

Whether covering traditional news beats or a using a new media approach, fundamentally all blogs operate with the same market dynamics as any other publishing entity: Publish content that attracts an audience, then sell exposure to that audience to advertisers, and use that money to pay the people who produce the content. Full-scale news companies have found success in the digital age, too, but their efforts require much more investment and up-front risk.

NEW MEDIA IS NOW BIG MEDIA

In 2011, a nonprofit online news site captured the Pulitzer Prize for national reporting. Jesse Eisinger and Jake Bernstein of ProPublica won the award for "Wall Street Money Machine," their series exposing questionable financial practices that contributed to the nation's economic meltdown. The project, pursued in partnership with NPR and Chicago Public Radio, used both stories and digital tools such as podcasts, interactive graphics and searchable databases to convey complex information—a strategy specially noted in the Pulitzer citation.

The prize to ProPublica was the second Pulitzer vote of confidence for online-only news, and for collaboration. The previous year, Sheri Fink of ProPublica had won the Pulitzer for investigative reporting in collaboration with the *New York Times* Magazine. That story chronicled the urgent life-and-death decisions made by one hospital's exhausted doctors when they were cut off by the floodwaters of Hurricane Katrina.

In recent years, startup news sites like the West Seattle Blog and MyBallard. com have won Online News Association awards alongside the *Washington Post* and CNN.com. In 2010, PhinneyWood, a news site that focuses on one Seattle neighborhood, won the national Sigma Delta Chi Award from the Society of Professional Journalists for deadline reporting on a series of arson fires.

Awards are not the only barometer of success, of course. Still, news startups winning major awards illustrate that it's still possible to achieve the highest quality of journalism while chasing the more critical components of success—financial viability and the ability to attract and engage an audience.

"We *are* the mainstream media," declares Tracy Record, founder of the West Seattle Blog. "People in the community look to us as the publication of record."

Increasingly, news startups have taken a place next to venerable journalism brands from a local to a national, and even global, level. The Huffington Post, the Drudge Report and Politico help set the national political agenda alongside the *Washington Post, New York Times* and *Wall Street Journal.* The Texas Tribune, California Watch and the St. Louis Beacon are each among their state's most influential news outlets. Local and hyperlocal startups like Baristanet, the New Haven Independent and the Voice of San Diego have quickly become the go-to source for news and information at the city and neighborhood level.

It's no longer necessary to work for a traditional news brand to be part of the mainstream media. Startups are finding commercial and journalistic success across a broad spectrum of markets. Let's take a closer look at some of the more prominent examples of this success to learn what makes them work.

▶ One path: Aim big, get big

We often think of startups as one- or two-person projects that are run out of a house, a basement or a garage. Silicon Valley is famous for producing huge, world-changing companies from such humble beginnings, including Hewlett-Packard, Apple, Yahoo! and Google. These companies grew very fast, following the popular entrepreneurial philosophy of "go big or go home." The entrepreneurs were determined to make it as big as possible— or die trying.

Sometimes, however, a company is launched to be big from the beginning. Once upon a time, not so long ago, CNN and *USA Today* were startups with audacious ambitions. CNN became the first 24-hour news broadcast channel when it launched in June 1980. Today it reaches 100 million households in the United States and many more people through CNN Airport Network, CNN radio and CNN International, which is seen in 212 countries.

Two years after CNN was born, Gannett launched *USA Today,* hoping to publish the "nation's newspaper" five days a week. For most of the early 21st century, *USA Today* boasted the largest circulation of any newspaper in United States, thanks in large part to its distribution in hotels and airports. The *Wall St. Journal* has overtaken *USA Today* to claim the top spot, due to its 400,000 online subscribers, but *USA Today* remained the widest circulated print newspaper in 2010.

In recent years, more news companies have launched with big ambitions, albeit more modest ones than those of CNN or *USA Today.* This time, the goal is to leverage the relatively cheap publishing platform provided by the Internet to amass a large, targeted audience to sell to advertisers.

Arianna Huffington, Kenneth Lerer and Jonah Peretti launched The Huffington Post in 2005 and raised $20 million in venture funding to grow operations. The site's original goal was to serve as an alternative to conservative websites. The Huffington Post has since expanded to cover everything from books and sports to green living and even divorce, linking freely to content elsewhere online. Before AOL bought the company for $315 million in 2011, The Huffington Post had a full-time staff of about 60, plus more than 3,000 volunteer writers and bloggers; since the merger, the company has hired several dozen more journalists. Incredibly, the site drew more visitors than either washingtonpost.com or wsj.com (the website of the *Wall Street Journal*) in 2009, and counted about 13 million unique visitors each month in 2011.

In 2007, Albritton Communications dedicated millions of dollars to launch the Politico newspaper and website. John Harris and Jim VandeHei left the *Washington Post* to lead the editorial efforts. Frederick Ryan, a former assistant to President Ronald Reagan, was president and CEO. The newspaper still accounts for the majority of the publication's revenue, but its online presence is what drives its influence. With a paid circulation of only 32,000 in print, Politico attracts 2.5 million unique visitors per month to its site.

Another example is The Daily Beast, founded by former *New Yorker* and *Vanity Fair* editor Tina Brown, and owned by Internet giant IAC. In late 2010,

Figure 2.7 ProPublica

the site merged with *Newsweek* to produce a new company called The Daily Beast Newsweek Publishing. It's a sign of the entrepreneurial times when a two-year-old website can merge with a venerable 75-year-old news magazine and take the lead in the name of the new company.

ProPublica, the Manhattan-based nonprofit news site that wins Pulitzers, employs a staff of 32 thanks to a funding source that exceeds most startups' fantasies. Herbert and Marion Sandler have given the site $10 million *per year* to perform "investigative journalism in the public interest" and provide the resulting stories for free to news organizations. The site published 138 stories in 2009 with 38 different news partners.

"I've always been critical of ProPublica's current reliance on funding coming from a wealthy source, which isn't sustainable," says Vadim Lavrusik, a former writer for Mashable and an adjunct professor at Columbia Journalism School. "However, I've been impressed that they have made their revenue more distributed and are now getting donations from elsewhere. I think that because they have already gotten so much exposure through winning the Pulitzer and partnering with big news organizations, they'll continue to have people interested in providing funding for them."

Big money funding big aspirations can happen on smaller levels, too. The Texas Tribune, the Bay Citizen and Civil Beat in Honolulu are examples of significant news operations launched on a local level. The Bay Citizen had $5 million to start with, while the Texas Tribune started with $4 million in funding. Pierre Omidyar, founder of eBay and someone with very deep pockets indeed, launched Civil Beat.

MinnPost (in Minnesota) launched as a nonprofit in 2007 with more than $1 million in startup funding and reached the break-even point in just three years. In its first year, the operation spent $605,000 more than it brought in. Corporate and individual donations, combined with earned income from events, advertising and sponsorships, quickly grew, however. In 2010, MinnPost spent $1.3 million and posted a surplus of $17,594. The founders, Joel and Laurie Kramer, called it a "tremendous vindication for our business model."[12]

Each of these new-era news startups has a different approach to the same business opportunity: publishing news on a topic area in a way that no one else is doing, then attracting an audience and becoming an influential voice. A business model can be built around the combination of audience and influence; we'll take a closer look at this and other revenue models in the rest of this chapter and others to follow.

▶ Another path: Pick a niche and go deep

Since the Web went mainstream, many independent organizations have succeeded in the business of news. ArtsJournal, Treehugger and other successful digital journalism businesses you may not have heard about have been making money for years by producing quality journalism in a niche topic area.

The power of the niche is one advantage of publishing news online. Targeting a certain segment of an audience, either topically or geographically, is a business model that makes sense in the world of the Web but is far more difficult—and expensive—through print or broadcast.

Consider Douglas McLennan, the ArtsJournal founder from earlier in the chapter. A former concert pianist and later an arts critic at the Seattle *Post-Intelligencer,* he knew very little about Web publishing and had only a "really vague idea" for a business model when he started ArtsJournal in 1999. He figured he'd attract 5,000 readers and then sell advertising—but he was disabused of this notion rather quickly.

Companies weren't advertising on small websites in those days, so McLennan started charging for feeds of his content. Eventually that income

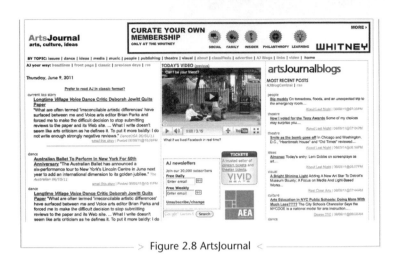

Figure 2.8 ArtsJournal

went away, so he started doing a premium newsletter that had 1,000 subscribers paying $28 per year in 2010, but he also had 38,000 subscribers to a free email newsletter

Now the ArtsJournal site has 250,000 readers each month and makes money from a combination of newsletters and classified and display advertising, bought by companies who want to reach the niche audience of people interested in the arts. "Be really flexible about where you're going to get your money," McLennan advises. "It's never been one place (for me). It's been a lot of different micro feeds of it. Sometimes one thing is going gangbusters and sometimes it's something else. You just really can't predict it."

Treehugger, as you might have guessed, targets a niche audience of people interested in environmental issues and living a sustainable green lifestyle. Graham Hill, who started the site in 2003, wanted to target the niche audience of "regular" people who were growing interested and needed more information about an eco-friendly lifestyle. The targeted audience was more general, larger and a better demographic than if the site had targeted extremely passionate greens. Those folks already had their network of blogs. Treehugger was meant for everyone else.

Hill ran the site as a solo project in the beginning, much as Ali, Marshall and Arrington did with paidContent, Talking Points Memo and TechCrunch, respectively. As the years progressed, the site grew in terms of audience, staff and advertising revenue. In 2008, Discovery Networks acquired Treehugger for $10 million and formed a new Planet Green Initiative. (The Discovery Network, which broadcasts the Discovery Channel, also acquired start-up websites Petfinder.com and HowStuffWorks.com—the latter for a whopping $250 million.)

While Treehugger and ArtsJournal targeted an audience with specific interests, other sites use location as their niche. In the first decade of the 21st century, so-called "hyperlocal" sites sprouted up seemingly everywhere, aiming to cover communities more intensively than traditional local news operations had ever attempted. The question has been, and largely remains, is it possible to turn these labors of love into profitable, sustainable, scalable businesses?

Tim Armstrong thinks so. He was a senior vice president at Google in 2008, when he helped fund a startup called Patch.com. With three local versions in New Jersey, these "Patches" aimed to blanket small communities with comprehensive news coverage, business directories and event calendars. A year later, Armstrong was named CEO of AOL. The company acquired the Patch platform for $7 million, then drew up ambitious expansion plans. In 2010, the company announced it would pour $50 million into Patch, hiring hundreds of journalists to serve as local editors to launch more than 1,000 sites in the United States. In 2011 AOL announced plans to hire as many as 800 more journalists so that each Patch site would have more than the single full-time local editor.

"I live in one of the most resourced communities in America," Armstrong said at the Online News Association conference in 2010, referring to his New Jersey suburb. "There are blogs in town, but they don't cover my needs as a (news) consumer. What's the consumer need in the town, and are you meeting it?"

That's what Patch is aiming to do on a very local level all across the nation. It's not alone. Big media companies like Yahoo!, Gannett, Tribune and Fisher Communications have also made significant investments in hyperlocal news. The opportunity to fill a local niche is no longer as wide open as it was in the last decade, but competition is a good thing. Big companies might struggle to replicate the success of a single local site across an entire network.

The advantage in local news and local business will still go to the people with local knowledge and local relationships. Those are difficult to replicate.

Be ethical—and show it

While traditional media have been slow to post ethics codes online to show what they stand for, some news startups are making transparency a virtue. As important as *having* ethics is letting people know that you do. Unlike a news organization with a long history, a startup has no track record to establish its credibility. As a journalism entrepreneur, it's crucial to be open about the goals and standards of your site, especially if the funding for your startup is a new model that the audience might not understand.

For example, the venture-backed startup Xconomy, which covers the biotech and high tech industries, proudly displays its ethical guidelines on the About page of its website. The ethics section begins, "[o]ur editorial principles are old-fashioned and simple. We believe that our content is only of value to our audience if we ensure that it is trustworthy." The section then addresses specific issues, such as forbidding writers to write about any company they invest in, and keeping editorial decisions independent of business operations.

Xconomy's guidelines spotlight many of the "ethical pressure points" that Kelly McBride of the Poynter Institute warns entrepreneurs to

▶ Target audiences for targeted advertising

Whether it's a topic or a location, the business model for niche websites is to find a targeted audience and publish content that attracts that audience. It sounds easy, but it's difficult to execute, especially as part of a larger business plan. You may find a niche that is relatively uncovered by existing publishers and think you've found a golden opportunity. Unfortunately, you may have simply found a niche that's too small to be a viable business. Or maybe there is a large audience interested in the topic, but no addressable market for advertising or other revenue-generating activities.

watch for. She says that news startups, which collectively she calls the Fifth Estate, should be especially vigilant in dealing with content, whether staff-created or user-created. The Xconomy site addresses several potential content problems, for instance by explaining the difference between content produced by professional journalists and opinion pieces produced by "the Xconomists," business leaders who are involved in the subjects they write about.

Content aside, McBride says conflicts between mission and revenue are the biggest source of ethical issues for startups. "You're responsible for upholding the standards *and* worrying about the bottom line," she explains. "You get to wear both those hats."

In the new media era, journalists are forced to deal with issues that, in a traditional news company, were the province of other departments. For example, tech writers and mommybloggers are often sent free products in the hopes that a glowing review on their website will lead to increased sales. If you're likely to be a target for these company giveaways, you need to figure out right from the start how you will deal with such situations. Draw a clear line, let your audience know what it is, and don't cross it.

The stronger the tie between the niche and a marketable opportunity, the better for the publisher. For example, Treehugger is a more powerful niche than ArtsJournal from a business perspective because the market for green products and services is huge. The market for products and services to a national audience of arts aficionados isn't quite as big. As a result, Treehugger has 10 full-time employees and is run by a multi-national corporation. ArtsJournal has one full-time employee and a handful of part-timers, plus dozens of volunteer bloggers, and is the sole enterprise of McLennan. Yet both sites have a dedicated community of readers who find their content indispensable, so don't confuse size with success.

"The Web favors things that are 'narrowly comprehensive,' " says Lisa Williams, founder of Placeblogger, a startup that aggregates hyperlocal news sites. "That is, everything about something. Newspapers, by contrast, are variety shows: something about everything, which I believe is part of the challenge to making them work on the Web. A site with some restaurant reviews is nice; a site with all of them is Yelp."

Williams asks would-be entrepreneurs, "What is it that you can commit to having ALL of?" When Treehugger launched in 2003, the term "green" was synonymous with hippie and was anything but mainstream. Hill, who launched the site as a one-man blog, saw an opportunity to cover all the news of this emerging market.

"I felt that if green was going to go mainstream, and that was the objective of the company, then it really had to become a lot more contemporary and urban and cool," Hill explained in a 2009 interview.[13] "I wanted to make green cool and convenient. We pushed hard so there was content every day—fresh, new, great content. From a global basis, people could really attach to it and step into this modern green future."

Hill, who has a background in product design, says he spent about $2,000 on design for the site and another $2,000 on programming. Then his

Figure 2.9 Treehugger

challenge was to find writers to contribute. He reached out to people through his networks or approached people directly. He eventually assembled a cadre of architects, chemists, biologists and designers, but admits that only a fraction of these were professional journalists. He paid them a certain price per post (starting out at $10 and $15 per post, but now pays them at a much higher rate) plus bonuses based on traffic. The site has had very little turnover.

He asked writers to commit to writing two posts per day, which was difficult in the early to middle part of the decade. Now, though, this goal is much easier to reach. "It illustrates the absolute explosion in green that we've seen," he adds. "Now we've got an editorial staff of around 10 full-time and 50 part-timers and a backlog of material. There's so many green products, services, news stories."[14]

If Treehugger could do great work, Hill was sure word would spread and people would come. He knew that advertisers wouldn't talk to them until the site had at least 500,000 pageviews per month. Before the site reached that tipping point, Hill created mockup ads on the site to show people what this new marketplace could be like.

"My vision is that the ads should be part of the content," Hill says. "You have a certain demographic that you're appealing to, and they're going to like certain brands. If you're looking at a magazine and it's well done, you're looking at the ads because the ads do pertain to you. They're relevant. We wanted cool, green companies. We got a lot of them and it was really great. The ads should be something you *want* to look at, not something you *don't* want to look at."[15]

McLennan would agree, saying, "Most of the advertising we do take, people end up seeing as content and actually seek it out." Overall, ArtsJournal's business model is flexible, with revenue coming from various sources. But when it comes to advertising, McLennan hangs tough: He won't take advertising that isn't related to the content. He feels that you can "pollute it a little bit" with a few unrelated ads, but once you pollute it too much, people will turn away. Most of ArtsJournal's advertisers are repeat customers, a testament to the effectiveness of the brand.

Hyperlocal sites also need a tight focus. A self-contained community with a large selection of local businesses who want to target nearby consumers is a better bet for business success than a community that is spread out, with fewer local businesses. The self-contained community has another advantage as well. In places where it's unclear exactly where one community stops and another starts, the location niche is more difficult to define for both editorial coverage and advertising sales.

West Seattle is a good example of a self-contained community. Separated from downtown Seattle by the West Seattle Bridge, it's easy for the 70,000 people of West Seattle to distinguish themselves from the 2.5 million people who live in the greater Seattle area. When a winter storm knocked out power for much of the community in 2005, West Seattleites had nowhere to turn for specific information. The newspapers and TV stations in Seattle covered the news from a broad, general angle. But all that the people of West Seattle really wanted to know was when their power was coming back on.

Tracy Record had recently begun posting a fairly random collection of notes and information on a new website she named the West Seattle Blog. A 30-year veteran of the local TV news business, she knew how to cover a breaking news event. During and after the storm, she used the blog to post updates on how the storm had affected West Seattle. Thanks to the name, search engines sent people who searched for "West Seattle" to the blog,

Figure 2.10 West Seattle Blog

and soon she had a growing audience. She kept posting news and updates after the fallout from the storm passed, answering reader questions about police activity and other hyperlocal issues. By 2007, local businesses were clamoring to advertise on this blog that everyone was talking about. Record and her husband, Patrick Sand, decided to convert their side project into a full-time business.

The couple runs the ever-growing business out of the house in West Seattle where they have lived since 1991. Their roots in the community were crucial in building relationships that led to both news and ads. Sand handles the ad sales, shoots photographs and occasionally gives Record a break on covering the news. They have a small stable of freelancers who cover events on a pay-per-story basis. The site is filled with community postings, from lost pets to garage sales; much of the news, from house fires to new businesses opening, is generated by tips from readers. Record is also a master at social media, leveraging Twitter and Facebook to engage deeply with her community.

Take away the digital nature of the operation, though, and you have a model that has been around for decades. "If you do this well, it's really like the community newspapers of yore," Record suggests.

Not every community could support a newspaper in the past, and not every community can support a news website today. Many can, however, and these are the markets of varying sizes waiting to be tapped. Once you find an untapped market, you can find success by publishing information that the community needs. The audience that your site draws will be valuable to local businesses that may have no other way, outside of direct mail, to reach this targeted audience.

Success in West Seattle means a projected 11 million pageviews in 2011 and more than $100,000 in annual advertising revenue. The site has about 60 advertisers at any given time and about 60 others that have advertised in the past.

The numbers that define success are different for each enterprise, even among hyperlocal sites. DavidsonNews.net in North Carolina, the Batavian in New York and Hartsville Today in South Carolina are three examples of the dozens of local websites that have carved out a niche and found a level of reporting, publishing and revenue that fits its particular mission. The benchmarks each site uses to measure success are tailored to its specific situation.

If your ideal startup is a local news site, Record says there's one simple secret: Know your community. Some critics of the hyperlocal approach suggest that the average neighborhood doesn't have enough interesting news to grow a significant audience. Record doesn't buy it. "There's so much to tell, even from what little I can do. There's so much that's publicly available, let alone if you have good sources."

Even the advertising potential "seems to be almost limitless," according to Record. Of course, that's possible only when a publisher has created a deep connection with a community, an essential ingredient for any niche information business.

▶ Check out the new app economy

Not every news-related startup involves reporting or blogging. The advent of the iPhone, iPad—and similar devices using the Android operating system—has changed the way millions of people get their news. This new ecosystem has also created opportunities for entrepreneurs to launch new projects quickly and cash in.

In the news category of Apple's App Store, big media brands make up only about half of the apps at the top of the lists for most downloaded and highest grossing. The rest are apps that were developed by startups. (At any rate, this was true in mid-2011; these lists change constantly.)

Apps are especially attractive to news publishers because of the familiar subscription model. A publisher can make the app free to download and then require a monthly subscription before the user can access the content. Or the publisher can charge a nominal one-time fee for the download of the app and make the content—or the service—free. On Apple products, these transactions are all handled in the iTunes Store, which means a clean experience for the user and a convenient way to collect funds for the publisher. It also means a 30 percent cut for Apple.

As you would assume, news publishers that already have great content stand a better chance of making money in the App Store, which is why the *New York Times* and CNN have topped the lists for news apps since their apps were first released. Entrepreneurs, meanwhile, have found success in the news app market by helping users read news from multiple sources. In 2011, Instapaper, Flipboard and Reeder were among the most downloaded apps in the news category for the iPhone and iPad.

These companies exemplify the different paths entrepreneurs can take to the same destination. Instapaper is a one-man company, founded and run by Marco Arment. The product is a minimalist, no-frills app based on a bookmarklet, something users install in a Web browser so they can save

Figure 2.11 Flipboard

long articles to read later. The app version of Instapaper, downloaded to an iPhone or iPad, organizes the links to articles that users have saved for later reading.

Flipboard is an iPad app that takes feeds from a user's social networks, and other news and information websites, and presents them in a compelling magazine-style layout. The company, launched in 2010 to much Web-based fanfare, within a year had raised more than $60 million from top-shelf investors in New York and Silicon Valley.

By contrast, Arment started small. He launched his iPhone app in 2008 with two versions: a free version and a paid version priced at $9.99. He lowered the price to $4.99 the following year. When the iPad launched in 2010, Arment provided only a paid app. Then he started experimenting with the iPhone app by pulling the free version intermittently. Sales of the paid app increased immediately.[16]

"I've made a lot of assumptions in the app market over the last three years that turned out to be wrong," Arment wrote on his blog. "Most frequently, I underestimate demand, both for my product and for others. The only way to figure any of this out is to experiment."

The challenge for entrepreneurs who are seeking to develop apps instead of—or in addition to—websites is the higher technical hurdle to clear.

Whereas anyone with the most basic computer knowledge can launch a Wordpress blog and start to build an audience, it takes much more technical expertise to build a mobile app for the iPhone, iPad or Android operating system. If you're not a technologist by trade, you will likely need a technical cofounder or enough cash to hire an app development company if you plan to enter the new app economy.

▶ Keep going when the passion wanes

Many successful news startups began life as a passion project. From paidContent to the West Seattle Blog, from Treehugger to TechCrunch, each company came into existence by the power of a single person. Whether you are a solopreneur or part of a two- or three-person startup, you will inevitably face a time when the excitement of your new project is challenged by the harsh reality of keeping that project afloat, especially when you have bills to pay and money is scarce.

It's a dilemma every entrepreneur encounters, even someone as successful as Evan Williams. In 1999, he started developing a tool to manage his personal blog. He dubbed the new platform Blogger and released it publicly. It rapidly attracted a large user base, but the company he built it from (Pyra Labs) barely survived the dot-com bust, with Williams remaining the only employee. Williams's perseverance paid off in 2003, when Google made Blogger its first acquisition.

"There were lots of points in 2001 that I seriously considered quitting," recalled Williams, who went on to become cofounder of Twitter. "Everybody I knew just thought I was crazy. And I was getting negative feedback on the Web; people who used to be my friends were posting negative things about me."[17]

Lisa Williams of Placeblogger says that the inevitable ups and downs, the rollercoaster of emotions, is something entrepreneurs should recognize and embrace.

"I almost always enter a period where I'm just not as enchanted by my project (indeed, I don't even want to look at it)," she confesses. "I'm tired and grouchy. I have no ideas, which is a strange and frightening state of affairs for me. Though it's happened many times, I'm always convinced I'll never have another idea again."

She says even her readers notice what Williams calls a seasonal progression: spring's florescence of ideas, summer's bursting into bloom, then harvest, then winter. While it would seem that "startup winter" is something to avoid, she has realized two things: She can't do anything to make it shorter, and she shouldn't even try. In its own way, this lull is vital.

"For one thing, while you were creating your startup, it's very likely that you did not a) pay your parking tickets, b) pay enough attention to your significant other, c) sort through that towering pile of mail you haven't opened, d) picked up your dry cleaning, or e) get your teeth cleaned . . . and on through Z," Williams says.

She recommends taking this down time to do those personal things. And, especially, sleep. And possibly take a short vacation. Startups create the illusion that they cannot survive without you, but you can't get suckered into that. Williams takes a vacation every November, at the conclusion of her busy season. She will go to Montreal with her husband, ignore email, and even occasionally leave her cell phone behind, which "is a little like teleporting to 1993."

Apart from allowing her to maintain her life and relationships, the break provides perspective. She says she always comes back to her work with greater clarity about the right direction.

The emotional connection to a project is important to cultivate. Kirkpatrick says it helps to win small victories most days. "Loving my writing and writing about an incredible period of democratizing technology and potential for goodness helps, too."

Justin Carder, a serial news entrepreneur and hyperlocal blogger, draws energy from his users. "I'm in a constant state of low-level anger, jealousy and fear of looking stupid," Carder says. "But I also really love the audience my work has attracted. Analyzing their behavior and their wants just gets more and more amazing, the more I can grow it and the longer I can make it last."

The answer for Carder is his Google Analytics account, which lets him track specific details about visitors to his site, like when they visit and what they read. He's amazed by having three years of his very own environment to study. "The learning is addictive," he says.

Some entrepreneurs don't need an outside energy source; they're blessed with an unflagging drive to push forward every day. Techdirt founder Mike Masnick, for example, says he hasn't felt the passion ever wane. "There's always something new to be excited about. If the passion is waning, then something's going wrong with the project, and it's time to figure out how to fix it."

While it's easy to get excited about the potential of new projects, it's sobering to realize that many other entrepreneurs are also out there—and just as excited. The challenge for new entrepreneurs is to draw lessons from previous successes and failures, but also to remain focused on their own idea without becoming distracted by all the noise. It's not easy, but even established news entrepreneurs warn others to not spend too much time analyzing the landscape. "The most important thing I tell people is, don't overthink it," says Record, who receives one or two inquiries each week about West Seattle Blog's secret to success. "I meet people at conferences and meetings who have spent months researching business plans and worrying about technology and the design of their site. To me, it's like the Nike slogan: 'Just do it.' But make sure you're setting out to fill a need that actually exists."

?? THINK: In this chapter you've seen various ways to measure a news startup's success. Filling a need is one important measure.

✓ ACT: Of the sites mentioned in this chapter, or others you've seen online, decide which one you think did the best job of filling a need that no one had previously filled. What exactly do you think the site did well, both in defining the need and filling it?

?? THINK: For a prospective entrepreneur, the people who build a blog or a small news website into a company can be a great source of inspiration.

✓ ACT: Pick the founder from this chapter whose role you'd most like to have had. What do you admire about that person and the way he or she does business? Write a description to keep as part of your inspiration file.

?? THINK: For every blog that becomes a big business, untold numbers of blogs are launched and then shut down. Others are published regularly without ever growing to the point where the publisher can make the site a full-time job. Think about what you'll do if your startup doesn't take off, or starts far more slowly than you'd hoped.

✓ ACT: Assess your strengths and weaknesses as an entrepreneur. In other parts of your life, where do you draw your energy? List three characteristics that you think will help you keep going when the passion wanes.

☑ **ACT AGAIN:** Interview someone in any field whose drive and stamina you admire. What attitudes and techniques might you adopt from that person?

?? **THINK:** When Rafat Ali, founder of paidContent, surveyed the media scene, he saw Mashable as a template for the future of online publishing. Look around at the news sites you most admire.

☑ **ACT:** Pick one site that strikes you as having a handle on the future of online news. Rather than just appreciating it as an audience member, analyze it as a businessperson. Where is its revenue coming from? How do the different components of the site work together to establish identity and credibility? What kind of audience interaction can you see on the site?

Notes

1. Dominic Ponsford, "Guardian accounts reveal £4m price tag for PaidContent," *Press Gazette*, Jan. 14, 2010.

2. Philip Meyer, *The Vanishing Newspaper*, University of Missouri Press, Columbia, Mo., 2004, 7.

3. Doctor interview.

4. From the Xconomy About page: http://www.xconomy.com/about/#Ethics

5. Galant interview with Rafat Ali on Venture Voice podcast, July 23, 2008. http://www.venturevoice.com/2008/07/rafat-ali-paidcontent.html

6. Mike Webb, "ProPublica Editor Paul Steiger Discusses Emerging Ethical Questions for Journalists," ProPublica.org, Oct. 21, 2010. http://www.propublica.org/article/propublica-editor-paul-steiger-discusses-emerging-ethical-questions-for-jou

7. Laura McGann, "Josh Marshall on Talking Points Memo's growth over the last decade: Moving from solo blog to news org," Nieman Journalism Lab Web site, Nov. 15, 2010. http://www.niemanlab.org/2010/11/josh-marshall-on-talking-points-memos-growth-over-the-last-decade-moving-from-solo-blog-to-news-org/

8. Fred Vogelstein, "TechCrunch Blogger Michael Arrington Can Generate Buzz . . . and Cash," Wired, June 22, 2007. http://www.wired.com/techbiz/people/magazine/15–07/ff_arrington

9. Vogelstein.

10. Douglas A. McIntyre, "The Twenty-Five Most Valuable Blogs In America," 24/7 Wall St., Nov. 10, 2009. http://247wallst.com/2009/11/10/the-twenty-five-most-valuable-blogs-in-america/

11. McIntyre.

12. Joel and Laurie Kramer, "A breakthrough year for MinnPost," Inside MinnPost, Jan. 24, 2011. http://www.minnpost.com/insideminnpost/2011/01/24/25093/a_breakthrough_year_for_minnpost

13. Greg Galant interview with Graham Hill on Venture Voice podcast, March 23, 2009. http://www.venturevoice.com/2009/03/graham_hill_treehugger.html

14. Galant interview.

15. Galant interview.

16. Marco Arment, "Why Instapaper Free is taking an extended vacation," from his blog marco.org, April 28, 2011. http://www.marco.org/2011/04/28/removed-instapaper-free

17. Livingston, 123.

CHAPTER 3

Make Your Money Plan

"Newspapers are dying."

"You can't make money on the Web."

"Journalism doesn't stand a chance in this new digital world, where content wants to be free."

Those were some of the "truths" that many journalists held to be self-evident when, like so many other newspaper journalists, Mary Vanac and Chris Seper took buyouts and walked out of their newsroom, *The Plain Dealer* in Cleveland, on Dec. 17, 2008.

Unlike many other buyout "victims," Vanac and Seper didn't despair or complain about the new world order. Instead, they took action. They set up shop in the corner of a marketing company the next day and began to build MedCity News, a news site and information service that leveraged their skills and experience. They had very clear goals—to do journalism *and* make money.

Rather than recreate their previous reporting jobs on the medical and business beats, the pair analyzed the media marketplace and thought creatively about the opportunities that were quickly emerging. They could see potential for a new brand of news service, so they set about writing a business plan and pitching it to investors. They knew they'd come face-to-face with finances in a way that they never had in the newsroom, but they figured their reporting skills had prepared them to ask good questions and learn.

The disruption that propelled Seper and Vanac out of the newsroom had overturned the old media order. With all the dramatic changes in technology

Figure 3.1 MedCity News

and people's habits, plus a proliferation of information sources, Seper saw an opportunity: a market that was wide open for "innovative, online, niche news media that meet the needs of targeted high-value audiences."

He and Vanac knew just the niche they wanted to target: health care, one of the country's top three fastest-growing industries. "Given its growing size, its economic significance and its diverse and valuable audience targets, the business of health care represents a natural vertical industry channel ripe for niche news reinvention," Seper states now, sounding like the businessman he's become.

Seper had been a technology reporter and medical editor, Vanac a business reporter specializing in the medical industry. They could easily have fallen into the trap that has ensnared so many entrepreneurs: trying to create the jobs they wanted instead of brainstorming what sort of company would have real growth potential. Instead, their creative thinking led them to discover a new way of doing something different with their particular expertise.

Seper describes MedCity News as a content company that delivers original reporting and custom content for organizations and individuals with a vested interest in health care. He sees the company as a solution—"for media companies and organizations that need content, stakeholders who need actionable information about the medical industry, and advertisers who want to speak to this valuable niche audience."

Vanac and Seper built the company in a way that leverages the emerging forms of online publishing, content production and targeted delivery. Instead of sailing into the wind, you might say that MedCity News has positioned its boat to catch the prevailing gusts. The company built a business model with low fixed costs; a creative, tiered content strategy; and an ability to quickly scale the tiers both geographically and by subject matter. The company, which began in Cleveland, now operates in Minneapolis/St. Paul and the Research Triangle area of North Carolina, as well as in five other cities. Seper expected to clear $500,000 in revenue in 2010, while drawing an audience of more than 100,000 visitors to the MedCity News website.

The diversified revenue model of MedCity News brings in cash in three distinct ways:

- **Syndication**: MedCity News Service operates like a niche version of the Associated Press, producing content on the economics of health care for any publisher to use, either through prenegotiated paid contracts or á la carte syndication deals.

- **Custom content**: Recognizing that in today's media environment everyone is a publisher, MedCity News Custom provides specific, made-to-order content to health care companies and hospitals. Experienced media professionals, who are managed by MedCity News, create this content.

- **Online advertising**: Niche audiences in the professional medical industry pay to advertise on MedCityNews.com.

The story of MedCity News shows the value of journalism skills, entrepreneurial passion and a creative approach to business models in the online world. It shows how motivated, focused entrepreneurs, whose experience is not in business, can learn what they need to know to start a company. Above all, it illustrates the importance of positioning your company correctly so that you stand the best chance to grow your revenue (the amount of money you bring in). More money means more resources, more employees and the ability to pursue more ideas.

Making money is not greed; it is the lifeblood of any company. Without it, you have a hobby, not a business.

For years, most journalists enjoyed the luxury of isolation from this reality. Those days are over. Businesses must make money to survive, even if they are performing a public service or defending democracy.

That means thinking and talking about money. Constantly. The best way to get comfortable with money talk is to learn some business and revenue basics. The faster you start bringing money in the door, the easier it will be to talk about it and think about it.

To that end, this chapter will show you:

- ▶ Different models that news businesses use to make money online.

- ▶ Ways to create revenue through various types of online advertising.

- ▶ Other revenue options you can mix and match.

YES, YOU *CAN* MAKE MONEY ONLINE

Fact: Many, many publishers make money online. Some examples of those who do so are Msnbc.com, the Gawker Media network, Mashable—but the list of online publishers employing journalists and ringing up big-time revenues is too long to include here.

Fact: Many, many journalists who have worked for newspapers, local TV news or magazines firmly believe that it is *not* possible to make money online. I've traveled to journalism conferences in every corner of the United States, and I can tell you this is accepted conventional wisdom. But it's wrong.

News startups big and small have discovered that advertising *can* fund journalism online. Michele McLellan, a fellow at the Reynolds Journalism Institute at the University of Missouri, hosts an annual conference in Chicago called Block by Block. She invited 50 publishers of locally focused news startups to participate and exchange ideas on how to build sustainable businesses. Then in 2011, she surveyed the 50 sites to find out how they were making a living.

Of the companies McLellan surveyed, more than 60 percent relied on some form of advertising for revenues; 25 percent realized 90 percent of their revenues from advertising. Having one source of revenue is a limiting strategy, however, and all of the sites that responded to the survey are looking to diversify their revenue model. A hybrid revenue model mixing multiple sources of income has been successful for a number of startups profiled in this book. Among the revenue sources fueling locally focused news startups are donations, grants, events, business services, merchandise and syndication. (See Fig. 3.2)

How much money are these sites making? Of the 50 sites that McLellan surveyed, fewer than one-third of them (13) achieved profitability (defined as earning more money than they spent) in 2010. About the same number (14) reported making more than $100,000. Ten reported making $80,000–100,000; 10 were making $10,000–80,000; and 10 were making less than $10,000.[1]

One revenue source you won't see in the chart is "pay wall." Many traditional journalists would love to charge for content and force readers to pay directly for the "product." After all, good content is expensive to produce, so it seems reasonable that people should pay for it. Unfortunately, that's not the way things work in the digital age.

"Sure, free news content is not a perfect system, but it's a lot like what Churchill said about democracy: It is the worst form of government except

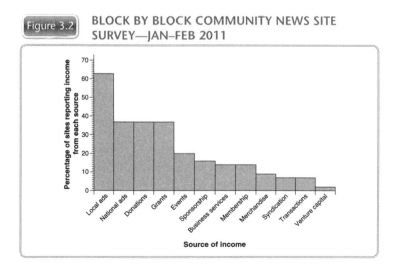

Figure 3.2 **BLOCK BY BLOCK COMMUNITY NEWS SITE SURVEY—JAN–FEB 2011**

all the others that have been tried," Arianna Huffington wrote in 2009. "That's the reality. Free content is not without problems. But it's here to stay, and publishers need to come to terms with that and figure out how to make it work for them."[2]

Huffington is one of many publishers who see multiple ways to make money online—the hybrid business model. In many cases, it comes down to creativity and innovation, a topic Chapter 4 explores. For example, TechDirt.com founder Mike Masnick is monetizing his engaged and highly informed community by turning them into "focus groups for hire," solving problems for companies. (More on this scheme later in the chapter.) Masnick definitely sees the financial glass as half-full instead of half-empty.

The only people complaining about the new world order in publishing, Masnick once wrote, "are those who represent the old way of doing things and don't want to change." These people, he said, "talk up all sorts of horror stories and moral panics about how 'journalism' or 'music' or 'movies' are going to go away—despite the fact that we actually have more of all three of those things happening today than at any time in history. Based on that faulty reasoning, they demand special protection not for 'journalism,' 'music' or 'movies' but for the old business models and old institutions that produced all three."[3]

As you'll see in this chapter, experimentation and a free market are inventing new and viable alternative business models for online publishers. Evolution is messy, though; you won't find a handy switch to flip that transports everyone from old media to new media in a clean and tidy way.

"Eventually, as these new business models and new institutions work themselves out, it'll suddenly seem obvious what the right answers were," Masnick says. "People will forget the hundreds if not thousands of different experiments—both good and bad—that went into developing the new model. It's a time of upheaval, for sure, but there's no indication that there's any real risk to the production of content. Just a few businesses that got big and don't want to change with the times."[4]

▶ Make peace with money

Before we go too much further into "the money chapter," let's face what many journalists see as the elephant in the room: dealing with money. Anyone who has spent time in a newsroom has been conditioned to look the other way when the issue of money arises—unless it's the subject of a news story, of course.

Being involved with corporate financial decisions makes many journalists feel tainted and, in extreme cases, corrupt. Even if their news coverage showed no favoritism to those who could provide financial gain, many journalists preferred living behind "the wall." The separation between the editorial and financial sides of the news business gave them comfort.

The promising startups featured throughout this book didn't need to tear down the wall between business and journalism. They never built one in the first place. Every businessperson must guard against the potential pitfalls and conflicts of interest, but mixing journalism and business in a principled way is not as difficult as some would believe.

Once you get comfortable with the concept of this mix, you need to get comfortable with actually dealing with money. This is easier said than done, for most journalists. Asking for money—whether as a grant or a product sale or an advertising solicitation, is an experience few people enjoy. Fewer still actually excel at "making the ask," which is why top-level sales reps and fundraising executive directors are paid so well.

The easiest path would be to hire one of those trained professionals to handle the asking and selling. That's not an option for most startups that have no money to pay their staff. To get money you'll probably have to rely on yourself or your business partner. So you'd better learn how to do what's needed. "If you can't make the ask, you're in the wrong business," says Rafat Ali, the founder of paidContent.

You're more likely to find people to write content for free than to sell ads for free. Even commission-only salespeople are tough to come by. The challenge of selling will likely be left up to you, the company leader, until the business grows and you can afford to hire sales or fundraising professionals. As a startup founder, you must first feel passionate and committed enough to sell your *idea* to people. Once you've done that, asking people to write you a check is not that big a leap to make.

How do you get comfortable asking for money? Well, you practice. Before the time when your company needs money, join a local nonprofit board. You'll be expected to help with fundraising, but here's the secret: It's much easier to ask for funds when the money you're asking for is not for you. If you're raising money for a local zoo or children's hospital, you can feel good about supporting a cause rather than feeling selfish.

Giving your time to a local board will give you experience dealing with and asking for money. This will free your mind enough to get you comfortable with the concept. It's also a good networking opportunity, as you're likely to meet other entrepreneurs, bankers, attorneys and others who could be good contacts for your business.

▶ Hook into the value chain

A business model is the method by which a company sustains itself—in other words, how a business makes money.

In business school, students learn about the value chain: Each company involved in making a product seeks to add value to that product so it can get paid. Think about a can of beans. One company makes the can, another company grows the beans, and a third company puts the beans in the cans, markets and distributes the product. The last company can charge the most because it's selling the final product. A can of beans is worth more than an empty can, after all.

If you run the company making the can, you could try to move up the value chain and buy your own beans, do your own marketing and distribution, and compete with the final company in our scenario. But that would mean significant added costs. If you're making profits in your current position in the value chain, a better strategy would be to find more customers to buy your empty cans. That would mean sticking with your current business model: buy aluminum at wholesale prices, manufacture cans according to certain specifications, then sell the cans and make a profit.

This is a simple version of a business model. A company produces a good or service and sells it to customers. If the money from sales exceeds the cost of making the product or performing the service, the company makes a profit.

In publishing and broadcasting, the value chain is more complex. Consider radio and local television programming, for example. For much of the last century, programming has been broadcast over the airwaves free to anyone with a receiver. The end customer doesn't pay for the product, yet companies throughout the value chain profit. How can this be?

The broadcaster is part of an intricate network of distributors, content creators, advertisers, advertising agencies and others. A broadcaster can create its own content by paying employees. News, for example, is expensive to produce; a TV station does it to attract a sizable audience that can then be sold to advertisers. The TV station adds value to the airtime by producing news programs. Then it extracts more money from advertisers during that piece of the value chain.

A local broadcaster can also buy syndicated programs and use them to attract viewers. The Oprah Winfrey show, for example, cost stations as much as $100,000 a week to air. The stations gladly paid that fee because they knew Oprah drew a big audience. Even if the stations couldn't sell enough advertising to cover those costs and turn a profit, they wanted Oprah's sizable audience on their TV channel directly in front of the 5:00 evening news. This lead-in was a huge advantage for local news stations, creating better ratings that, in turn, become a significant advantage over competitors when selling advertising.

That's a complex business model, for sure.

Many publishers, especially those with newspaper experience, still believe that charging for news is the only way to fund a sustainable business in the digital age. By 2011, different forms of pay walls had sprung up everywhere and attracted industry press as possible solutions to the revenue challenge for news publishers. Most of these experiments, however, were different versions of the same old thing—likely to produce supplemental revenue but not to have the significant impact on the bottom line that online publishers truly need.

The pay wall idea doesn't work for startups because they lack the established, well-known brand that people will pay for. The first challenge for a news startup is to build an audience. A barrier to entry like a pay wall is more likely to scare away audience than to grow it.

▶ ▶ *Mix and match online business models*
Fortunately, you have plenty of other business models to consider when launching a news startup. You don't have to pick just one; you can mix and match what best fits with your overall mission. And you don't have to try them all at once. Consider a phased approach where you prioritize ideas based on your prediction for success, then roll them out when you are able.

Many experts believe that digital information will not only give rise to new business models but also reinvent and alter some tried-and-true models. Auctions are a perfect example, according to Michael Rappa, a professor at North Carolina State and creator of Managing the Digital Enterprise, a website devoted to the study of management in the digital world.[5] In the same way eBay or Priceline changed how we think of auctions, news startups will find new approaches to age-old practices and some of the stock business models we've grown comfortable with.

According to Rappa, the basic categories of online business models include the following:

- **Brokerage**: Brokers are market-makers. They bring buyers and sellers together and help facilitate a business exchange. Commercial equivalents are Amazon, eBay, or Orbitz.

- **Advertising**: The online advertising model is usually an extension of the traditional media model. The broadcaster or publisher—in this case, a website—provides content (often for free) and services (email, IM, blogs) mixed with advertising messages such as banner ads or text ads.

- **Infomediary**: Information intermediaries collect data about consumers and their consumption habits, then carefully analyze the data to target marketing campaigns. Some firms function as infomediaries assisting buyers and/or sellers in a given market. Edmunds.com is an example of an infomediary.

- **Merchant**: A digital version of the retail business model. Merchants buy goods and resell them at a profit. These merchants can be virtual (Amazon), catalog (Lands' End), click-and-mortar (Barnes & Noble) or "bits brokers" (Apple's iTunes).

- **Manufacturer (Direct)**: This model means a compressed value chain since the manufacturer doubles as the distributor and retailer. Examples are Dell and Nike.

- **Affiliate**: While still technically advertising, this is a pay-for-performance model. A site runs ads for a merchant on its website, but if the affiliate does not generate sales, it represents no cost to the merchant. Variations include banner exchange, pay-per-click and revenue sharing programs.

- **Community**: User loyalty drives the community model. Wikipedia, public broadcasting and open source software consultants are the most famous beneficiaries and examples of this model.

- **Subscription**: Users are charged a periodic (daily, monthly or annual) fee to subscribe to a service. While this model has been around for decades, the Web has given it new life. Think of Netflix, Pandora or eHarmony. Publishers are also able to mix free and paid content easily on the Web, so the *Wall St. Journal* and *Consumer Reports* can offer free content in the hopes of enticing users to subscribe.

- **Mobile applications**: Increasingly, publishers are finding success by packaging their content into convenient apps for use on mobile phones and devices. Often these are free downloads, but this market is evolving quickly and paid apps are growing in popularity. The *Miami Herald* developed an app for Miami Dolphins fans in 2009, which sold 25,000 downloads at $1.99. In 2010, the new Dolphins app was free to download but cost $4.99 for 12 months of access to the information.

The models can be implemented in many different ways. As a publisher, for example, your first instinct may be to combine advertising and a subscription model, which many other publishers have done in the digital world. But the ideal way to plan for revenue, especially in the early stages, is to explore as many options as possible.

▶ ▶ *Subsidize your journalism*

Rappa's list of models applies to news sites as well as to all other websites. When it comes to business models specifically for news startups, New York University professor Jay Rosen prefers to focus on methods of subsidy. "News production has always been subsidized by someone or something," Rosen notes. "Very rarely have users paid directly for the costs of editorial production."[6]

In 2009 Rosen published a list of promising business models, or potential "sources of subsidy," that circulated on the Web and became a rallying cry for news entrepreneurs. Here is a partial sampling of that list; follow the endnote for a link to the rest of the entries.[7]

- **Philanthropy**: Examples of grant-funded journalism are ProPublica, The New Haven Independent and Texas Tribune.

- **Advertisers**: As NYU professor Clay Shirky notes, Best Buy never signed up to fund the Baghdad bureau. It used to be when a company advertised in a national newspaper or on a national news broadcast, it didn't have a choice. Now, in a different way, companies do. They can go directly to consumers and become publishers themselves.

- **Entertainment value**: Entertainment content can generate revenues to subsidize news production, as in the early days of network television, when the news divisions lost money.

- **Features**: Similarly, soft news or features can subsidize hard news, for example successful travel and food sections that help to pay for investigative reporting and breaking news coverage in other areas.

- **Professional information**: Professional services such as research and specialized data can drive a specific form of journalism and be sold as a product to subsidize that journalism. Bloomberg and Thomson Reuters both make big money this way. The *Economist* has an "intelligence unit," which works in a similar way. Another related business would be selling Web services—help setting up a website or using social media tools—to "the people formerly known as the advertisers."

- **Nonprofit funding**: Non-governmental organizations (NGOs) are increasingly likely to sponsor or support journalistic work, often in partnership with traditional news producers.

- **Live events**: Live events can create revenue through admissions charges. Magazines have done this for decades while, more recently, tech sites like GigaOm, paidContent, Mashable and Techcrunch have found success with this model.

- **Lead generation**: Lead generation means providing contact information to businesses about people who are likely to buy—for a fee. A form of sponsorship, leads can be generated through an opt-in scenario during the registration process for a website or contest.

Rappa and Rosen have given us a broad overview of many possible business models for publishers. Now let's take a closer look at some of those models in action and focus on how different publishers make them work.

MAKE MONEY WITH ADVERTISING

Advertising is the most popular business model for content publishers. It's not the only one, but whether it's used alone or mixed with other forms of revenue generation in a hybrid model, most news companies use advertising to pay at least some of the bills.

Call it the "attention economy"—a term I happen to love. Your startup will create content that people will want to read or watch, which means you'll earn their attention. The attention of those content consumers is worth paying for, which is why traditional media (newspapers, TV, radio, magazines) have been powered by advertising for decades.

In the digital age, fragmentation has disrupted the advertising industry. While companies are spending more money on advertising today than at any other time in history, they also have more places to spend their advertising budget. This has created massive competition for publishers but also massive opportunity, especially for publishers whose content finds a niche or target audience that's attractive to advertisers.

John Gruber has found such a niche with Daring Fireball, a website about anything related to Apple and its products and services. Daring Fireball generates $15,000 to $20,000 a month in advertising while serving 2 million page views.[8] Sure, Gruber picked the right market, since an audience that can afford hot consumer products like the iPad and iPhone is probably more desirable for advertisers than the average consumer. But how does Gruber do it?

Daring Fireball has several advertising products and approaches. (This chapter will look more closely at advertising mechanics later in this chapter.) The site is part of an ad network, which means it makes available certain ad positions on its pages to an ad seller, and splits the revenue with the seller. Daring Fireball also sells sponsorships on its RSS feed and has a membership subscription plan.

John Lampard, a blogger and online publisher, looked at Daring Fireball's business model and estimated that "an independent online publisher could make a reasonable, self-supporting income from around 30,000 unique visitors a day."[9] While the number (30,000) is a ballpark figure, the lesson is clear: Build an audience and you will have a chance to turn a profit. You'll probably need a combination of different revenue streams, but once you have the audience, you have a chance.

Advertising, of course, has supported publishing for centuries. It's perfectly logical to pay for a commercial message to appear adjacent to content that is already attracting an audience. A business looking for customers wants its message to appear where the audience goes and will pay for the privilege.

Internet advertising is based on the same business mechanics as traditional offline advertising, with a few significant differences. For starters, online ads are sold in two forms: by impression or by action. (These terms are defined below.) The way online advertising is measured is different, too. With newspapers and magazines, advertisers can know how many copies are sold, but they have no idea how many people actually view a particular ad. Similarly, with television and radio, advertisers can know only the potential audience—how many people *usually* watch or listen to a program. They can't know in advance how many people will actually tune in to the show on which their ad airs, or will actually pay attention to the ad if they do tune in.

It has been famously said (John Wannamaker and Henry Ford are the two people credited with this piece of wisdom) that with traditional advertising, half is effective and half is wasted. You just never know which half.

Online, however, every view of every ad can be tracked with precision. This can be a good thing or a bad thing. If your advertiser wants a lot of clicks, you face a challenge. The average rate of click-through for a banner ad online is about 0.1 percent. One-tenth of 1 percent doesn't sound very impressive, of course, so most online advertising is sold as a brand-building endeavor, much like the billboards on the highway or the side of a city bus. It's about the number of people who see the message, not the number of people who click on the ad.

Online advertising takes many forms, and successful publishers often piece together several ad "products" to offer potential advertisers a number of options. One ad position on a single page isn't usually enough to fund an online publisher. The combination of many ad positions on many pages, from different sources, can be a recipe for success. Many online publishers go overboard and litter their pages with too many ads, which can hinder the chances for any one ad to cut through the noise and reach the audience.

"In year one, focus on early adopters—people who are advertising because they believe in you as much as for an opportunity to reach customers," says Seper of MedCity News. "Then keep asking: Who would *want* to reach my audience? Also, find ways to leverage special packages that go beyond banners. Can you deliver programs that include content, events, widgets, etc.?"

Now knowing that advertising is an important source of revenue for online publishers, you will need to get up to speed on advertising terminology and techniques. The more you know about advertising, the more likely you'll be able to build a sustainable content business.

▶ Learn advertising terms

While you won't have to learn an entirely new language, understanding some frequently used advertising terms will help you make advertising work for your business. Here's a quick look at some of the most important terms. For more advanced terms, download the Internet Advertising Bureau's glossary of interactive advertising terms at www.iab.net.

Creative: In advertising, this is a noun referring to the graphics and words that make up an ad. When a local business asks to place an ad your site, one of your first questions should be: "Do you have some creative?" In other words, "What do you want your ad to look like and include?"

Impression: Each time an ad is displayed online, that's one impression. If you have one ad on the homepage and it is displayed 10 times (usually, when 10 people visit the page), you've given the advertiser 10 ad impressions. Early in any advertising negotiation, a potential advertiser will ask, "How many impressions can you supply in one month?" The more page views your site generates, the more inventory—in the form of ad impressions—you have to sell.

Fulfillment: The process of delivering the ads that a customer has purchased. Fulfillment also includes the billing and reporting, too. An advertiser that pays $100 for 1,000 impressions on your homepage will expect the fulfillment to include an invoice billing the advertiser for $100 and a report of when and where the ads were displayed. Fulfillment can also include processing the payment from an advertiser, either by credit card or check. Figuring out fulfillment as early as possible is an important step in the process.

Display versus classified: A classified ad is mostly text, maybe with an accompanying photo, and runs in a special section that is nothing but other classified ads. Think of craigslist or the section of the newspaper with the ads for jobs, pets and houses for sale. Classified ads are less expensive than display ads and do not need to be creative; they're just a description and a photo of a product or service. A display ad, on the other hand, is usually a larger format, built with creative—which online can include video or interactive features—and runs throughout a publication. Display ads cost more to produce and run because they are mixed within the content areas of the site.

Click-through rate: The rate at which users click on a specific ad. If one out of 100 people who look at a page click on a particular ad, that ad has a click-through rate of 1 percent. The industry average is around 0.1 percent, meaning only one person in 1,000 clicks on the average online ad.

Pay-per-click: An advertising program where a customer pays only when a user clicks on an ad. Google built its massive empire on pay-per-click ads through its AdWords program. (Google's algorithms are really good at delivering contextually relevant ads next to search results.) An advertiser can set a cap on the amount to spend on a given day, week or month to be protected from going over budget. Think of this as a good way to start spreading the word about your new site. Yes, it will be an expense instead of a revenue item, but you can control the amount of money you spend.

CPM: Impressions are usually sold in groups of 1,000, and the rate is referred to as CPM (cost per thousand; M is the Roman numeral for 1,000). If you sell your ads at a $10 CPM and an advertiser has $100 to spend this month, you can deliver 10,000 ad impressions. An "effective CPM" refers to the average of all ads across an entire website. News websites generally charge $3 to $10 for "run of site" ads, or $10 to $20 for targeted ads that are segmented by the content or the demographic of the reader. (Keep in mind that all ad rates are variable and based solely on what the market will bear.)

Remnant: Publishers frequently employ some form of remnant advertising to fill out the available impressions on their websites that haven't been directly sold by their sales staffs. Remnant advertising is less valuable, but at least a publisher makes *some* money with it. (These are the low-quality, often annoying ads you see on websites.)

▶ Leverage advertising networks

An ad network is a collection of publishers sold together as a group by a third party. The ad seller takes a cut of the revenue, then shares the rest with the publishers in the group. Most of the ads you see on websites today are bought, sold and displayed through advertising networks. The basic concept is simple: Bundle together many publishers' sites as one advertising "buy," allowing an advertiser to place an ad on many different sites with one deal.

The two main forms of ad networks are agency-represented networks and what I call self-serve networks. To use an agency-represented network, you work with a company that has built a network by bundling ad impressions on as many websites as possible, and then sells those impressions to advertisers or ad agencies. The network can negotiate better rates and work with bigger advertisers, thanks to the larger scale of its offerings, than if the individual websites were selling their inventory separately. The network is more efficient for the advertiser or agency, too. Instead of dealing with dozens or hundreds of separate websites, they can work with a handful of networks and get their ads placed on just as many sites.

A self-serve network is a model where you, as a publisher, sign up through an online interface, then place a code on your Web pages and watch the ads roll through. Google's Adsense, the most popular form of automatic network, accounts for a significant percentage of all of the advertising on the Web. Individual advertisers or agencies buy ads in the network. When those ads are published and/or clicked on, the advertiser is charged, and Google shares some of that revenue with you, the publisher of the site where the ad appeared and was clicked. (The amount of the revenue share is a closely guarded secret.)

Both forms of ad networks have their advantages. Agency-represented networks are more lucrative, but have a higher barrier to entry. Google's offerings, and competing services like AdBrite, are so easy to implement that you could be up and running in the time it takes to read this chapter. The downside is how little you make, in many cases, from the revenue share. Some publishers are also frustrated by the lack of control: They have no say over which ads are displayed on their site and don't know how much revenue Google is making from their audience. If Google sends you a check for $100 for a particular month, you will wonder how much of a share Google took.

Other forms of self-serve or automated advertising networks include in-text advertising with companies like Kontera, and affiliate programs with companies like Commission Junction. In-text advertising automatically creates a double underline on words in your copy that are contextually relevant to an advertiser. Affiliate programs offer actual products through Web retailers like Amazon and eBay. When one of your site visitors clicks an ad for a product and follows through on the purchase, you receive a small cut of what the user spends.

MedCity News relies on four different networks: GoogleAds, 24/7 Real Media, Health Ad Net and Good Health Media. Like many content based websites, it also does direct sales, meaning the company's own sales reps sell ads. The MedCity lesson is a good one: The ability to make money with online advertising often means taking a diversified approach, even if advertising is only one piece of your diversified revenue pie.

"Keep searching for ideal ad network partners that will bring you higher revenue than GoogleAds," Seper says.

For example, Daring Fireball, the Apple enthusiast site, is part of a private advertising network called The Deck. The sites in this network have sizable audiences in a similar demographic: creative, technical and design-oriented professionals. At one point in 2010, 26 advertisers were paying almost $8,000 per month to advertise across 43 member sites. Even after The Deck takes a cut, that's still a healthy $208,000 to divvy up.[10]

Daring Fireball also claims 400,000 subscriptions to its RSS feed. That's a huge number, especially for such a niche website. This level of interest allows Gruber, the site's publisher, to sell an exclusive weekly sponsorship at $5,000 a slot.[11]

To qualify for the best agency-represented networks, sometimes called boutique ad networks, your site needs to have a sizable and desirable audience. BlogAds, BlogHer, Federated Media and The Deck are examples of boutique ad networks that work with publishers who target a very specific niche or have millions of page views.

By the time your site is ready for a boutique ad network, you'll have the option of handling the sales yourself by hiring additional staff. The question you'll have to answer is whether the extra money you would make by selling your own advertising is worth the effort and hassle of hiring sales reps and managing the process.

If your site has an intensely local focus, direct sales may be unavoidable. The scale of network advertising is more difficult on a local level, but local ad networks were popping up in a few markets, such as Sacramento and Seattle, at the end of 2010. You'll want to engage local businesses and have their presence on your site for the credibility they will bring (in addition to the money).

Selling directly to advertisers means you need to serve and track the ads. Let's look at some of technology options available to publishers who sell ads directly to customers.

▶ Let advertising platforms help you manage inventory

In its most basic form, running an ad on a website means taking the creative and putting it on the specific pages the advertiser paid to have it run on. If you have only a few ads, handling them manually is pretty manageable, but as your site attracts more advertiser traffic, the work piles up. Technology can help, in the form of an ad-serving platform.

Large-scale websites use enterprise-level advertising platforms that cost too much and offer more functions than a startup needs. Fortunately, free, high-quality options exist for serving and tracking ads on your website. It's easy to load the ad onto the platform and tell it how often to run on which pages. You can also see the history of the ads and know how many times they've run and how many people have clicked on them.

Google's AdManager and OpenX are two options for serving and tracking your own ads. Setting up either solution on your website involves a fairly steep learning curve, but remember—they're free. You can also find ample information online that will help you to figure these platforms out.

In 2010, OpenX was serving 350 billion ads a month for 80,000 publishers. OpenX offers hosted packages (which means you don't have to install any software) and downloadable packages for free, as well as an advertising marketplace to help publishers fill their remnant space.

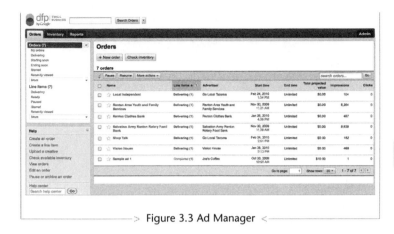

> Figure 3.3 Ad Manager <

MedCity News relies on the free version of OpenX and a WordPress plugin called Ad Manager to serve and track its ad inventory.

Google's Ad Manager became DFP Small Business in 2010, after the company completed its purchase of advertising giant Doubleclick (DFP stands for Doubleclick For Publishers). DFP is a hosted solution, meaning there is nothing to download and install, it manages ad inventory, provides excellent tracking and is integrated with Google's Adsense and Google Analytics. If you choose this for your startup, you need only register an account and copy and paste some code onto your Web pages to get started.

▶ Seek mobile advertising opportunities

If you spend any time on public transit, you know how ubiquitous the mobile device has become. On trains and buses and nearly everywhere else, people have put down their printed newspapers and magazines and picked up their iPhones, BlackBerries, Kindles and iPads.

It follows that advertisers want to capture that audience. As in the early days of the Web in the 1990s, however, that transition is going more slowly than publishers would like. Many advertisers, especially small businesses, find mobile advertising too complex and limiting to justify. Some traditional advertisers are frustrated by the small size of the advertising message on a mobile device, much smaller than in any other format. Of course, that's unavoidable, given the smaller screens involved. (Tablet devices like the iPad are poised to dramatically change this, however.)

HELLO METRO

http://hellometro.com

(1,500 individual city sites like hellochicago, helloboston, etc.)

STARTED: 1999.

FOUNDER: Clark Scott, bachelor's degree in business and master's degree in health care administration.

MISSION: Help the audience get to know a city through news and listings. Encourage community engagement through ratings and reviews posted by more than 4 million daily users.

STAFF: 12 full-time and 25 part-time journalists in the field.

STARTUP CASH: Self-funded.

MEASURE OF SUCCESS: By 2011 had grown to an international network of 1,600 city guides with 5 million unique visitors a month.

TOP BUSINESS TIP: Get a college minor or major in journalism, and work for a newspaper or other publication for at least a year, even if it pays next to nothing. Then you can call yourself a journalist and start your own online or offline publication.

TOP CONTENT TIP: A quality journalist, even at a high cost, is better than free bloggers. With content mills that pay $5 an article or lure people to post blogs for free, quality can be low. There's no way to verify facts and no one to go after if information is wrong or self-serving.

Even so, going mobile has many advantages for advertisers. The growth in smartphone adoption has been meteoric; smartphones began outselling personal computers and laptops in 2010. The mobile device is also the most personal form of digital media: People rarely share their phones with anyone and usually keep them right nearby. Mobile is also synonymous with local, since many devices now have location-based GPS technology and many mobile users rely on their mobile device for localized information.

SCVNGR, Foursquare, Gowalla, Yelp, Urbanspoon and even Facebook have been battling with many other companies in the field of location-based services. This is the holy grail for local advertisers: to reach potential customers at the precise moment when they are looking for your type of product or service *and* are in your neighborhood and ready to buy. If a user is looking for a pizza joint within a mile of where he or she is standing right now, an advertiser would love to dish up an ad, or maybe even a coupon, to that mobile device user at that very moment.

That's the potential power of mobile advertising. According to projections by research firm BIA/Kelsey, U.S. mobile local advertising revenues will increase from $213 million in 2009 to $2.02 billion in 2014.

A number of companies host ad networks for mobile, much like the web-based networks. Because of the complexity of the technology involved, your best bet is to partner with such a company to get a mobile advertising program started. One such company is Where.com, which served more than 1 billion mobile ads per month in 2010, and is growing exponentially.

"The intersection of mobile, location and commerce is widely viewed to be the next revolution for local advertising," said Walt Doyle, CEO of Where Inc.[12]

AdMob (which Google acquired for $750 million in 2009), Third Screen Media (acquired by AOL in 2007) and Apple's iAds were some of the other big players in this rapidly changing space in 2011. They were among dozens of companies eager to help you sell ads on your mobile content. Like other digital ad networks, they will take a cut of the revenues, so it's probably worth your time to do some comparison shopping and talk with other publishers to learn more.

▶ Access affiliate marketing programs

You've seen them all over the Web; those little ads hawking products from Amazon.com or eBay or other online retailers. Did you know that in most cases, those ads are free?

They are free because they are served as part of an affiliate marketing program instead of as traditional advertising. Affiliate programs are done on a cost-per-action basis, rather than the cost-per-impression basis for most advertising online. Cost-per-action means that, as a publisher, you'd agree to place the ads free on your site, then receive payment from the advertiser only when a user clicks the ad and, in many cases, makes a purchase. You'd get a small cut of the money the user spent with the affiliate.

Affiliate marketing has become quite sophisticated. The ads are highly targeted based on the content of a Web page or, in some cases, the Web viewing habits of the user.

You might be wondering why you'd choose to run free ads for a chance at making some money, versus selling that spot for actual, reliable dollars. In most cases, publishers use affiliate-marketing programs as a supplemental revenue stream. They reserve the best placements on their pages for paid advertising, then fill out other spaces with affiliate programs.

Gatehouse, a company that owns hundreds of small community newspapers throughout the East and Midwest, launched an aggressive affiliate marketing program in 2010. Dubbed RadarFrog, it was marketed in dozens of areas where the company publishes newspapers and news websites. The idea was simple: Attract an audience with special deals from dozens of retailers and product brands, then take a share of the revenue every time a user purchased a product or redeemed a coupon.

"We've been pleased with our results thus far. The revenue line that has been strongest is the one that is tied to merchants placing their coupons online for a fee," explains Shannon Dunnigan, CEO of RadarFrog. "The other, more non-traditional lines (commission from online deal purchases and from premium membership fees) that we had planned for haven't met expectations."

Dunnigan says the RadarFrog project has reinforced the company's belief in innovation, which is itself beneficial. Building something new and different has also invigorated the staff. The creation and success of RadarFrog shows how a startup mentality can permeate a corporate news culture. The fact that it is an affiliate marketing program is secondary to the excitement around building something new and innovative. Both are positive for Gatehouse in this case.

EXPLORE ALTERNATIVE REVENUE STREAMS

While advertising remains the predominant way to make money online, you have other options for bringing the dollars in the door. Many online publishers have found mixing some advertising with other revenue-producing initiatives to be their best bet for success.

Figure 3.4 GigaOm

The GigaOm network, for example, mixes at least four different forms of revenue-generation to support its network of technology-related blog sites. Om Malik, a former reporter for *Business 2.0* magazine and others, started with a blog that grew into a company with an ambitious vision to become a one-stop information resource for technology innovators. He hired professional business managers, who in turn hired advertising sales people. As of 2011, the company was publishing five sites under the GigaOm umbrella, employing 25 people and "humming along nicely," according to Malik. Revenue doubled in 2009 and 2010.

GigaOm generates revenue through several channels:

- **Advertising**: The site is part of several ad networks and also has direct sales reps.

- **Pro subscriptions**: For $200 per year, users get access to more than 400 reports on specific technology topics, all created by the staff.

- **Corporate research subscriptions**: Companies can subscribe to an all-you-can-eat plan for GigaOm research.

- **Events**: GigaOm hosts five conferences each year, using its influence to attract top-shelf speakers, who bring in the paying audience. An exhibitor hall features dozens of companies who pay to pitch their wares to this audience, too.

The company wants to grow even faster. In 2010, it secured $2.5 million in its fourth round of venture funding.[13] This hybrid business model, where several revenue sources combine to sustain a company, is a smart but challenging approach. While you can see the logic behind diversification, it can be difficult to get one thing going, let alone several.

Some independent publishers have been even more creative in their business models. A prime example is Techdirt, which publishes news articles and analysis on topics largely outside the traditional world of technology journalism. Techdirt eschews breaking news and rumors of mergers and acquisitions, choosing instead to cover the impact that technology is making on society and business. Its audience is passionate—and active. The readers discuss and argue concepts and trends that are otherwise neglected. The result is a site that exhibits a sophisticated comprehension of the Internet and chronicles the changing landscape for technology and business that goes beyond mainstream technology news sites. The site has succeeded in attracting an audience that is intelligent, critical, loyal, generous and committed to the project.

> Figure 3.5 Techdirt <

Attracting such an audience isn't easy. Monetizing it is even more difficult. Sure, advertising is one option, but founder Mike Masnick decided to pursue a creative revenue stream that would honor the core mission of his site. The community on Techdirt spends a fair amount of time discussing how the concept of free has disrupted business models all over the Internet. It made sense for the Techdirt to experiment with new forms of revenue on a free model.

Masnick developed a seemingly wacky formula that has proven to be genius. The formula is CwF+RtB = $$$, and here's what this equation stands for: Connect with Fans (CwF) and give them a Reason to Buy (RtB). It's not just a slogan, it's a primary link on the website. The idea is to offer readers as many volunteer opportunities as possible without constant nagging. It is a pay-what-you-can, when-you-want model.

The list of items on the CwF+RtB page is eclectic, to say the least. You can pay to put a "Techdirt Insider" badge on your profile, or pay to have Techdirt review your business plan or pay to have Masnick speak at your event

"I still think (CwF+RtB) is a bit short of a full business model, but is getting closer," Masnick says. "Based on our experiences with it, we're getting more and more ideas on how to fund not just journalism, but all sorts of content creation."

One such idea is the Insight Community, which provides an opportunity for individual Techdirt readers to work together on particular problems faced by companies/clients, and for Techdirt's parent company (Floor64) to make some money along the way. Corporate clients like Dell and Oracle sponsor conversations that "pose challenging and relevant questions to the community," according to the InsightCommunity.com site. The companies pay Techdirt for the access to its influential audience, while built-in bonuses for users help drive the quality of the conversation and, hopefully, insights.

Techdirt's innovative model generated $37,000 in one particular month.[14] However it continues to evolve, the creative approach to making money is already paying dividends, both for Techdirt and for other online publishers who will learn from their experiences. Masnick calls his own entrepreneurial experiences an "accidental success story."

Accident? Maybe, but like other entrepreneurial "accidents," it illustrates the importance and power of adaptability in startup companies.

One at a time, let's take a closer look at some of the other popular ways that a news entrepreneur can make money online.

▶ Charge for content, access

Publishers who choose a hybrid business model often attempt to sell content directly to readers or charge for access to portions of their site. As part of a supplemental revenue stream, this can be an effective strategy. As a sole business model, it's mostly unproven.

In the "freemium" model, some content is available for free and some is available at a premium. The ratio of what's free and what costs depends on the content and the target audience. The *Wall Street Journal* and *Consumer Reports* frequently receive praise for their ability to charge for content. When you consider that their content is largely aimed at helping investors make money and consumers save money, you quickly realize these publishers enjoy a different value proposition from most.

Startup publishers pursuing a freemium model must first determine how to produce content that customers would consider valuable enough to pay for. The next step is to determine how *much* a customer would be willing to pay. Here are some ways that companies are charging for content:

- *Consumer Reports* offers overviews and email newsletters for free but charges $26 for an annual subscription to view all of its content.

- *Pittsburgh Post-Gazette* started a premium section in 2009 called PG+. For a few dollars a month, it features bonus content, mostly sports-related for a sports-crazy town.

- ESPN has offered an Insider section of premium content for years. Access costs a few dollars a month and comes with a subscription to *ESPN Magazine* in print. In 2009, ESPN reportedly had 350,000 subscribers to its Insiders service.

- CivilBeat, a Honolulu news startup focusing on public affairs that is the brainchild of eBay founder Pierre Omidyar, has pushed the freemium model from its start in 2010. News coverage and discussions are considered premium content that users must pay $20 per month to access.

An alternative to having a "pay wall" around all premium content is the metered approach. Some newspapers have experimented with this model, in which a certain number of clicks by a single user prompts the pay wall to appear. The *New York Times* launched its metered pay wall in

2011. Lancasteronline.com, the *Lancaster Intelligencer Journal*'s website, experimented with a metered model for its obituaries, allowing readers to view seven notices per month before it asked them to pay up.

Darren Rowse, author of the ProBlogger website, which focuses on helping bloggers make money for their efforts, says that before you can start charging for some of your content, you have to take a hard look at what that content is and what it does. He offers this list of requirements for the content to meet before "a certain percentage" of readers will open their wallets:[15]

- It saves them time

- It's unique; it can't be found elsewhere for free

- It comes from someone they perceive as having expertise

- It's directly useful; it helps audience members in some area of their lives

- It comes from someone to whom they feel loyal

Even if your content meets these expectations, however, Rowse says you'll still face obstacles:

- **Competition**—Information is everywhere. Can your content be unique and exclusive?

- **Critical mass**—You'll need a large readership to find enough paid subscribers.

- **A culture of "free"**—People expect content to be free and may hold it against you if you attempt to charge.

- **Established expectations**—If something that previously was free suddenly carries a price tag, customers may balk.

- **Blocking the link**—The interlinking nature of the Web is a powerful form of distribution and marketing. If some of your content is behind a pay wall, you could hurt its ability to spread to new audiences.

Charging readers of your website is only one way to generate revenue from your content. You can also follow the traditional path of syndicating (selling) your content to other publishers, or follow a new path of creating mobile applications that readers will buy in order to access your content.

Challenges, advantages for women as entrepreneurs

Women own more than 40 percent of the companies in the United States. But less than 5 percent of those companies benefit from venture capital, which remains largely a man's world. (According to *Forbes,* only 10 percent of venture capitalists are women, which definitely influences the climate.)

Whether or not you're seeking venture capital for your business, this data begs the question of what challenges—and advantages—women face in starting a new media news company

First, the advantages: Studies from all corners of the Internet show that women spend more time on social networking sites and shop more on e-commerce sites. Women, in fact, are driving the explosion of digital companies. Using social media to market your startup is critical, and studies have shown that women are more likely to incorporate a sense of community into their business plans.

"Women have a lot of creative ideas and are very good at spotting doable information opportunities," says Jan Schaffer, executive director of J-Lab. Between 2008 and 2011, the New Media Women Entrepreneur program sponsored by J-Lab received 1,579 applications and gave 14 awards of $12,000 each. "There is no question the applications have gotten more sophisticated in recent years," Schaffer said. "Women are applying who have more tech skills and business skills."

Schaffer says New Media Women grants allow entrepreneurs to develop a "proof of concept" that they can then leverage into other support. Even if they don't win, women have told her

▶ **Syndicate your content**

Syndication is one of the oldest business models for publishers, broadcasters and other content creators. It's a simple model, too: You create the content, then set a price that will bring in the most customers, that the application process gives them practice articulating their idea and developing an elevator pitch.

"Still, I think it is hard for women to penetrate the world of nerds and geeks, even if they themselves are programmers and engineers," Schaffer says. "That is true for VC money. It is true for foundation money. And increasingly foundations are enamored of the cool juice coming from places like Facebook and Google, so even proven women-led projects are losing out."

The challenges, outside of pursuing venture capital, may stem from the age of "Mad Men" when women were expected to serve the drinks, not drive the innovation. Much as we'd all like to think that society has transcended such stereotypes, most women can describe business meetings where supposedly open-minded men dismissed their ideas or made it tough for them to speak, even when they were the one who'd set up the meeting.

Nonny de la Peña, who founded a virtual video editing startup called Stroome, says people used to address emails solely to her male co-founder, even after she made it clear they were equal partners. Overall, though, "My experience has been very different, including watching several of my female college pals ending up as high-powered Hollywood executives," she wrote on a PBS blog. "One went from sleeping on my couch and working as a temp secretary to ultimately becoming president of a major cable television network. Whatever the difficulties of that path, the fact that there were others around her on a similar journey had to make it feel less impossible."

then make the transaction. The best deals are recurring. If you are a columnist or cartoonist, for example, you promise to turn out a column or cartoon every week. Your customers then pay a monthly rate, expecting to receive four columns or cartoons every month.

As we have already seen, MedCity News has made syndication a lucrative stream of revenue. Among new media startups, it is not alone. When Julia Scott left the *Los Angeles Daily News* in 2009 to start Bargainbabe. com, syndication quickly became one of the promising revenue streams that would help get her fledgling site off the ground. She pulled together content from her blog posts and created a savvy shopping column, then sold it to print publications.

Scott views this kind of syndication as "an untapped resource." It sounds good on paper to market your content and charge a fee for republication, but she warns that the logistics are time-consuming.

Investigate West is one of a number of investigative journalism startups to launch between 2008 and 2010. While many of these organizations are grant-funded, many also supplement that foundation support by syndicating individual story projects to other news publishers. For example, a newspaper or local TV station might pay a few hundred dollars for a story, photographs and multimedia piece. Ideally, the investigative journalism startup would offer the story on a non-exclusive basis and be able to make additional sales, increasing the total take from a particular story.

"Syndication is very important," said Rita Hibbard, Investigate West's founder. "With a high demand for content, a 24/7 news cycle and depressed budgets, news organizations are less interested in exclusivity than perhaps they were previously. So we make all kinds of distribution deals."

The Rocky Mountain Investigative Network positioned itself as a wire service to entice the *Denver Post* to sign a five-figure syndication deal in 2011. Founder Laura Frank launched the startup in 2009, and landed a $100,000 grant from the Ethics & Excellence in Journalism Foundation in 2010, but included syndication as part of her business plan from Day 1. She described it as a "three-legged stool": Grants and syndication are two legs, training and services are the third.

There have always been freelancers and wire services. Opportunities for new services are emerging, thanks to regional investigative news organizations and other creative new media operations like Spot.us. At their core, though, all of these are still businesses with the same challenges as more traditional operations.

"Finding customers is a big part of what I do," Hibbard says. "It's a lot of work. It's the business part of the job that is a learning curve for any journalist launching an entrepreneurial venture."

▶ Consider apps, software and services

Experience with software, mobile platforms and social media is critical for practicing interactive journalism, and those skills can lead to new business models.

Dozens of successful software companies, many started by former journalists, cater to news organizations. Often, these companies began when an entrepreneur started building something to solve his or her own problem and then realized that others who shared that problem might pay for the solution. Thus, a business was born. Here are some examples:

- **Publish2**: Founded by Scott Karp, a former director for the *Atlantic* magazine website, this service powers social bookmarking for journalists.

- **Apture**: Tristan Harris started Apture, which supplies publishers with in-page search technology, while he was an undergrad studying computer science at Stanford. Connecting with journalists serving Knight fellowships at Stanford helped him launch the company.

- **Outside.In**. This company's platform aggregates hyperlocal blogs by location for publishers, including CNN. It was founded by bestselling author Steven Johnson and its CEO is Mark Josephson, a veteran of new media businesses including About.com. (AOL acquired Outside.In in 2011.)

- **Second Street Media**: Matt Coen once worked on the website of the *St. Louis Post-Dispatch*. Now he helps run Second Street Media, which powers online contests and photo reprint sales for publishers.

These are **B2B business models**, meaning business-to-business (instead of business-to-consumer, or B2C). Syndication, which we discussed earlier, is another B2B business model for journalism. Companies large and small have served the publishing business for decades with products and services. So when you're thinking about where to get the money to fuel your startup, keep your eye out for both publishing models, and B2B opportunities.

In addition to software development, the rise of smartphones and tablet computers has created new opportunities for publishers, especially those whose content is well-positioned for mobile delivery. From a publishers' perspective, the app business model is attractive because mobile consumers are accustomed to paying for apps. True, most news apps remain free, but some news organizations that built truly special apps have had success in charging users. CNN, the *Guardian* newspaper and *Wired* magazine, for example, all reported healthy sales of their mobile apps in 2010.

Whether you charge users to download your app or not, you can also find potential revenue with in-app advertising. As discussed earlier, mobile advertising networks can help you get going.

For most publishers, revenue from mobile app downloads or advertising will be supplemental to their Web revenues, at least in the beginning. As the growth of mobile consumption for news and content starts to outpace the use of PCs and laptops, mobile apps will become more than a supplemental source of revenue for tomorrow's digital publishers.

As exemplified by MedCity's three streams of revenue, startups have long relied on services to augment their revenues. Consulting services are the most popular among startups, especially technology-based companies. Performing side projects for hire, building websites or doing custom development for cash is a good way to keep the rent paid while you're bootstrapping your startup.

Some news publishers are putting a new twist on the services business model. The Sacramento Press, for example, is a news startup that launched in 2008 and regularly assists its advertising customers with their social media plans and execution—for a price. The folks running SacPress have become experts in social media while building their news website from the ground up, so why not cash in on that expertise? It's a good plan that is paying real dividends for SacPress, as almost half the company's revenue in 2010 came from these outside services; the rest came from advertising. (See SacPress chart.)

 SACPRESS CHART

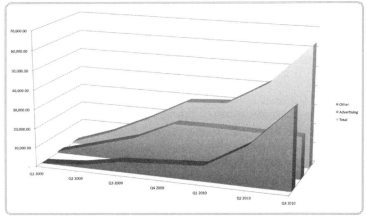

How does it work? Marketing and business development specialists for SacPress guide local and regional businesses in developing new, nontraditional ways to market themselves through outlets such as Facebook, FourSquare, Twitter, YouTube and more. SacPress collects consulting fees for its guidance.

Larger media companies are also tapping into consultancy for additional dollars. Gannett and Hearst, for example, have trained their advertising reps to help clients with search engine optimization, placing ads on big Web players like Google and Yahoo! *and* placing ads on the Gannett and Hearst websites. It's quite a departure from just a few years ago, when sales reps would do everything they could to prevent clients from advertising anywhere else.

What expertise do you have that someone would pay for? While it may not be enough to build an entire business around, it might be enough to provide you with some supplemental income as you grow your startup business. You can find piles of books and plenty of websites to help you make the most of your knowledge and turn it into a consulting business.

Alan Weiss, author of *Million Dollar Consulting,* says the great news about consulting—and also the horrible news—is that the field has no barrier to entry. The key is identifying how you can help someone who has the means to pay for that help.

"A consultant is someone who provides value through specialized expertise, content, behavior, skill or other resources to assist a client in improving the status quo in return for mutually agreed-upon compensation," Weiss writes. "A consultant improves the client's situation."[16]

▶ Host events, sell merchandise

In 2010, The Texas Tribune and the St. Louis Beacon, two nonprofit local-news startups, each cleared more than $200,000 in revenue from hosting sponsored events. Events have grown in popularity for online news organizations in recent years. Without question, they are time-consuming to organize and host. But for news sites that have already established an online audience and have the influence necessary to attract speakers who can draw a crowd, hosting events can be a double winner: An event brings in new revenue and raises the site's profile at the same time.

This business model isn't new, of course; trade magazines have been hosting conferences for decades. *Inc. Magazine,* for example, started its "500 | 5,000" conference in the 1970s as a way for the magazine to honor the 500 fastest growing companies in the United States and allowed its readers to meet and share ideas about how to build their businesses. The magazine's influence helps it attract a credible cast of speakers—most of whom speak for free—and then charge the audience a fee to attend the conference. The magazine also charges sponsors a fee to set up booths in the exhibit hall to pitch their wares, creating another lucrative revenue stream.

Technology websites, such as TechCrunch, paidContent, GigaOm and others, have adopted this business model, holding national conferences and contests that build their brands while bringing in new dollars. Events can be organized on a regional and local level, too.

NewWest, a regional news site covering development, land use and public policy issues for the Rocky Mountain region since 2005, hosts several conferences each year. The goal for the conferences is to foster discussion about changes in the region, but the publisher also makes money. NewWest and another local news startup called The Terminal in Birmingham, Ala., each generated more than 20 percent of revenues from events in 2010.

Spot.us, the crowdfunded journalism project discussed in Chapter 2, started holding events not long after it launched in 2009. "We've had a few, and they are great fundraisers," says founder David Cohn. "But they also require a lot of time."

As Cohn cautioned, it's important to recognize the investment in time that hosting an event will require. You'll have to find a theme, choose and schedule the speakers, rent a venue, buy food and beverages, promote the event and manage the registrations. The money that comes in may or may not be worth the time and expense.

A quality event will help build your brand, so factor that into your cost-benefit equation. In fact, quality should be your original goal—not to make piles of money. It's unlikely you'll host a really profitable event right away. Start with something manageable and build from its success. Eventually, you'll be able to charge more and attract better sponsors, which will help your bottom line.

Whether at a conference or just online, selling merchandise is another supplemental revenue stream to consider. Newspapers have made money for decades by selling reprints of news photographs. In 2006, when I was at The News Tribune in Tacoma, Wash., we sold more than $100,000 of photographs from a tall ships festival through our website. (That was an anomaly, of course.)

In recent years, publishers and broadcasters have become more creative. CNN turns its weird news headlines into T-shirts, which are comic relief for the customer and effective branding for CNN, since the T-shirts all say "I saw it on cnn.com." Fox News has an extensive catalog of hats, coffee mugs, apparel and more for sale on its website. CNBC takes it a step further, with retail stores in several airports throughout the United States.

In creating unique merchandise, consider taking advantage of crowdsourcing. For example, The View From Your Window started as a daily photo feature on the Daily Dish, a popular blog edited by the *Atlantic*'s Andrew Sullivan. Many among the blog's million monthly readers send in pictures of the window they look out of each day—"as a way to capture the reality of actual life in a virtual world." In 2009, the *Atlantic* published 190 of the photos—representing more than 80 countries and all 50 U.S. states and ordered from dawn to dusk—as a softcover book and sold it on its website for more than $30 a copy.

Other examples of crowdsourcing include the efforts of The Poynter Institute, which sold thousands of books that reprinted the front pages of newspapers from around the United States with the headlines from Sept. 12, 2001, the day after the largest terrorist attack in history. And the humor blog Icanhascheezburger.com, the famous purveyor of LOLcats (funny photos of cats with humorous captions), has published several books with the images and captions its audience has created. The blog sells the books in a section on its website called LOLMart, "the one stop meme shop."

If your startup's content or audience lends itself to merchandise, you can find companies to help you get these products made and fulfill the orders, including processing the shipping and credit card transactions. They will take a cut of the proceeds, of course, but these operations are worth outsourcing. You don't have time to figure out how to make T-shirts, let alone process credit cards and ship products to customers.

▶ Go nonprofit—but don't forget to make money

Many would-be entrepreneurs, especially in journalism, mistakenly believe that starting a nonprofit business will relieve them of the pressure of making money. Not so. Any business, whether nonprofit or not, must bring money in to survive. Nonprofits simply go about it differently. The advantages of a nonprofit are the tax exemptions and the ability to accept grants from foundations, while also allowing individuals to make tax-exempt donations.

This is the business model of the most successful news nonprofit, National Public Radio. Its famous pledge drives occurring several times a year raise about one-third of the annual income for its member stations directly from local listeners. Businesses that pay for "sponsorships," which include on-air mentions but are not considered advertising, represent about 20 percent of the revenue. Universities, grants and funding from the Corporation for Public Broadcasting make up another third of NPR's income. (Miscellaneous revenue sources account for the remainder.)[17]

"The good bet from 2005–2010 was nonprofit," says Paul Bass, founder of the New Haven Independent and creator of the Online Journalism Project, which serves as a fiscal agent to other news startups. "There's never been one solution and that's still true. Different models work in different places. For-profits seem to be figuring out some models, though."

The nonprofit model has been a good bet because many forms of traditional journalism, from public affairs reporting to investigative journalism, aren't easily monetized by commercial revenue models such as advertising. This is why many news entrepreneurs go the nonprofit route.

Nonprofit sites focusing on investigative reporting are proliferating throughout the United States, a development that Charles Lewis calls "historically stunning." Lewis, who founded the nonprofit Center for Public Integrity in Washington, D.C., believes we are witnessing the dawn of a new investigative journalism ecosystem in which the most ambitious reporting projects will be conducted by nonprofits, instead of private, commercial outlets.[18]

For example, the Investigative News Network, a consortium of nonprofit watchdog sites, had more than 50 members as of 2011. Each of these startups was individually launched and run on a local level, and each had the challenge of finding enough sources of revenue to keep the lights on.

It sounds enticing to ask a big foundation to write a big check once a year and then spend the rest of your time doing journalism. Too bad it's not that easy. Simply becoming a nonprofit requires you to master the time-consuming rules and policies under which nonprofits operate, or the regulations and bureaucracy of a university if you partner with one. And once you are "official," writing grant proposals and schmoozing potential funders is no less taxing than trying to sell advertising.

Large nonprofit publishers need a grant-writing team, which is comparable to the advertising sales team at a similarly sized for-profit company. For nonprofits, finding funding is a nonstop, year-round process.

Of course, the nonprofit model does have advantages. You can solicit and accept grants and foundation support, plus avoid income taxes. Andy Hall and Brant Houston, coauthors of the "Launching a nonprofit news site" Web module for the Knight Citizens News Network, suggest that you look for a pro bono lawyer to help you navigate the complex issues of starting and running a nonprofit, and maybe to assist with such basics as libel protection or intellectual property.

Hall and Houston also encourage you to seek help from others with experience, since "the nonprofit world is a unique community that often helps others who aspire to join it."[19]

Even after you are legally certified to accept checks, finding someone to write them is a challenge. McLellan suggests nonprofit founders take the time to inventory local foundations and research their issues. "Find connection points—topics they are interested in that you are interested in covering and for which you believe there is an audience need that is not being met," she said. "Find examples of local foundations that are funding similar projects to yours and use that to pitch local foundations."

Whether you are a for-profit or a nonprofit startup, you need to build and grow a network that includes potential community partners and people who have access to wealth. "If you don't have strong and broad community connections, you likely are not going to succeed," McLellan said.

▶ ▶ *Options for running a nonprofit*
Nonprofits have several ways to raise money and several options for structuring:

- **Become a 501(c)(3) entity**. The name is a reference to a section of the federal tax code, this entity is the most common form of nonprofit business. To qualify, you must have a charitable or service-driven mission, and your organization cannot be active politically. (For more information, visit the IRS website).[20] Be warned, though. Acquiring a 501(c)(3) exemption is not an easy or fast process.

- **Partner with a university or college to piggyback on that institution's nonprofit status**. This has become more common in recent years, but requires clearing tall hurdles in the world of academia.

- **Find a fiscal agent for the purpose of obtaining grants**. Going through an agent allows you to accept grant funding without being a 501(c)(3). Look for an organization that shares the same mission.

The goal is to be able to accept funding in the form of grants from foundations and other charitable organizations. The structure you choose will probably not affect your ability to attract those grants. The vision and execution of your plan is what will win you foundation dollars.

Filing to become a 501(c)(3) is the cleanest path to nonprofit funds, but it's tricky. The IRS, of course, is not the easiest organization to work with. To apply, you will need a tax identification number, articles of incorporation, bylaws and a conflict of interest policy and include those as a part of your application. Once you submit all of the required documents, it can take six months—or longer—for the IRS to approve your application.

▶ ▶ *Revenue models for nonprofits*
Accepting grant money as a nonprofit does not legally prevent you from experimenting with and using other business models, including advertising. You may have more trouble attracting grant money if your website is littered with logos and banner ads like a NASCAR entry, but holding nonprofit status does allow for other forms of revenue.

In addition to the ability to accept grants from foundations, not having to pay federal income taxes is the other primary benefit of going nonprofit. If, however, your revenue through advertising or other business models exceeds the expenses it takes to run the business, you will be forced to pay taxes on the difference.

Finding grant opportunities is time-consuming and complicated. Many foundations have strict application deadlines and may make awards only once or twice a year. One place to start is by finding other nonprofit journalism startups online and determining where their money came from. Knight, Ford and McCormick are some of the more prolific funders of journalism projects. New sources seem to be appearing more frequently during this time of upheaval for journalism, so do your homework and search out organizations with money to give.

Once you've identified a potential source of money, you'll need to submit a grant proposal. This can be a lengthy process that requires planning and preparation, so do not delay until the day before the deadline to get started. (Perhaps you know a few journalists who procrastinate until the last possible minute?) Various books and websites, including Non-Profit Guides (npguides.org), will guide you through this arduous process.

Another model that has shown early promise is establishing a "trust," instead of relying on grants. One of the first journalism trusts was established in 2010 when a writer and retired businessman named Bill

Schubart formed the Vermont Journalism Trust to fund operations for a news startup that focused on state political and civic issues. That site, VTDigger.com, came to life in 2009. Like Seper and Vanac in Cleveland, founder Anne Galloway had lost her newspaper job in a round of layoffs (she was with the *Sunday Rutland Herald and Times Argus*) and saw an opportunity to provide the type of coverage that her former employer—and other newspapers in the state—were cutting back on.

Also like Seper and Vanac, Galloway knew from the start that she needed to put money as a priority. "Money is just as important as the journalism," Galloway says, "because without the money there is no journalism." Bass offered his Online Journalism Project's 501(c)3 status to Galloway to help her get going. Having a fiscal agent allowed Galloway to benefit from nonprofit status without having to go through the time-consuming process.

Then she met with Schubart, and a short while later Schubart created the Vermont Journalism Trust to serve as the fundraising engine for VTDigger. The two organizations merged in 2010 and VTDigger received more than $80,000 in the first quarter of 2011 from the trust. The plan calls for the trust to help fund VTDigger for three years. After that, Galloway hopes VTDigger will have built its own pool of sponsors and donors and be able to fund operations independent of the trust.

> Figure 3.7 VTDigger

If traffic and audience can be an indicator of future performance, the early signs are promising. In the first year of publication, VTDigger drew an average of 1,500 unique users to the site. In 2010, that number grew to 14,000 and, early in 2011, the audience had ballooned to 40,000 unique views per month.

▶ ▶ *Be relevant and useful*

Can journalism be pursued with a blind eye toward the market realities of current business models? Not if journalism is to have a future.

When digital entrepreneur Elizabeth Osder visited the University of Southern California in 2009, she spoke frankly to journalism students about this new world. According to a summary posted by *Online Journalism Review,* Osder presented the following recipe for entrepreneurial journalism:

"Start with the impact you want to have. Figure out how what audience you need to assemble to have that impact. And what kind of content is needed to do that. Then price it out: How much money do you need to do it?"

After one student complained that this advice felt too much like business school, Osder defended her approach as bringing a necessary discipline. "It forces you to be relevant and useful versus arrogant and entitled," Osder said.[21]

If you are relevant and useful to an audience, you gain the satisfaction of helping people and fulfilling your mission. You also stand a much better chance of being solvent in your business. Thinking about content—and journalism—goes hand-in-hand with exploring your money-making options. You can't have one without the other.

BUILD YOUR BUSINESS **Stage 3**

When you begin analyzing business models, it helps to think like the consumer you already are. Start there to begin exploring how your startup might bring in revenue.

?? THINK: Do you pay for music downloads or mobile apps, buy items on auction sites like eBay, or use freemium services like Evernote or Dropbox? What are your favorite services that you get for free? What are your favorite services you pay for?

☑ ACT: List your top three favorite paid services and top three favorite free services and note why you think the paid ones are worth your hard-earned money. If these particular free services started charging, would you pay?

?? THINK: Paying for content is often considered the holy grail of business models for publishers. What content do you pay for right now? If you subscribe to a newspaper or magazine, is it because of the content or for some other reason?

✓ ACT: List any content—news, music, movies, etc.—that you pay for on a regular basis. Include for each category the reason you think that the content is worth the price.

3

?? THINK: Look at Michael Rappa's list of online business models on page 76. Which two or three do you think are most promising for a content-based website?

✓ ACT: Write a quick description of how each of the models you selected might work. If you have an idea for a startup, explore how the models could work with the particular audience and content you're envisioning.

?? THINK: What kinds of ads attract you as a consumer? Spend some time looking at the ads on sites you visit regularly. Then look for sites whose content or audience are similar to the one you'd like to start.

✓ ACT: Write a quick analysis of a site whose ad program you admire. What did you like about the content, placement, method of activation of the ads? What ideas would you like to "steal" from this site for your own?

?? THINK: From the advertising information in this chapter, what do you understand and not understand about how you'd get an ad program going, and keep it going, at your company?

✓ ACT: Choose a news site that takes advertising—*not* a site you'll be competing with when you start your own—and find the name of the person who seems to be in charge of selling. Ask for a little of that person's time to answer your questions about how online advertising works. Demonstrate that you're worth this person's time by referring to specific programs and platforms. Make a note of your three big takeaways from this conversation.

?? THINK: Reread the section on supplemental revenue opportunities. What expertise do you have, or will you be gaining as you get your startup off the ground, that you might be able to market as a consulting service?

✓ **ACT:** Check the many websites that help people market consulting services. Design an ad that would let potential users know what your consulting service does. How would you target the audience for this ad?

?? THINK: What nonprofit (.org) sites can you find that you think do a good job fulfilling their mission? Look especially for sites that are doing something similar to what you'd like your own startup to do.

✓ **ACT:** Choose two nonprofit sites and explore where their money comes from. List funding ideas from those sites and any others you've seen that might hold promise for your own startup. What would you need to do to get the money?

Notes

1. Michele McLellan, "In local community news space, advertising rules but it's not the only revenue source," from the News Leadership 3.0 blog on the Knight Digital Media Center site, April 14, 2011. http://www.knightdigitalmediacenter. org/leadership_blog/comments/20110413_in_local_community_news_space_ advertising_rules_but_its_not_the_on/

2. Arianna Huffington, "Journalism 2009: Desperate Metaphors, Desperate Revenue Models, And The Desperate Need For Better Journalism," Dec. 1, 2009. http://www.huffingtonpost.com/arianna-huffington/journalism-2009-desperate_b_374642.html

3. Mike Masnick, "There Are Lots Of Ways To Fund Journalism," Techdirt.com, Nov. 20, 2009. http://techdirt.com/articles/20091118/1552456997.shtml

4. Masnick.

5. Michael Rappa, "Business Models On The Web," Jan. 17, 2010, http:// digitalenterprise.org/models/models.html

6. Jay Rosen, "Quote and Comment," Nov. 14, 2009.
http://jayrosen.tumblr.com/post/243813457/sources-of-subsidy-in-the-production-of-news-a-list

7. Rosen.

8. John Lampard, "An online revenue model for independent content producers," April 12, 2010. http://www.disassociated.com/2010/04/12/an-online-revenue-model-for-independent-content-producers/

9. Lampard.

10. Lampard.

11. http://daringfireball.net/feeds/sponsors/

12. "WHERE Ads Deliver 1 Billion Hyper Local Advertisements in 30 Days and Adds 100th Publisher," company press release, Sept. 21, 2010. http://where.com/site/ where-ads-delivers-1-billion-hyper-local-advertisements-in-30-days-and-adds-100th-publisher/

13. Om Malik, "Okay, We Got More Money," Oct. 22, 2010. http://gigaom. com/2010/10/22/okay-we-got-more-money/

14. Hirsch.

15. Darren Rowse, "Blogs charging for content—can it work?" from the ProBlogger.net blog, March 6, 2007. http://www.problogger.net/archives/2007/03/06/blogs-charging-for-content-can-it-work/

16. Alan Weiss, *Million Dollar Consulting* (New York: McGraw Hill, 2009), 4.

17. NPR, "Public Radio Finances," from its web site. http://www.npr.org/about/aboutnpr/publicradiofinances.html

18. Charles Lewis, "10 rules of the road for nonprofit centers," *IRE Journal,* Spring 2009.

19. Brant Houston and Andy Hall, "Launching a nonprofit news site," from the Knight Citizens News Network website, Sept. 2010. http://www.kcnn.org/launching_nonprofit_news_site/

20. Comprehensive information available at http://www.irs.gov/charities/index.html

21. Geneva Overholser, "Focus on 'what,' not 'where,' in planning your journalism career," *Online Journalism Review,* Oct. 9, 2008. http://www.ojr.org/ojr/people/Geneva/200810/1542/

CHAPTER 4

> **Don't Wait; Innovate**

D avid Boraks moved to Davidson, N.C., in 1993 after taking a job as a tech columnist at the *Charlotte Observer*. He came to the newspaper with an extensive journalism background, having worked as an editor at the *Hartford Courant* among other stops in a career that spanned more than 30 years. He loved news—as a reporter, editor and reader.

In 2006, when Boraks returned to North Carolina after spending a couple of years at *The China News* in Taipei, he noticed that news about his town of Davidson was getting harder to find. The *Observer* had never covered Davidson extensively, and when the paper reduced its overall coverage of the areas surrounding Charlotte, Davidson coverage shrank even more. Boraks recognized an opportunity.

"I found a vacuum in Davidson, and I said, 'Someone needs to do something about this,'" Boraks recalls. "It's a town of only 10,000 people, but I still believed there was a place for what I was thinking."

To help fill the void in local news coverage, Boraks started an email newsletter and sent it out weekly to several dozen people that he knew from the neighborhood where he lived. When the newsletter quickly became popular, he looked for the next step. Through blogging in China, he'd discovered the power of this interactive platform for journalism. He knew it would be easy to try, so he launched a Wordpress blog called DavidsonNews.net in 2006, before many of the now successful hyperlocal news sites had appeared on the scene.

He didn't have a model to follow, just some vague ideas on how to serve the local news needs of his town through an Internet-based publication that would be more hobby than profession. "I thought this was something I'd do as I retired, but the website took off," Boraks says.

Figure 4.1 DavidsonNews

By 2007, his hobby had transformed into a business. Boraks incurred new expenses as he expanded DavidsonNews.net to provide more coverage for the community. As the enterprise grew, managing it became a struggle. He had extensive experience as a writer and editor, but a lot to learn about running a business.

Quickly realizing that new expenses required new revenue, he started selling classified ads and experimenting with a donation model similar to what he'd heard on public radio. In 2007, donations brought in $15,000, which represented 100 percent of his income. Boraks knew he needed to evolve his business model if he wanted to grow his business and publish the kind of news Davidson needed. He wanted paid advertising to support the site and felt that local businesses would be interested because no other outlet met their needs.

He moved the site off Wordpress and implemented a new system for displaying ads using the OpenX platform. In 2008, a former technology sales representative offered to help him sell ads—and quickly sold every ad available on the website. Boraks hired an ad designer and additional writers.

By early 2011, Boraks said the site had about 16 people involved in various paid, but mostly part-time, positions. The business was "more than breaking even," but that didn't include his salary. He chose to reinvest everything he could in the company and was looking for investors to help him expand operations and launch new sites in adjacent communities.

"Journalism is an entrepreneurial venture," Boraks said. "We're not the future, we're the present of local journalism."

Out on his own, with no model to follow, Boraks had hit upon the first rule of entrepreneurship: Don't wait; innovate. Whether you're working from inside a company or starting something new, you will be only as successful as you are creative.

Slowly but surely, traditional media organizations have realized they need to move forward as fast as possible to survive—and hopefully thrive—in a digital age where the rules are still being written. But in this age of disruption, journalism startups have a significant advantage. As smaller, leaner operations, they can change direction quickly. They have less workplace culture to overcome and a greater appetite for new initiatives.

Whether you work for a mainstream news organization or you're planning a journalism startup, innovation will be the engine powering your future. The idea that "anything is possible" is exciting—but if you don't have experience with innovation, it can also feel overwhelming. Here's the secret: Just as you can learn to write a great lede or shoot a compelling photograph, you can learn to innovate. It just takes some background knowledge and then some practice.

Innovation can be taught. It can be learned. It can be practiced and honed. And it can be applied to operations of any size, including an everyday workplace and even a 24/7/365 operation, such as a newsroom.

So let's get going. In this chapter we'll focus on:

- ▶ What innovation means.

- ▶ How innovation is taught and practiced.

- ▶ How you can work creatively when you're working on your own.

- ▶ How to innovate from inside a business.

DON'T WAIT FOR AN EPIPHANY

If innovation were sold at a store, it would be one of the most popular products in business. The fact is, innovation is difficult to define and design and often difficult to divine.

Scott Berkun wrote *The Myths of Innovation* in 2007 to help people understand innovation by recognizing what it is *not*. (An expanded and updated edition of the book was released in 2010.) Assumptions and stereotypes color the concept of innovation, creating an aura of mystery that some people want to think is magical. Others want innovation to be a mechanical process, something tangible that can be reliably repeated when necessary.

Done well, innovation produces something productive and substantive. But it has to be done every day, not just once in a lifetime. Practicing everyday innovation, Berkun argues, is like solving a 1,000-piece jigsaw puzzle. Only when you put the last piece in place does the entire creation become visible. So the last piece becomes the story, the "epiphany"—even though the previous 999 pieces were equally important.

Isaac Newton, for example, didn't discover gravity by getting hit on the head with an apple, even though that's the story that has been passed down through generations. Newton worked for 20 years to explain gravity, but a long, arduous journey of intellectual curiosity isn't as juicy as that falling apple.

"It's entertaining more than truthful, turning the mystery of ideas into something innocent, obvious and comfortable," Berkun wrote. "Instead of hard work, personal risk, and sacrifice, the myth suggests that great ideas come to people who are lucky enough to be in the right place at the right time. The catalyst of the story isn't even a person: it's the sad, nameless, suicidal apple."[1]

Waiting for an epiphany to help you with your business strategy is about as effective as waiting for an apple to bonk you on the head. Instead, you can jump-start the process by studying—and practicing—innovation as you would any other subject.

▶ Elements of innovation

Innovation is invention. It can be inventing a new product like the iPod or a new service like PayPal, or inventing a new way to do something old, as eHarmony does by using a complex computer algorithm to match prospective mates. Either type of innovation requires four essential elements: creativity, risk, hard work and optimism.

Creativity: Inventing something new means envisioning what does not exist. Taking a new approach to an old problem means seeing beyond business as usual. Both require creativity. And encouraging creativity in an individual or an organization means valuing open thinking and flexibility.

Figure 4.2 Wine Library TV

Without creativity, the founders of eHarmony would never have considered using a scientific approach to matchmaking. A clinical psychologist and a research scientist developed the 400-question survey and the matching algorithm that brings people together. In 2010, according to the company, matches that began on the site resulted in more than 200 marriages each day.[2]

Gary Vaynerchuk was thinking creatively when he took over his family's wine distribution business in the late 1990s. At the time, the company brought in about $4 million a year in revenue. To grow the business, Vaynerchuk took to the Web. In 2006 he created a "show" called Wine Library TV, which was simply Vaynerchuk in front of a camera, drinking wine and talking about it. He didn't try to promote his business; he simply shared his knowledge of wine by posting his videos on YouTube. When Twitter and Facebook emerged almost 10 years later, Vaynerchuk jumped on those platforms and continued to build his personal "brand" and, by extension, his business.

He recorded and posted more than 1,000 videos on Wine Library TV before retiring the show in 2011—on subjects as unexpected as what wine to pair with Lucky Charms cereal—that have been viewed millions of times. Vaynerchuk also has some 900,000 followers on Twitter. Vaynerchuk's wine company's annual revenues, meanwhile, topped $60 million.

Vaynerchuk has written two books about his creative business approaches: *Crush It* and *The Thank You Economy*. You'll find both listed in the section on resources for entrepreneurs at the back of this book.

Risk: People and (especially) organizations are hard-wired to resist change. But it's impossible to be innovative by protecting the status quo. By definition, a new idea or new approach means taking a risk; you have no way to know whether you will succeed or fail.

The founders of PayPal were determined to build their business around security of transactions with a PalmPilot or by email. (The company received its first funding when investors "beamed" $4.5 million of funding to one co-founder's PalmPilot in a restaurant.) The founders' initial fear of performing financial services prevented them from seeing the spectacular business opportunity in front of them. Only after recognizing that most users were trying to do transactions on their website, instead of with a PalmPilot, did the company change course and become the preferred method of paying on the Web. (In 2002, eBay purchased PayPal for $1.5 *billion.*)

Risk is part of the business plan for Civil Beat, the civic-affairs news site launched in Honolulu in 2010 by eBay founder Pierre Omidyar. The site is very new media and heavily uses Twitter and Facebook,

Figure 4.3 Civil Beat

blog-style reporting, topic pages, and lots of engagement. It also features a subscription price. In an era where many startup news sites struggle to gain a significant audience, Civil Beat is planning to grow and monetize an audience from scratch.

Omidyar founded eBay in the mid-1990s and made it turn a profit much sooner than most dot-coms. Now he's bringing the same approach to this news experiment. "If it's valuable, they'll pay," Omidyar says. "And if it's not valuable, they won't pay and we'll learn from the fact that they're not paying."[3]

It's a risk that will bring reward, either in the form of a sustainable new business model or the knowledge and experience of why that model didn't work.

Hard work: John Wooden, the legendary UCLA basketball coach, was considered a great leader, not a great innovator. But winning 10 NCAA titles required finding a new way to do something old. His primary innovation might be the Pyramid of Success he developed for his leadership. A cornerstone of the pyramid is Industriousness, which Wooden defines as "Work hard: Worthwhile things only come through hard work."

The founders of Pandora, the popular online radio service, spent almost 10 years developing their technology and business model, originally building kiosks for record stores. The creators of Guitar Hero traveled a similar road, spending almost 15 years working on their concept for an air guitar video game before becoming an "overnight success."

Brad Flora started Windy Citizen, a social news site for Chicago, in 2008 with no funding and no business plan. The site allows users to submit links to news stories from all over Chicago, to comment on them and then vote them up or down.

Fueled by passion and a steady diet of ramen noodles, Flora survived his first year on just $11,000 in income, near the official poverty level. His persistence paid off, though. In 2009 he hired his first advertising sales rep and started to see his business make money. In 2010 he landed a prestigious Knight News Challenge grant to pursue an innovative advertising idea using real-time ads and Twitter.

Optimism: Unless genuine excitement is driving your innovation, it's likely to die on the vine. Passion for improvement is a necessity for creating something new or finding a new way to do something old. Without that passion, the hard work and risk of innovation will be difficult—probably impossible—to sustain.

> Figure 4.4 Metropolis <

Wooden built this idea, too, into his Pyramid of Success. The other cornerstone, in addition to Industriousness, is Enthusiasm: "Work without joy is drudgery."

Tom Ferrick spent more than 30 years working as a reporter and columnist for *The Philadelphia Inquirer*. He lost his job in a round of layoffs in 2008, but wasn't ready to give up on journalism for the Philadelphia area. Deciding the time had come to "stop worrying about the future of local journalism and start creating it," he applied for several grants to launch his own site. He didn't win any of them.

"It's a story of failure, mostly, but I can't help that," Ferrick told a group at the 2010 Online News Association conference in Washington, D.C. Lacking grants, he figured, "I failed with Pew, I failed with others; I think it's time I failed on my own."

Using $13,000 from his retirement savings and pension, he launched Metropolis in 2009. Because the site stresses commentary and investigations rather than coverage of breaking news, he envisions it not as a daily experience but as a place readers will visit a few times a week. As a writer, he felt he should pay all his writers, an idea that he acknowledged "has fallen out of favor these days."

Ferrick is committed to carrying out his vision, his way. Like the other entrepreneurs in this book, he has the optimism and enthusiasm to make his project possible. In 2010 he received support from the Public Media Lab, an organization devoted to bringing the best in news and information to the Web, and the William Penn Foundation.

▶ Have creativity, will innovate

All problems are opportunities. The bigger the problem, the bigger the opportunity. That was the headline from a presentation by Tina Seelig at the Stanford Entrepreneurial Leadership Lecture Series. It comes from Vinod Khosla, one of the co-founders of Sun Microsystems, who became a general partner of the venture capital firm Kleiner, Perkins, Caufield & Byers in 1986.

"No one will pay you to solve a non-problem," Khosla says in a video that Seelig shows to her classes. When it comes to mainstream journalism and the news business, it would be hard to find anyone who doesn't believe the industry has a problem. And there are plenty of people who would pay you to solve it.

Seelig, the executive director of the Stanford Technology Ventures Program, teaches a course on creativity and innovation. To help students become comfortable with solving problems, she starts with small problems and then gradually assigns the class bigger and bigger problems so that by the end of the course, the students are ready to tackle anything.

Students in Seelig's course tackle mind-bending exercises to spur creative thinking for entrepreneurial strategies. In one, she divided a class into teams and gave them $5 "seed money" and two hours to make as much money as possible. One team made more than $200 pumping up bike tires—and didn't even win the contest. Other classes were given paper clips, and the outcomes were amazing.[4]

"We frame problems way too tightly," Seelig said in the lecture. The news industry certainly has done so, continuing to frame its economic problems so tightly that conversations that started in the 1990s, about deep linking and charging for content, continue today.

Instead, think about problems in new ways—"If we keep unpacking them and unpacking them," as Seelig says,—"we realize we have resources that are more valuable than we ever imagined."

Creativity leads to innovation that solves real problems. In a 2010 survey conducted by IBM, 1,500 CEOs from 60 countries and 33 industries rated creativity as the most important skill for effective leadership.

Tony Schwartz, a CEO who blogs for *Harvard Business Review,* urges CEOs to use their own creativity to encourage innovation throughout the company. That means giving employees the freedom to find their own paths. "Define what success looks like and hold people accountable to specific metrics, but as much as possible, let them design their days as they see fit to achieve those outcomes," he wrote in a 2010 post titled "Six Secrets to Creating a Culture of Innovation."

Two of Schwartz's tips for CEOs are good advice for entrepreneurs as well: Nurture your passion and make the work matter.[5] The last point—that a compelling mission keeps people motivated—is what can help startups achieve higher levels of creativity than bigger companies. The people who founded the company or work there believe deeply in the mission, so they're inspired to do whatever it takes. (Remember Mike Orren's description of his "pirate ship" crew with Pegasus News in Chapter 1?)

▶ How innovation is taught

Business schools have been teaching entrepreneurial philosophies and practices for decades, preaching the virtues of creative innovation and market adaptation. Recently, journalism and communications schools have taken up the topic, hiring professors with news and entrepreneurial experience to teach courses on starting new companies or new business units within companies.

Going from journalist to entrepreneur requires a change in the way you think. As Shutterfly CEO Jeff Housenbold told students at the Entrepreneurial Thought Leader series at Stanford, entrepreneurship is a state of mind, one that can be practiced and cultivated in the largest corporations and the smallest companies.

"How do you create things that people haven't envisioned before?" Housenbold asked.[6] "How do you aggregate the resources, motivate people and execute against that vision? Entrepreneurship is really about creating new products, new markets, new ideas and new businesses to capture some of the economic benefit from the vision and the hard work."

From USC to Syracuse, from Columbia to Missouri, entrepreneurial journalism has become a focus for college journalism programs. At Arizona

State it is a required course for all journalism students. At the City University of New York (CUNY), students work on real journalism startups and the faculty have published business models, complete with spreadsheets, for news startups.

In addition to the basics of starting a business—market research, competitive analysis, and plans for product, revenue and distribution— CUNY courses push students to be innovative. "Why does the world need this thing?" Jeff Jarvis asks about each startup idea. Students have to decide who the customers for their business would be, then do some reporting and talk to those customers. "The better their reporting, the stronger their businesses," Jarvis says. "I've had many students change or even abandon their plans after learning from the market."

At Northwestern University's Medill School of Journalism, innovation-focused classes are organized as team projects. This enables all students to contribute and taps into the strengths of different class members. "It's very helpful if the enrollment can be as interdisciplinary as possible," says Rich Gordon, director of digital innovation and associate professor at the school. "It's great if there are computer science students or marketing students along with those from the journalism school."

Gordon tries to frame an interesting problem or challenge for the class. Some real examples from past semesters include:

> Figure 4.5 Northwestern <

- When would journalism delivered based on your physical location be better or more compelling?

- How can we enable better conversations and interactions around local news?

- What kind of print/Web news product would appeal to teenagers in a small metro area in Iowa?

- To what extent can news coverage in a suburban community be provided by the citizens themselves?

Students research the topic area, collecting available information and conducting original research, from one-on-one interviews to formal surveys. The goal is to learn as much about the target audience as possible. Then it's time to brainstorm ideas, develop mockups and prototypes and test them with potential users. This process is very similar to what you might find at a Silicon Valley technology startup.

"Typically students are required to address not just the content and design/functionality of their innovation, but also the potential business model(s)," Gordon explains. "I find that making journalism students think about the business side ensures that their idea has real-world possibilities."

Gordon requires students to summarize their ideas in written and presentation formats; the act of writing a report or organizing a presentation focuses the work. "Often, I like to have the class maintain a blog about their project as they work on it," Gordon says. "This helps keep them focused on the project and requires them every so often to reflect on an interesting development or reach some tentative conclusions." The process is fairly structured, which is intentional. By giving the students a structured approach to innovation, Gordon hopes to give them tools that they can use again in the future.

At Arizona State, students have developed iPhone apps and new websites for news coverage, working through the New Media Innovation Lab and the Knight Center for Digital Media Entrepreneurship. "We're looking to build more cool digital multimedia products," notes Christopher Callahan, dean of Arizona State University's Walter Cronkite School of Journalism and Mass Communication. "Traditionally, journalism schools have not been built like this. Journalism schools have lagged behind the tech industry."[7]

MARKETWATCH

www.marketwatch.com

STARTED: 1997

FOUNDER: Larry Kramer, previously a reporter and editor at *San Francisco Examiner* and *Washington Post*.

MISSION: Provide real-time financial data to investors, combined with the latest news and analysis.

STAFF: More than 100.

STARTUP CASH: $500,000 from friends and family.

WROTE A BUSINESS PLAN?: Yes

MEASURE OF SUCCESS: More than 4 million monthly unique visitors. Acquired by Dow Jones for more than $500 million in 2004.

TOP BUSINESS TIP: What's happening today is as big as the invention of the printing press. The biggest problem is companies trying to protect their business models, not their products.

TOP CONTENT TIP: You need to be in the free universe to be searched, to be all the things that cause you to grow and gain stature in the world today.

STARTING SMALL, OR STARTING ALONE

Large organizations have trouble with innovation. The considerable inertia created by multiple layers of management often makes it difficult for new ideas to emerge. Even managers who know they need to "think outside the box" often run into barriers to creativity. Between too many meetings and too much email, it's all they can do to get the basics done each day. Big organizations often can't seem to get out of their own way.

If you're fortunate enough to find yourself on the outside of a large organization, either working independently or for someone else's startup, you have a distinct advantage: the freedom to experiment and quickly launch new ideas. Of course, you probably have fewer resources to *execute* those new ideas, but that's the tradeoff. When you're small and nimble, it's easier to do little experiments to see what works.

▶ Make innovation a strategy

To become a news entrepreneur, you'll need to learn how to practice active innovation on your own, and then how to foster and promote innovation among the people you eventually hire. Both types of innovation require a culture, strategy and infrastructure.

Culture: Usually people apply the word *culture* only to organizations. But looking at your own habits through an organizational lens can help you see whether you're allowing yourself the freedom to innovate. If it will take **creativity, risk, hard work and optimism** to be innovative, how do you make it happen?

- **Make it a priority:** The momentum of any organization serves to protect the status quo. Carly Fiorina, the former CEO of Hewlett-Packard, says it's incumbent on leaders of an organization to drive change. "Collaboration produces change, but leaders drive change," she states.[8] On an individual level, change happens when you set goals outside your personal comfort zones. Challenge yourself to do something you've never done before, if only to give yourself the confidence that comes with it.

- **Make failure acceptable:** Telling yourself or your organization to take risks is one step, but making failure acceptable means putting your money where your mouth is. Change that leads to progress cannot occur without failure. Nowhere is this concept more apparent than in Silicon Valley, home of the leading technology advancements from the digital age. Craig Newmark, founder of craigslist, recognized this in July 2009 on a trip to the UK. "I was struck by the repeated comment that failure is stigmatized in UK business culture. In Silicon Valley, failure is just a normal phase of one's career. You might succeed in your first endeavor, but probably not, so you're ready to persist in subsequent efforts.

"Widespread innovation and success requires the acceptance of failure, and then a readiness to move on," Newmark added.[9]

Or as Winston Churchill said: "Success consists of going from failure to failure without loss of enthusiasm." This is true for both organizations and individuals. If you want to start a news business, you'd better get comfortable with the idea that things won't always go perfectly.

Strategy: Simply wanting innovation won't make it happen. Setting goals and tracking progress are important tools, for an organization or an individual.

- **Set goals:** Technology companies like Microsoft and Google have goals for the number of patents they will file during a given time period. The more specific the goal, the better. But the engineers and managers at these companies know that innovation usually blossoms in unexpected places, so placing too fine a focus on goals can be limiting. Goals should be "ideas to be tested," not inflexible solutions. Pursuing an idea sounds less daunting than finding a solution.

- **Be Agile:** Agile is a popular project management method in the software development world.[10] The core values that make Agile a successful way to manage IT and software projects can be applied to any innovation assignment, since the outcomes of both are uncertain:

  - Individuals and interactions over processes and tools.

  - Working software over comprehensive documentation.

  - Customer collaboration over contract negotiation.

  - Responding to change over following a plan.

Valuing the first item in each pair over the second will help your innovation project avoid the "vacuum" effect that occurs when new ideas are fully developed by an individual or committee without ever being tested by outside "customers."

Infrastructure: Even an individual can benefit from a system for communication, and from project management tools to keep any innovation project moving in the right direction.

- **Communication:** If only we would just talk to one another! Simple, honest, direct communication is critical to innovation. Unfortunately this is a fundamental weakness for most people and, according to Malcolm Gladwell's book *Outliers,* has actually led to thousands of deaths in the airline and healthcare industries. Be sure that your team allows any member, regardless of rank or position, the ability to speak openly and directly to anyone else. And as an individual, be sure that you have advisers or colleagues who will give you unfiltered feedback on your innovation ideas.

- **Tools:** Project management and collaboration software will make it easy to track any innovation project and will alleviate many of the communication problems just mentioned. See Chapter 7 on harnessing technology to discover free services from Google and Zoho or popular paid services like Basecamp and Backpack. These tools will make you, or you and your team, more efficient and more accountable.

- **Accountability:** People and organizations who believe innovation happens by epiphany don't tend to hold themselves accountable. After all, you can't control when lightning will strike next. You can avoid this trap by setting what experts in project management call SMART goals: Specific, Measurable, Attainable, Realistic and Timely. Then devise a system that will track progress and hold people—or just yourself—accountable. If you're striking out on your own, you'll essentially be acting as your own supervisor, so you don't let yourself give up on your goals too easily.

▶ See innovation as a product

In business today, innovation has to be a product that is produced with the same commitment as any other core product the company offers. In the digital age, also known as "the era of creative destruction," change is a constant, and every kind of business—including big news companies and small startups—must become more nimble.

"The pace of change is just so fast that the only thing you can be sure of is your business has to look different tomorrow than how it looks today or you're going to be in a whole boatload of trouble," Scott Anthony, author of *The Silver Lining,* told *Business Week.*

Anthony acknowledges the difficulty of predicting the future. "You simply cannot gather enough data that tells you what the right answer is because data, of course, is backward- looking."[11]

Companies must free themselves of needing to know that an idea will work before pursuing it. Traditional newsrooms have had an even steeper hurdle

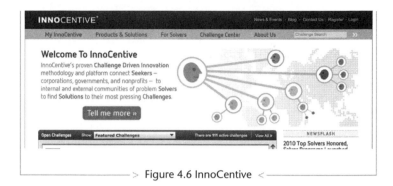

> Figure 4.6 InnoCentive <

in this regard because for many years newsroom culture demanded that an idea be proven in another market before it could even be considered.

InnoCentive CEO Dwayne Spradlin puts it this way: "Culture eats strategy for lunch." So no matter what great ideas you have or can collect from staff, if you or your company can't commit to innovation, then those ideas will mostly be dead on arrival.

"Most organizations don't think about structure and how it impacts innovation," Spradlin suggests. "And now that we're in a more open, innovative world, where organizations can invite in customers, users, employees they don't easily reach today—anybody in the world—to work on their innovation problems, it completely smashes the paradigm as we know it today."[12]

Spradlin should know. His company, InnoCentive, is an amazing example of "open innovation," where the largest companies in the world bring their research and development problems in engineering, computer science, math, sciences and business, and open them up for anyone to solve. Cash awards motivate outsiders to provide the best solutions.

What if news innovation included a contest where anyone and everyone could enter? Every community is stocked with smart people, from college professors to engineers to art directors. A news company could create a contest with an award that would motivate these outsiders to work on the company's problems. The public could also be tapped to vote on or rank the ideas, providing even more brainpower to the process. Many news organizations have already tried something similar with open-source reporting projects, by collecting public views on how to balance the city budget or solve another local problem. Asking the public for help on bigger issues such as what kinds of reporting the organization should be doing would be a more positive step for these news organizations.

▶▶ *Stop planning and start doing*

Brainstorming new ideas is easy. Changing corporate culture and launching successful new projects are difficult.

Most companies—and especially most newsrooms—have the added disadvantage of being staffed by people who are more interested in planning than progress, especially at the managerial level. Scott Porad, the chief technology officer at the Seattle-based company behind a network of humor websites like FailBlog.org and icanhascheezburger?, says that even in a startup, it takes work to cultivate and maintain a startup culture.

"Over an eight-year period, my last startup grew from a startup into a corporate environment with several hundred employees and layers of management," Porad wrote on his blog. "For the last five or six years of that, I felt like we spent 80 percent of our time planning and only 20 percent of our time doing stuff. To me, this was very frustrating. I enjoy just doing stuff, and I felt like all my time was spent discussing/debating/arguing with others about what we should be doing, instead of just doing stuff to see what worked. A lot of the time it felt like we were just paralyzed in planning . . . literally gridlock."[13]

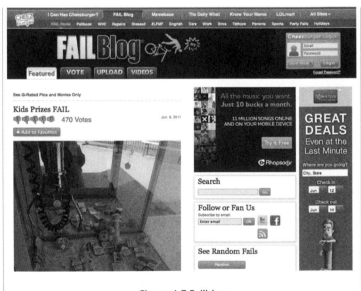

Figure 4.7 Failblog

Anyone who works for a news organization (or any large corporation, for that matter) can weave tales of woe around all the planning, brainstorming, off-site retreats and other groupthinks that led nowhere. But isn't it ironic that news companies, given a breaking news event, quickly break out of "paralysis by analysis" and move at breakneck speed to cover the news, print extra copies and provide bonus coverage on the air or online?

Porad estimates that his current startup spends 5 percent of its time planning and 95 percent doing. "I think the most important difference is that we have a very clear vision of what we want to do," Porad says. "This allows us to make decisions about what to work on, quickly and easily. I always thought my old company was paralyzed because there wasn't a very clear vision or plan or strategy. We couldn't just do stuff because nobody could even agree on the general direction that the stuff should be headed.

"But there were other reasons too: The company had a culture that was risk-averse and punished failure. Success was the only option."

▶ ▶ *Practice Innovation*
InnoCentive is proof that contests can spur innovation. Competition can be the key to innovation inside a company or among total strangers.

Individuals can learn to be innovative with practice. Reasonable people give up their free time to participate in different innovation events all over the United States like Startup Weekend, which brings together people with technology, business, legal and marketing backgrounds to build a company in three days. Business students compete in the worldwide Entrepreneurship Week contests that started at Stanford, where students are given something random (Post-It Notes, rubber bands, etc.) and compete to create the most value from the random object. Some states and cities also have innovation meetups, like Mass Innovation Nights in Massachusetts.

Search your local events calendars and look for opportunities to practice innovation. Once people get a feel for actually participating in innovation events, they are able to expand the scope of what innovation can do. This is a concept Christian Terwiesch and Karl T. Ulrich, professors at The Wharton School of Business, write about in their book *Innovation Tournaments: Creating and Selecting Exceptional Opportunities*.

Innovation isn't always about new technology or new products, the authors argue. It is a new match between a need and a solution, or taking an existing solution and applying it to a previously unrecognized problem.

INNOVATING FROM THE INSIDE: BE AN "INTRAPRENEUR"

You don't have to be a one-person show or work for a small startup to be an entrepreneur. Innovation is happening in the largest news companies today, as all news organizations adapt to the rapidly shifting media landscape. Some have found success weaving best practices from software and tech companies into their corporate structures.

An *intrapreneur* is someone who makes innovation happen inside a large organization. Whether it happens in a large or small organization, innovation still comes down to developing new ideas for new products or solving existing problems in new ways. Google and its "20 percent time" is one of the most famous examples. Employees are expected to spend 20 percent of their work time developing new ideas that may or may not be related to their other projects.

Google's goal is to get smart people working on ideas that interest them. Sometimes the ideas mature into products that Google adopts and develops for the marketplace. (Google News is an example of a "20 percent" project.) But company leaders know that even when ideas don't turn into products, the company benefits because employees grow and become energized by working on their own ideas.

Many companies—not just news companies—need more intrapreneur-ship these days. Guy Kawasaki offers several ways to foster the spirit of intrapreneurship from within a company in his book *Reality Check*. Here are my favorite Kawasaki methods:

- **Kill the cash cows**. The purpose of cash cows is to "fund new calves." Kawasaki, who started his career at Apple, points out that Apple killed the Apple II, then asks where the company would be today if it had protected that product.

- **Reboot your brain.** If everything you learn and do inside a big company is wrong for "intrapreneuring," then take a page from George Costanza of *Seinfeld* fame and "do everything the opposite."

- **Stay under the radar.** Repeating the age-old advice to "seek forgiveness, not permission," Kawasaki recommends keeping a low profile on your brainstorms until upper management asks for new ideas. Then try to make them think your ideas are really theirs.

When I was running the website for *The News Tribune* in Tacoma, we talked about new ideas as "pilot projects," which really helped lower the barrier for support from the managers and acceptance by staff. A pilot project sounds like a trial that is temporary, and that makes the innovation easier to support.

Don't be fooled by Kawasaki: He is directly suggesting you rock the boat. "Trust me, you will get in trouble . . . This is because the higher you go in most organizations, the thinner the air, and the thinner the air, the more difficult it is to support intelligent life."

All kidding aside, the intrapreneur's dilemma is obvious. Those who rock the boat are seen as troublemakers. When the idea works, no one remembers whose idea it was, but everyone remembers who made the trouble.

So be aware of the risks, and then realize that the rewards are worth it. By innovating, you will help your company grow, evolve and adapt. On a personal level, you'll overcome challenges and grow. The fulfillment you'll feel from seeing a new idea through to implementation at an established organization—despite all the culture that tried to kill it—will make the trouble all worthwhile.

▶ Innovation does happen at big news companies

Lack of innovation by big news companies has had a variety of negative impacts, as we saw in Chapter 1. Now some of those companies have learned the hard lessons and are trying to change. Adapting to the changing needs of digital audiences has forced news executives and managers to place more emphasis on flexible work cultures and an environment that supports experimentation, research and development. While these traits have been native to other businesses for decades, they are relatively new in news companies.

The *New York Times,* Gannett and Hearst are three of the more innovative news companies operating in the United States. The *Times* launched a Research and Development group in 2006 to explore innovative ways that people might consume news in two to 10 years. The group experiments with e-readers, tablet computers, electronic paper and other futuristic technology that may—or may not—change the way people consume the news.

Hearst Magazines opened an "App Lab" at its New York headquarters in late 2010. The lab serves as a think tank and headquarters for consumer focus groups. Eventually, the space will be opened up to consumers as a showcase for Hearst's iPhone, iPad and tablet "products."

> Figure 4.8 MomsLikeMe <

Gannett, meanwhile, created a group called Innovation & Design in 2007 that leads innovation projects across multiple divisions. The owner of 82 local daily newspapers and 23 local television stations, Gannett empowers its local affiliates to experiment and serve as R&D test centers. The company also works with Innosight, a consultancy created by Clayton Christensen, author of *The Innovator's Dilemma*, and IDEO, a famous global design firm.

One of the first innovations that Gannett is famous for (in the media industry) is the Information Center concept, which launched in 2006. The company blew up the traditional newsroom structure and replaced it with a multimedia, constant-publishing approach aimed at providing more local info, more databases and more interactivity. Gannett has launched external innovations, too, such as MomsLikeMe, the network of niche community websites for mothers.

Finding the right ideas for innovation is a challenge. A significant part of any innovation effort at Gannett are "questions on how people are living their lives and how we can keep a razor focus on their evolving needs," according to Jennifer Carroll, Vice President. "With Moms, we worked with local sites in Cincinnati and Indianapolis to carefully test concepts and talk to moms on what they want and need. We launched based on extensive personal feedback and testing in these two sites, learned much and began expanding throughout the company."

Measuring success is critical for a big company attempting innovation. But it's not easy. Carroll says Gannett continues to learn, especially from companies such as Innosight and IDEO, that markets that don't yet exist can't be measured and analyzed. "In other words, we can quickly kill an emerging idea or business by applying metrics used for the core business and/or forecasting metrics based on unrealistic expectations. By starting small, we can fail quickly, recover and build."

In Innosight language, Carroll says, innovation wins through simplicity, convenience, accessibility or affordability. "We don't have to be best; we have to target jobs that consumers need done. And we try to keep it simple; complexity can suffocate as we try to research and iterate on new experiments."

As Thomas Edison famously said, "I have not failed. I've just found 10,000 ways that won't work."

▶ Bring startup culture to your newsroom

It can be difficult to stop planning and start doing, especially if you are an "intrapreneur." One method to explore is the "demos, not memos" philosophy. Matt Waite credits this mantra for the success of Politifact, an interactive project that he and Bill Adair developed at the *St. Petersburg Times* to fact check the presidential campaign. After PolitiFact won the Pulitzer Prize for its 2008 election coverage, it then expanded to fact

> Figure 4.9 PolitiFact

checking Congress and the White House. But in the beginning, just getting anyone to pay attention to this innovative idea was a challenge.

Adair and Waite were both reporters, so they approached their new idea as they would a story project, writing pitch memos and asking for meetings to talk about the memos. The reactions were positive but ho-hum—the kind of reactions that meant, "We like it, but we don't get it," according to Waite. So the two decided just to go ahead and design what the site might look like. They didn't waste more time writing *about* their idea; instead, they spent that time *developing* it.

They built the first iteration on a computer server that was on its last legs, headed for the recycling bin. The mockup was crude—"ugly as homemade sin," according to Waite—but its impact was instantaneous.

"We took that functional demo to the same people who got the pitch memo, and it was a completely different experience," Waite says. "They lit up, they were far more engaged, they started forgetting about the 'should we do this' and started focusing on 'how will this work, and how will that work.' It completely changed the dynamic. And we walked out of those meetings and said, 'Wow, demos really matter.'"

Launching demos instead of writing memos doesn't guarantee success, but it does allow you to see much more quickly whether an idea has legs. "Sometimes just trying to build it reveals what a giant hairy ball of pain your idea is going to be," Waite wrote on his blog. He can list more than a dozen demos that went nowhere, but he still believes each project was worth the time. "You won't learn that from a memo. In a memo, everything is easy. Which is why demos matter."[14]

Waite created the first file for PolitiFact on May 24, 2007, and the site went live on Aug. 17. That's a really fast turnaround—especially at a newspaper company—but Waite says that the site could have been done even faster if he had as much programming experience then as he does now.

Regardless, that pace is possible only when you stop planning and start doing.

News organizations haven't been able to transform from a perfectionist, command-and-control culture into a free-thinking startup-like culture, though some have tried through programs like The Learning Newsroom. Many news editors and managers wish for a more nimble, action-oriented workplace. If you have some say over how your newsroom operates, here's how to take a few small steps in the right direction.

- **Divide and conquer:** Pick two or three small teams and give them decision-making authority. In other words, allow them to launch anything the whole team agrees is worth trying. But pick the right people. Remember, certain types of people prefer planning to progress. They're not the people you want on these teams.

- **We report, you decide:** Use the weekly or monthly meetings that normally serve to seek clearance on new projects as a progress update. So instead of saying, "We'd like your blessing to try this new approach," your message would be "We decided to try this new approach, and this is what we've seen so far."

- **Don't let money stop you:** If it's a service that costs money, don't waste time traveling up the chain of command to get approval. Ask the vendor for a free trial (good service providers will be flexible, especially in this climate). If what you want is an online technology, look for an open-source solution or a free demo period, or find another news organization that will share some code.

Holding a companywide competition is another way to inspire all staff members to think like innovators. And that means the entire company. Newsrooms should open up any innovation contest to all departments in the company, and even consider inviting ideas from the public (as in the InnoCentive model).

Here are some guidelines to follow to maximize results and minimize costs of an innovation contest within a company:

- Make participation mandatory.
- Pick a slow time of year.
- Assemble small, diverse teams.
- Keep it loose, make it fun.
- Reward the best ideas.

It takes commitment to make innovation a priority in large organization. It's important to make that commitment.

▶ New news jobs—and more of them

Did you go to journalism school to become an online community and social media manager? Probably not, but that's one of the hottest jobs on the market these days; you can't launch a successful digital news business without it.

The era of specialization is dead, but a new class of jobs and roles at new-era news businesses offer exciting opportunities for journalists and communicators who are interested in new thinking and new approaches.

In terms of jobs, journalistic occupations are outperforming the overall economy, according to Michael Mandel, former chief economist at *BusinessWeek* and founder of Visible Economy LLC. That certainly seems counterintuitive to anyone who has heard about, or directly experienced, layoffs at newspapers and TV stations in recent years. But a shift in journalistic employment to nontraditional companies such as Yahoo! and AOL, plus an increase in self-employed journalists, has created surprising growth.

Drawing from numbers based on the Current Population Survey, a monthly survey of roughly 60,000 households conducted by the Bureau of Labor Statistics and the Census Bureau, Mandel found the overall number of employed journalists increased by 19 percent from 2007 to 2010.[15]

Over a comparable time period, Mandel notes, employment in newspaper publishing has fallen 26 percent; periodical employment is down 16 percent; and radio and television broadcasting is down 11 percent. So journalists are getting jobs—just not as often in the traditional industries or at the companies you would expect.

And those traditional news companies that *are* hiring? They aren't looking for the same old thing any longer. A spirit of innovation is mandatory; lots of experience is not. If you are willing to learn new ways of communicating to—and with—an audience, including inventing some ways of your own, you're ready for a job in a new era news business.

Luddites need not apply. New skills can be learned, and people who have shown a previous proclivity toward trying new types of digital communication will separate themselves from the pack.

Here's an excerpt from a July 2010 job posting on the Tribune Co. website:

> The TV revolution is upon us—and the new Tribune Company is leading the resistance. We're recruiting a solid team of anti-establishment producer/editors, "preditors," to collaborate on a groundbreaking morning news/infotainment format unlike anything ever attempted on local TV. Don't sell us on your solid newsroom experience. We don't care. Or your exclusive, breaking news coverage. We'll pass. Or your excellence at writing readable copy for plastic anchorpeople. Not interested.

Sell us on this:

—Your personal relationship with the internet, blogs, video-sharing, iPads, Droids, Blackberries, Blueteeth, Facebook & Twitter, and all things Modern Culture

—You're in sync with the pulse of the streets, not the PC, Capital "J" journalism world

It's a new era, whether you're looking for work in journalism at a traditional company, ready to explore the emerging world of journalism outside newspapers and TV stations, or heading out to go into business for yourself. The career path is no longer well defined. In addition to new skills, you will need a new adaptability to find your way. Just know that, if you have an open mind and an innovative spirit, the possibilities are out there.

BUILD YOUR BUSINESS **Stage 4**

Innovation happens because an individual or an organization is willing to try lots of ideas. The more ideas you generate, the more you can try and the faster you'll find one or two that actually work.

To get going, individuals and organizations must adapt to a world where change is constant. Welcome to the new normal, where you must expect tomorrow to bring different challenges than today. As Fiorina, the former CEO of Hewlett Packard, told a group of graduate students at Stanford, if you apply Darwin's theory of evolution to innovation and leadership, you understand that it's not necessarily the strongest or the smartest that survive. It's the organism (or individual or organization) that can adapt the best.[16]

Because innovation is so important, here's an extra helping of questions to try:

?? THINK: What was the time in your life when you felt most creative? What did creativity feel like? What did it lead you to do? What factors do you think combined to make this a period of innovation for you?

✓ ACT: Fill in the blank: I can be creative when _____.

?? THINK: Reflect on the way you work. What does your "inner critic" say and do—and in what situations does that critic kick in—that stops you from thinking creatively? What hurdles do you set up for yourself?

☑️ **ACT:** Take a cue from Guy Kawasaki and reboot your brain. Pick a day and tackle each task in ways you've never tried before. Start with something as simple as driving or walking along a different route, then move on to harder stuff. Write some notes about what happens and what you notice.

❓❓ **THINK:** Who are the two most talented, creative people you know? If they're creative in areas you know nothing about, so much the better.

☑️ **ACT:** Ask them how creativity comes to them. Regardless of whether they have a news background or dance the tango, ask them for their wildest ideas about a news product they would like to see created. Express no skepticism about anything they say; just keep asking for more.

❓❓ **THINK:** What resources do you have, either within your company or on your own, that might help create a startup culture?

☑️ **ACT:** Decide who are the most creative people in your company, and how you might tap into their ideas.

❓❓ **THINK:** Taking your cue from DavidsonNews.net and PolitiFact: Is there some part of your idea that could be up and running—right now?

☑️ **ACT:** Once you've defined that segment for immediate implementation, decide how you would present it. Even at this early stage, how could you start moving from memo to demo? Make a rough sketch of what your presentation might look like. Don't worry if it is—as Matt Waite of PolitiFact said—"ugly as homemade sin." Show it to a few people and see if they grasp your basic idea.

The goal here is to get going, regardless of circumstances. Ryan Thornburg, a professor at the University of North Carolina who previously worked at *U.S. News* and the *Washington Post*, argues that innovation isn't enough. He urges newsrooms to get past the idea of "innovation" and adopt a more defined experimentation approach. He even offers a "failure form" that can be used by reporters and editors who want to pursue a crazy idea.[17] While crazy ideas may not save the news industry from continued job cuts, they are an important first step toward a culture of innovation.

Notes

1. Scott Berkun, *The Myths of Innovation* (Cambridge, MA: O'Reilly, 2007).
2. eHarmony About page: http://www.eharmony.com/about/eharmony

3. Ben Markus, "Online News Service is eBay Founder's Next Bid," NPR.org, April 22, 2010. http://www.npr.org/templates/story/story.php?storyId=126183424

4. Tina Seelig, "The Art of Teaching Entrepreneurship and Innovation," Entrepreneurial Thought Leader Lecture, May 27, 2009. http://ecorner.stanford.edu/authorMaterialInfo.html?mid=2219

5. Tony Schwartz, "Six Secrets to Creating a Culture of Innovation," *The Harvard Business Review*, Aug. 10, 2010. http://blogs.hbr.org/cs/2010/08/six_invisible_secrets_to_a_cul.html

6. Jeff Housenbold, "Entrepreneurship that clicks," April 2008. http://ecorner.stanford.edu/authorMaterialInfo.html?author=288

7. Emily Gersema, "ASU Cronkite School focuses on innovation, entrepreneurship," azcentral.com, Aug. 17, 2010. http://www.azcentral.com/community/phoenix/articles/2010/08/17/20100817asu-cronkite-school-journalism-innovation.html

8. Carly Fiorina, "The Difference Between Management and Leadership," Entrepreneurial Thought Leader Series, Stanford Technology Ventures Program, May 2007. http://ecorner.stanford.edu/authorMaterialInfo.html?mid=1718

9. Craig Newmark, "The acceptance of failure as a spur to innovation ," July 14, 2009. http://www.cnewmark.com/2009/07/the-acceptance-of-failure-as-a-spur-to-innovation.html

10. Kent Beck, et al., "Manifesto for Agile Software Development: http://agilemanifesto.org/"

11. Scott Anthony, "Transformative Innovation: Why Change Is Good," June 15, 2009. http://www.businessweek.com/mediacenter/podcasts/innovation/innovation_06_03_09.htm

12. Dwayne Spradlin, "Building an Innovation Culture: Thinking about internal innovation," June 10, 2009. http://www.businessweek.com/mediacenter/podcasts/innovation/innovation_06_10_09.htm

13. Mark Briggs, "How to bring startup culture into the newsroom," June 10, 2009. www.journalism20.com/blog/2009/06/10/how-to-bring-a-startup-culture-into-the-newsroom/

14. Waite.

15. Michael Mandel, "The Evolution of The Journalism Job Market: We May Be Headed Into A Golden Age," republished on The Wire, Aug. 3, 2010. http://www.businessinsider.com/the-evolution-of-the-journalism-job-market-2010–8

16. Fiorina.

17. Ryan Thornburg, "The One Tool Your Newsroom Needs Right Now: A Failure Form," June 10, 2009. http://www.ryanthornburg.org/blog/2009/06/10/the-one-tool-your-newsroom-needs-right-now-a-failure-form/

CHAPTER 5

Turn Your Idea into a Business

After working at Court TV, Fox News and CNN, Jessica Mayberry knew about news and knew about video. As she watched the citizen journalism revolution take hold, it troubled her that in so many places around the world—places where important stories happened and people needed to know about them—citizen journalists lacked the training and equipment to start reporting on their communities. In 2003 Mayberry founded Video Volunteers, a nonprofit with a mission to empower people to do digital storytelling in poor, rural areas of developing countries.

"With the advent of citizen journalism and changing viewing habits thanks to the Internet, the world is hungry to see content they've never seen before," Mayberry explained. In the far-flung places where the mainstream media rarely go, she wanted to give local residents the tools and experience they needed to tell their own stories.

Mayberry definitely had the passion, but at first she had no way to know whether her idea would work. Inspiring tales of entrepreneurial adventures often begin this way: with an unproven idea. But the idea alone is never enough. Ideas become sustainable only when they are transformed into a product or a business—and that's a constant process of development, marketing and improvement.

Video Volunteers aimed to democratize the media—not just finding and training video journalists, but helping them learn to support themselves. "Going into this project, one of our concerns was whether we would be able to find people who were entrepreneurial, and who would want to run their own video business," Mayberry wrote. "The reality is that other jobs are less satisfying, but they can guarantee work. We had our doubts about

Figure 5.1 Video Volunteers

whether entrepreneurship could be taught, so we needed to find that drive in our fellows/producers."[1]

Mayberry won a 2008 Knight News Challenge grant and traveled to Brazil in 2009 to find people with entrepreneurial promise and help them start their own video businesses. In 2010, Video Volunteers launched IndiaUnheard, a network of community correspondents. "Our producers are in places that the mainstream media cannot or does not access, so this is a window into the real India,"[2] she says.

The business model for Video Volunteers is complicated and evolving. More traditional journalism models—where you publish news, attract an audience and sell advertising—are daunting enough, yet they seem simple compared to Mayberry's concept. She wants nothing less than to change the world, to build a more democratic and sustainable global media landscape. As lofty as her goal sounds, she is steadfastly convinced that her idea will work.

What makes a good idea? No two entrepreneurs will answer in the same way because no two share the same passions. But here's a test: When you think about your idea, do you feel a rush of excitement? The energy created by a great idea is the fuel that drives entrepreneurs. Developing an idea takes patience, persistence and a lot more time than you ever imagined. You're going to need the fuel generated by passion to keep you from getting discouraged as the process unfolds.

Mayberry knows that simple truth on several levels, both for herself and for the people she trains. "Business skills are easy to teach, but personal drive or motivation is another thing," she adds. "Not everyone is an entrepreneur." As her projects have developed, she's been excited to see the new community correspondents gaining in skills and confidence. "All are committed to a career in video," she describes the newly empowered journalists. "All are committed to developing their own creativity, and to working for their communities."[3]

Make no mistake; starting a business is hard work. It takes courage, persistence and dedication. Though he was speaking in 1910 in Paris, Theodore Roosevelt might have been issuing a rallying cry for 21st-century entrepreneurs:

> It is not the critic who counts, not the man who points out how the strong man stumbles, or where the doer of deeds could have done them better. The credit belongs to the man who is actually in the arena, whose face is marred by dust and sweat and blood; who strives valiantly, who errs, who comes short again and again, because there is no effort without error and shortcoming; but who does actually strive to do the deeds; who knows great enthusiasms, the great devotions; who spends himself in a worthy cause; who at the best knows in the end the triumph of high achievement, and who at the worst, if he fails, at least fails while daring greatly, so that his place shall never be with those cold and timid souls who neither know victory nor defeat."[4]

That's rousing stuff! Congratulations on having the daring to get this far. The hard truth is that not every idea deserves to go further. In this chapter, you will learn the difference between an idea and a product or business. Since the goal is for you to take your good ideas and make something out of them, you will also learn how to:

- ▶ Listen to potential customers—but not too much.

- ▶ Evaluate possible revenue sources.

- ▶ Size up the market and find your place in it.

- ▶ Draft your plan of attack.

DO YOU HAVE AN IDEA OR A BUSINESS?

Where do ideas come from? Often they come from one person who has discovered an unmet need in his or her own life, a need closely aligned with that person's interests or talents. You may think the world needs an SUV that runs on vegetable oil, but if you're a journalist, you probably don't have the expertise to design one. Instead, you're more qualified to start a blog or a website focusing on cars and green energy.

Steven Berlin Johnson, author of *Where Good Ideas Come From,* says great ideas rarely rain down from the sky, magically landing on a random person—a process rather like a winning lottery ticket. Instead, he says, the network in your brain connects bits and pieces from different areas to make something new; most new ideas are actually pieces of existing ideas cobbled together. The first connection happens in one person's brain, and then is improved as that person bounces the idea off other people.

Great innovators and entrepreneurs, Johnson found, are constantly tinkering and exploring; their appetites and temperament help them tap into their own ideas. They're also comfortable with what Johnson calls "the slow hunch," the long incubation period that many ideas require.

"A lot of great ideas linger on for a long time, sometimes decades, in the backs of people's minds," Johnson says.[5] They have a feeling there's an interesting problem, but they don't yet have the tools to fully recognize or figure out what to do about it.

Scott Berkun, author of *The Myths of Innovation,* agrees that ideas are made from other ideas. Often, he suggests, they come to us when we least expect them—say, in the shower. Why? Because your conscious mind is quieted when you're in the shower, or on a walk or mowing the lawn. Then your subconscious mind awakens, and ideas emerge.

"But part of the mythology around ideas and showers is somehow a truly great idea will, on its own, make you rich and change the world—a fantasy I can promise has never happened," Berkun elaborates. "Ideas are easy to find once you understand the basics of how they work. But it's always what you do with your ideas after you get them that matters."

Take a cue from the great innovators and learn to tease out the ideas lurking in dark corners of your mind. Depending on how your particular brain works, sit with a blank sheet of paper or a blank computer screen and start brainstorming words that capture your idea. Or sketch rough mockups of what your idea might look like. This is how you'll force your idea through an essential first filter—and that is your own intuition. Your head and your gut will work together and tell you whether your idea passes the first "sniff test."

If your idea has real potential, this brainstorming process will feel easy, maybe even fun. It will get your creativity flowing and you'll get excited as additional ideas start popping into your mind. If your idea wilts when it hits the real-world air outside your brain, you'll soon feel that.

This is the first step in the process of discovering whether your idea is worth pursuing and, more important, whether it has the potential to become a business. Make no mistake; *process* is the operative word. Ideas do not develop themselves; they need a lot of help to become reality.

▶ Ideas are cheap; execution is everything

Here's a reality check: Ideas are everywhere, and most of them really are a dime a dozen. It doesn't take a Thomas Edison to come up with an idea for a new product or service. People from all walks of life have ideas about a new product, a new business (often a restaurant) or a way to improve an existing one. Since most people are not entrepreneurs, most of these ideas live a short life.

It's the execution that determines the true value of an idea. "I think the key quality is determination," says Paul Graham, a serial entrepreneur who helps other entrepreneurs though the startup incubator Y Combinator. "The founders who do the best are the type of people who just refuse to fail. Most startups have at least one low point where any reasonable person would give up. That bottleneck is the reason there are so few successful startups. The only people who get through it are the ones who have an unreasonable aversion to failing."[6]

Developing a great idea into a successful business is like pushing a boulder up a hill. The best entrepreneurs—those who successfully reach the top—get to watch the boulder roll down the other side. That's the fun part, when momentum makes the business go faster than you can control. At that point, the daily challenge becomes dealing with growth: hiring new employees, filling customer orders, answering interview requests from the media.

You should be so lucky. Right now all you've got is that boulder at the bottom of that steep hill. You can't even see the top or know how far you'll have to push. Congratulations!

"The world is a very malleable place," says Netscape founder and Silicon Valley legend Marc Andreessen. "If you know what you want, and you go for it with maximum energy and drive and passion, the world will often reconfigure itself around you much more quickly and easily than you would think."[7]

▶ Solve a problem or cure some pain

"Solve your own problem" is a common theme among entrepreneurs. Personally experiencing the "pain" or the problem creates a unique passion that will drive you as nothing else can. Unfortunately, unless others—hopefully many others—share your pain, your idea will not become a product or service.

At the outset, you need to understand the distinction between an idea that is merely interesting and an idea that will create a business. Investors talk about looking to invest in "painkillers"—not "vitamins." One pill is nice to have; the other is something people *must* have.

Hotmail, Blogger, Yahoo! and craigslist are all examples of successful companies that were started by individuals solving their own problems. Hotmail's founders were building a Web-based personal database that they called JavaSoft, when they grew frustrated that their employer's firewall prevented them from accessing their personal email accounts. Sabeer Bhatia and Jack Smith thought they should be able to use their email from anywhere, so they came up with the idea for Hotmail, a service that allowed users to anonymously access email from any computer connected to the Internet. Just a year later, in 1997, Microsoft acquired Hotmail for $400 million.[8]

Figure 5.2 Hotmail

"Let me tell you one other thing about the Internet: There are thousands of such ideas under our noses even as we speak," Bhatia told Jessica Livingston for *Founders at Work*. "In our case, we had a need. That's what triggered the idea. Sometimes ideas are born out of necessity: you solve a problem for yourself, and hopefully solve it for a number of other people, too."[9]

Starting a company from scratch is hard. To stay motivated, you must truly believe in what you're doing. It easier to do that if you're creating something that solves your own problems.

▶ Don't keep it secret; socialize your idea

Some entrepreneurs keep quiet about their great business ideas for fear that someone will steal them. But remember: It's not the idea that counts; it's the execution.

"The most brilliant idea, with no execution, is worth $20," says Derek Sivers, who founded CD Baby to help his musician friends sell their music. The company grew to become the largest seller of independent music on the Web, with over $100 million in sales for over 150,000 musician clients. Sivers sold the company for $22 million in 2008—and not, he admitted, because of the idea. "The most brilliant idea takes great execution to be worth $20 million. That's why I don't want to hear people's ideas. I'm not interested until I see their execution."[10]

Figure 5.3 CD Baby

This doesn't mean you should call up the competition and show them your business plan. Be smart with whom you share your ideas—but definitely share them. Ask questions and really listen to what you're told. Obviously, you'll want to talk with people who know the product or business you're trying to start, the people with domain expertise. If you're planning to publish news online, find people who know about online news publishing; if you're envisioning a locally focused site, find people who know that community.

Having a business plan, or at least an executive summary, will give you something specific to share and details to discuss. (We will look at how to do this later in the chapter.) Don't spend too much time trying to write the perfect plan, though. Bhatia wrote the business plan for Hotmail with one all-nighter. (Seeing how tired he was the next day, his boss assumed he had been partying and sent him home to rest until after lunch.)

"Make sure you write a business plan because it will crystallize your thoughts to communicate your ideas to someone else," Bhatia says. "Make sure that once you have written your business plan, you have someone else read it and critique and ask questions."[11]

In addition to bouncing your idea off people with some expertise, look for others who don't know much about how your industry works but could potentially be part of your target audience. You'll spend more time talking to these folks later, as your product develops, but it's a good idea to get their input early. The main benefit of talking to nonexperts is that you'll be forced to explain your idea without industry buzzwords. This will help you simplify the concept to its most basic core principles, which will help you stay focused as you get going. If you can't explain the idea clearly and concisely to your spouse or sister or brother, simplify it and try again.

This process is called "socializing your idea." It's extremely helpful for an entrepreneur who is excited and passionate about a new idea to test it with other people. Your ability to quickly explain the idea and gauge the reaction and enthusiasm from other people will tell you whether you have a product or business or just a neat idea.

IDEA OR PRODUCT? MONEY IS THE DIFFERENCE

Simple fact: An idea doesn't make money until it becomes a product or business. Wanting to serve the public in a unique way, as Jessica Mayberry did, is a wonderful thing. Unless that wonderful idea turns out to be sustainable, however, you can't pay the rent or buy groceries—or keep performing that service you think the world needs.

Everything starts with the idea. Fully develop that idea in your mind and the minds of your partners, before you begin trying to transform it into a product or business. Will your idea "stick"? Test whether your idea will "stick" by using principles from Chip and Dan Heath's book *Made to Stick*. It's a great resource, with numerous examples of "sticky" ideas and astute analysis of what makes them stick.

The Heath brothers found that six principles link sticky ideas of all kinds (note that these are not just in business). "Sticky ideas won't have all six, but the more the merrier," they wrote. For example, President John F. Kennedy's idea to put a man on the moon in a decade had all six of the principles (denoted by the acronym SUCCES).[12]

a. **Simple.** Having a single, clear mission.

b. **Unexpected**. Putting a man on the moon is an excellent example. It seemed like science fiction at the time.

c. **Concrete**. Defining the parameters. For example, success was defined very clearly with the moon mission—no one could quibble about man, moon or decade.

d. **Credible**. Speaking as an authoritative source. In the case of the moon mission, the president of the United State behind the project.

e. **Emotional**. Having an appeal to the imagination. The moon mission appealed to the aspirations and pioneering instincts of an entire nation.

f. **Story**. Having a compelling narrative. The story of the Apollo mission was an astronaut overcoming great obstacles to achieve an amazing goal.

Take your idea and run it through this "sticky" exercise. Is it **simple** and **concrete**? These are probably the two most important qualities. Is it **credible**? Or rephrase the question to ask are *you* credible? If you realize your credibility in your chosen area might be lacking, can you partner with someone who carries more credibility? If your idea is **unexpected**, it is probably also "innovative." Naturally, the more innovative your idea is, the better your **story** will be. Finally, finding an **emotional** charge to your idea is the icing on the cake.

If your idea is sticky, it's time to develop it into a product (or service) and find some customers (or an audience).

Developing a new technology, a new gadget, a new tool or even a new website takes a time, energy, effort and, most likely, money. That's why seeking some return for your idea—in the form of customers paying for a product or service—is one of the most basic business needs.

CHOOSE CUSTOMER DEVELOPMENT BEFORE PRODUCT DEVELOPMENT

There is a traditional progression for how new and innovative companies go from an idea to a business success. A particularly famous model among entrepreneurs comes from Silicon Valley, where Internet companies have minted many millionaires but also countless flameouts and failures. The model starts with an idea or concept, gets developed as an "alpha" and then a "beta" website or service, then it is launched to the public as something called a "first customer ship."

Steve Blank, a serial entrepreneur, author and instructor at Stanford, says this model overemphasizes product development at the expense of customer development. Anyone can make a product, but unless it fits into a market that wants it or needs it, money won't change hands and you won't have a sustainable business. The business term for this concept is "product-market fit." The only way to start learning whether you have a market for your product or service is to talk to actual customers about your idea. Or, as Blank says, "get the hell out of the building and test it."

"Unless you have been working in a particular market for the past 20 years, anything you're thinking about customers and markets is nothing more than a guess," Blank says.[13]

"The first step is go out and test some of the fundamental hypotheses that you have about your business. There are two that are absolutely essential: One is that you believe you're making a product or service that solves a problem or a need that a customer has. Great, I'll believe you. Now show me that there are customers out there who have agreed with you," says Blank, who is also author of *Four Steps to the Epiphany*, an excellent book for entrepreneurs.[14]

We will discuss "product-market fit" in more detail in Chapter 8.

▶▶ *Make something people want or need*
The reason to talk to customers early in the process is to see whether anyone needs or even wants what you are building. The idea that a business should be making something that people actually want seems so simple, but when you start by solving your own problem, you have a tendency to assume others have the same problem (or need).

Paul Graham started Y Combinator to serve as an incubator for startup companies. The aspiring entrepreneurs admitted to the program get a little seed funding and a lot of guidance. They also get a T-shirt with the slogan, "Make something people want."

Customer development takes assumptions and tests them with real people. As Blank says, the goal is not to discourage you from becoming an entrepreneur. "The goal of a customer development process is simply to take the hypotheses about your business and product, as-is, and see if there are customers and a market outside the building."[15]

And what is the most direct way to gauge whether people want what you have? Just ask them. Finding people and asking them to give up their time to give you feedback is not easy or efficient, however. You don't want to talk to 1,000 people about your new idea. That would take too long. Start with a handful of friends and colleagues and be respectful of their time.

If your startup will be a news and events website, ask these people general questions. How do they get their news and information? What kind of information are they most interested in? What kind of advertising are they most likely to respond to? Build a few user profiles based on the responses you receive, and if someone is likely to be in your target market, ask them if you can talk to them again when the website, product or service launches.

People want to save money, save time and get smarter. These are "jobs" that need to be done, and customers will buy products that help them get these jobs done. Not all jobs are functional, though, like shaving or feeding your kids breakfast in the morning. The book *What Customers Want* defined three types of jobs that customers are trying to accomplish most often: functional, personal and social. Functional jobs sustain our lives (they're related to food, fuel or shelter). Personal jobs make us feel better, smarter and more attractive. Social jobs make us feel connected to and appreciated by other people.[16]

It's important to consider all three types of jobs. And if your product or service can help people accomplish more than one, you stand a better chance of succeeding.

▶ ▶ *Learn when not to listen to the customer*
Do you remember New Coke? If so, then you already know one of the most cautionary tales in business about the uses of customer input. Almost 200,000 consumers were interviewed during the process of developing New Coke—at a cost of about $4 million. All that energy and expense produced one of the most embarrassing product failures of all time.[17]

Figure 5.4 iPad

The iPad, on the other hand, was developed with no outside input, no focus groups, no surveys, nothing. (Just the inspirational genius of Steve Jobs and a bunch of really smart people who work for Apple.)

Like so many aspects of business, listening to customers is a balancing act. Unless you've got the confidence and the staff of Steve Jobs, you don't want to develop your idea all alone. Talking to *too* many people, however, can bring its own problems. The more people you talk to, the more ideas you will receive. You need to learn how to assess each suggestion, pull out the information that matches your vision, and discard the rest. The goal is not to get ideas from these potential customers about new directions to pursue, but to learn about their "problem points" so you can come up with your solution or way of making their lives better.

The idea and the company is your vision. Listening to potential customers should help you shape your vision and help you figure out where it might need fine-tuning. Just don't let too much outside influence derail your original idea.

Evan Williams, who co-founded Blogger and Twitter, issues these words of caution: "I think one of the things that kills great things so often is compromise—letting people talk you out of what your gut is telling you. Not that I don't value people's input, but you have to have the strength to ignore it sometimes, too."[18]

▶ Money has to change hands

"Show me the money!" Yes, it's time to channel Jerry Maguire. Unless money is changing hands around your idea, it will be difficult to sustain or fully develop. This is the reality, and not merely greedy thinking. For a business, money means more than profit. It's a resource you need to cover expenses, hire staff and provide you with an income so you can support yourself and your family. It's what allows you to fulfill your mission every day. Money is the oxygen of business. Without it, businesses die.

Chris Anderson's book, called *Free,* illustrates how businesses are making money every day—and lots of it—with a form of "free" in their pricing. "Even within the commercial meaning of 'free' there is a wide range of meanings—and business models," Anderson wrote.[19]

This is an important concept for Web publishers especially, since the root of most online business models is some form of free. Usually it's free content in return for attention that can be sold to advertisers. There are others, of course, that this chapter later examines. Just realize that money can—and should—change hands even if the original product is essentially available for "free."

It's much easier for money to change hands if you're making or providing something people want. Graham, who has helped dozens of startups get going at Y Combinator, says, "If you make something users want, they will be happy, and you can translate that happiness into money."[20]

When thinking about your idea in the initial stages, try answering the following questions to assess whether you just have a neat idea or the makings of a viable business.

▶ ▶ *Will customers pay for your product or service?*
If you're developing a website or news service, it's probably not feasible to assume readers will pay directly for the content. While a few sites do charge for content—or try to—the predominant business model for Web publishing is free content.

It's a simple case of supply and demand. There is seemingly no limit to the supply of free content online. At the same time, the demands on viewers' attention continually grow. The result is people have less attention to give to ever-growing amounts of content. That competition defines the "attention economy."

If you can identify a type of content or a service that is in short supply and high demand, and you can produce it, then consider charging for it. If your content or service will draw people's attention but not their money, then you'll have to explore other money-generating options. Don't worry, though. Capturing the attention of users and customers is hard enough. If you accomplish that much, you're way ahead of the countless websites that produce content without drawing much of an audience.

▶ ▶ *Find startup funding until you grow your audience*

For a website or news service, the common sources of revenue are selling advertising and sponsorships, syndicating content or performing professional services. To generate revenue from any of these models, you must grow an audience first, meaning you will likely need money to get going. This is called "startup funding" or "seed capital," and it can come from a variety of sources.

"Having enough money is crucial for the success of a startup, and insufficient funding is one of the top reasons why new businesses fail," Audrey Watters wrote on ReadWriteWeb, one of the leading news sites for technology startups. "Too often entrepreneurs underestimate the amount of money they'll need—not just to get started but to keep running."[21]

We'll explore funding options in greater detail in Chapter 6, but here are options for your startup's early funding:

- **Self-fund** your startup using your own assets, equity and credit. This is dangerous territory, of course, since we're talking about a second mortgage, tapping into savings, liquidating investments and retirement funds, or using credit cards for business purchases.

- **Bootstrap** your business by spending only what you earn. This often means going without a salary and asking others to as well. If your business will generate cash flow quickly, this is an ideal because once the money starts coming in, you'll have no debt to pay off and you won't have given away equity to investors.

- Ask **friends and family** for money. "While you can choose to offer them equity, you can also simply ask for a loan," Watters writes. "Regardless of whether it's a loan or an investment, it's always advisable to put the terms of your agreement in writing— even if you're borrowing from your mom."[22]

- Seek **angel investment**. Angel investing has grown markedly during the past few years and is now nearly as active in the number of deals (though not the dollar amounts) as venture capital. Angel investors ask for equity in your company and expect a return of three to five times the amount they originally invest. That means you'll need an "exit strategy," a plan to sell the company for a big payday. To find angel investors, Watters recommends checking out Venture Hacks' curated AngelList site. "Look for public events sponsored by angel investors in your area (at www.angelsoft.com) and cultivate business relationships that might introduce you to potential angel investors."[23]

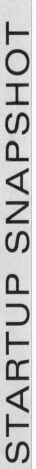

STARTUP SNAPSHOT

I-NEWS: THE ROCKY MOUNTAIN INVESTIGATIVE NETWORK

www.inewsnetwork.org

STARTED: 2009.

FOUNDER: Laura Frank, previously an investigative reporter at the Rocky Mountain News and a 20-year veteran of daily newspapers, radio and TV.

MISSION: Increase access to in-depth news and information of public importance, and enhance civic engagement.

STAFF: 3.5.

STARTUP CASH: $100,000 grant from the Ethics & Excellence in Journalism Foundation in 2010.

WROTE A BUSINESS PLAN?: Yes.

MEASURE OF SUCCESS: In its first year of producing collaborative multimedia investigative reports, more than 20 media outlets used its content, which is having impact and leading to proposed changes in laws and policies.

TOP BUSINESS TIP: Establish the value of your products and services both by proving their worth and by drawing price comparisons to similarly valued products and services. (For example, don't sell your high-impact, multimedia, investigative reports for the going price of a quick-turn freelance piece.)

TOP CONTENT TIP: Establish your niche. I-News is successful because we work collaboratively with other media to help them produce a specific kind of high-quality investigative report that would be difficult or impossible to do alone. We focus on high-impact stories that require technical skills (such as data analysis), and we help our partners develop those skills internally.

THE BASICS OF PRODUCT DEVELOPMENT

You're convinced your idea has a market, and you've found a little cash to get started. Now what? Your next task is to determine a direction and then develop your product.

While it probably seems backward to start working on a plan after you've already built something and talked to potential customers, that's actually the most effective order of events in growing a new business. Yes, you can mix up the order and draft a plan first, but by *doing* first and *planning* second, you limit the number of assumptions in your plan and it is less of a fictional work.

In fact, if you've already launched a product or service and received feedback, chances are pretty good that you've already altered your original idea. The feedback you received, and the data you compiled from your early testers, will bolster your plan and solidify the direction in which you're taking your idea. Once you've identified the problem that needs solving, the opportunity for a niche in the market, and the product or service you think will make money, it's time to check out the competitive landscape.

Obviously, the best direction to take your product is the one with the most potential for revenue and audience. At the same time, it's important not to stray too far outside your area of passion and expertise.

Bestselling author and marketing guru Seth Godin advises that no matter which way you go, go with gusto. "Do your best to pick a direction (hopefully an unusual one, hopefully one you have resources to complete, hopefully one you can do authentically and hopefully one you enjoy) and then do it. Loudly. With patience and passion. (Loud doesn't mean boorish. Loud means proud and joyful and with confidence.)"[24]

▶ Measure your idea

Determining whether your idea has potential as a business is a fairly simple equation. This test will also help you determine how big your business could be, whether it's a two-person shop or a company with 20 employees.

- How much will it cost to produce your product or service?

- How much will people pay for your product or service?

- How many people will pay for your product or service?

Of course, the test is really not so simple at all. Experts advise you to be overly conservative in your estimates of how much people will pay—and how *many* people will pay—for your product or service. And you should expect your costs to be twice as much (at least) as you start out thinking they'll be. That's just the way things work.

If you want to start a news site where the people who create the content will be your greatest expense, try to project how much content each full-time employee (FTE) will produce, then try to determine how many employees you will need to execute your vision. Or maybe it's a team of freelance writers whom you'll pay per article. How many writers and how many articles do you need each week or each month? And how much will you pay for each article?

You know where this is going, right? The bottom line: If it costs more to produce your product or service than people (advertisers?) are willing to pay, you don't have a business. As you work through the product development process, look for opportunities to increase the amount of revenue you're seeking and decrease the costs.

Thinking about money in this strategic way does not mean you're greedy. *Not* thinking about money, or thinking about it too late, is the real problem. Jason Fried, author of *Rework* and co-founder of 37 Signals, spoke at SXSW Interactive in 2010 about the realities of running a business and the danger of assuming that money will come later.

Technology companies, Fried said, tend to consider themselves excused from needing to make money early. "There is no such thing as a startup," he cautioned. "Every company needs to adhere to the basic physics of business, no matter what stage. Make more money than you spend. And make a product people will pay for."

If you're not yet convinced that you have a product, don't stop. Many businesses start out spending more money than they make, or doing one thing and later finding success doing something else. Adapting your original plan is essential to succeeding in business. The list of famous companies that started out doing something different from what brought them success is long and includes such names as Microsoft, Groupon, PayPal and Flickr.

Even Fried's own company started as something else. Originally a Web design firm, 37 Signals now develops Web-based software tools like Basecamp and has millions of customers.

Often entrepreneurs find that customers or audience react to their product or service differently from what was expected, so they change course to meet the newly discovered demand. More often, the original vision isn't shared by enough customers, so the original idea can't support a business. This causes a setback, but it's never the end.

"Entrepreneurs fail, learn from it, and move on," says digital media expert Steve Outing. "They don't give up."

To discover whether your current idea can develop into a sustainable business, follow these basic product development steps.

▶ Build and deploy your product or service

While it's not recommended that you build out your entire idea at first, it's important to build and launch at least part of it. You can think of this portion as a prototype, or an alpha or beta test. No matter what term you use, it's important to launch something and see how potential customers or an audience responds. You naturally make assumptions on how people will use your product or service, but you can't know for sure until you put it in front of the users.

If you're planning some type of news website, your prototype could be something as simple as a Wordpress blog designed with one of the many freely available Wordpress themes. (We'll take a closer look at publishing technology in Chapter 7.) You can use the prototype to publish the type of content you plan to create once the business gets going, or simply use it to test your content ideas. Months before Pegasus News launched, Mike Orren launched and updated a blog about the idea for the site and conversed with the potential audience. With that conversation he fine-tuned the vision and discovered his future audience.

Once you get to the actual development, keep things as simple as possible. You may have ideas about different types of content, a mobile version and many other features that you'd like to include in your website. Rather than focusing on what you *can't* produce in the short term, focus on what you *can* produce right now. That means taking the KISS approach: Keep It Simple, Stupid.

"Once you decide what business you're really in," Jeff Jarvis writes in *What Would Google Do?*, "once you settle on your strategy, once you figure out how to execute it in the new architecture and realities of the Google age . . . there's one more important thing to do: simplify."[25]

Simple is better. Picture the Google homepage. Remember that a new iPhone ships without a user manual in the box. Think about how little time it takes to get going on Twitter. At a time when you probably don't have the resources to do anything complicated, embrace the concept of simple and make it your mission.

French writer and aviator Antoine de Saint-Exupéry captured this sentiment perfectly, even though he died in 1944, decades before the Internet: "A designer knows he has achieved perfection not when there is nothing left to add, but when there is nothing left to take away."

Indeed, Evan Williams was surprised by the success of Blogger because the idea was so simple. (The same could be said for Twitter, which Williams also co-founded.) "How far you can get on a simple idea is amazing," he said. "I have a tendency to add more and more—the ideas always get too big to implement before they even get off the ground. Simplicity is powerful."[26]

▶ ▶ *Pick the right name*

Naming your business, never an easy task, has grown far tougher now that you also have to worry about registering the corresponding domain name. Because squatters or other companies have gobbled up the vast majority of "normal" domain names, picking the right name in the digital age can be both a great creative outlet and a form of torture.

"I spent far, far more time naming GeekWire than I did naming my son," says GeekWire co-founder John Cook. "It's sad, but true."

Figure 5.5 GeekWire

Cook and co-founder Todd Bishop were business reporters at the *Seattle Post-Intelligencer* who left a year before the paper ended its print edition in 2009. They'd known for a long time that they wanted to launch their own site and wrote several memos to the paper's management about the idea while they worked there. They had a clear vision of what their business could do as *the* source for technology and startup business news in Seattle and the Northwest. They knew there was a tangible need for this information in the marketplace, and they felt they could serve an audience that would be attractive to advertisers.

They just didn't know what to call it.

Cook says they spent almost a month constantly brainstorming, constantly searching for the right name. His wife would often troll for ideas on her iPhone while the couple was driving around town. The process consumed massive amounts of time and energy. They were looking for a two-word name, but every combination seemed to be taken.

Eventually they created a list of 30 to 50 names and formed an ad hoc judging panel of 15 to 20 people they knew well and hoped would be part of their new audience. They were looking for a name that would resonate with the tech community but also conveyed their self-image as professional journalists.

The word *tech* was in a number of options, but Cook and Bishop deemed it too boring and too similar to many other sites. "Geek" had an offbeat tone that Cook and Bishop appreciated. They even created a Venn diagram to define the word, which they summarize this way: Geek equals Intelligence plus Obsession minus Social Ineptitude. And *wire* is the opposite of offbeat; it had the credible, newsy feel they wanted, to convey the company's mission.[27]

Not everyone liked the name GeekWire, according to Cook. In fact, some hated it. The founders didn't mind.

"As long as it was a name that was easy to say and spell, it could work," Cook says. "Everyone, whether they liked it or not, they remembered it. It's a very strong name."

Like it or not, GeekWire wasn't available as a domain name, as is frequently the case for a new business. In fact, none of the names that Cook and Bishop considered were available, and the price to buy them ranged from $250 to $10,000. GeekWire was "somewhere in the middle" according to Cook, and available on the Premium Domains section of Network Solutions' website.

If you have some money to spend on a domain name and can get the one you want without breaking the bank, it very well could be worth the investment. The right domain name and business name will go a long way to helping you establish your company. It's the first impression every new potential customer will have, so it's worth doing whatever you can to make sure it's good. This is not a place to cut corners. (Be sure to check the U.S. Patent and Trademark Office to see if the name is trademarked, too: http://www.uspto.gov/trademarks/.)

The more your company name communicates to potential audience members or customers, the less you'll have to explain. If your business has a local focus, you'll want to include the town or neighborhood in the name. But don't limit yourself if you might want to expand later.

If you don't have money to spend on a domain name, your next best bet is "inventing" a new word. Gawker, Engadget, Fark and Mashable are examples of invented words that are now recognizable brand names for content companies. If possible, follow the model used by GeekWire when choosing a name:

- Brainstorm as many ideas as possible.
- Unless you're a nonprofit, choose only .com names (steer clear of .biz, .info and even .net). If a nonprofit, you can go with a .org.
- Make it memorable and short.
- Make sure the name is easy to type and say.
- Try to convey both your business's mission and its tone.
- Form an ad hoc group of potential customers to help you evaluate the options.

In the end, Cook says, the name GeekWire worked because people remembered it. For any business, that contributes to a successful start.

▶ ▶ *Get user feedback*
You've solicited feedback on your business idea and feedback on your business name. When you reach the prototype stage, seeking feedback is even more important. Once you have any part of your project up and running, tap your network and persuade people to take a look and tell you what they think.

You have several options for soliciting and collecting feedback, especially when the product or service is online.

- **Set up an online survey:** You can create a simple form with predetermined questions for free through a service like SurveyMonkey or Google Docs. Responses to the survey will be automatically entered onto a spreadsheet.

- **Email and conversation:** One of the most effective forms of feedback is actual conversation. Try setting up a call or a face-to-face meeting, using an email that contains a link and basic introduction.

- **Digital feedback:** Set up a third-party service on your site that solicits and receives feedback from users as they are visiting the site. GetSatisfaction.com is one of the leading services for digital startups but it costs a few dollars per month.

- **Tracking users:** Test your website with a Web service to see how people are using it. Services like userfly.com, loop11.com and usertesting.com will show you how people are clicking around a site so you can learn whether they are actually behaving the way they say they are in surveys, or the way you assumed they would.

Tech startup marketing expert Sean Ellis recommends one critical question that any user testing surveys or email should ask:

How would you feel if you could no longer use [this product or service or website]?

- Very disappointed.

- Somewhat disappointed.

- Not disappointed (it isn't really that useful).

- N/A—I no longer use [it].

This question gets to the essence of making something people want. "If . . . you find that around 50% or more of your users are saying that they would be 'very disappointed' without your product, there is a great chance you can build a successful business on this 'must have' product," Ellis says.[28]

It's also a good idea to include some basic demographic questions, such as age, gender and zip code. This will give you a head start when it comes time to identify your target market in Chapter 8.

▶ ▶ *Learn from your mistakes*
"Innovation is not an event. It's a process," says author Guy Kawasaki. "An innovator doesn't worry about shipping an innovative product with elements of crappiness if it's truly innovative."

The good news is that if you're setting up a website or other digital information service, the costs to deploy are extremely low. Hosting is cheap, open source software is freely available. So there's no reason to hold back.

"I'm saying it's okay to ship crap—I'm not saying that it's okay to *stay* crappy," Kawasaki adds.

An Internet-based business will go through several iterations, meaning the sooner you get that first version out there, the sooner you'll get to the version that works.

"Being willing to be wrong is a key to innovation," Jeff Jarvis wrote in *What Would Google Do?*. "Mistakes can be valuable; perfection is costly. The worst mistake is to act as if you don't make mistakes."[29]

Almost every new service Google launches is a beta, Jarvis writes. It's a "test, an experiment, a work in progress, a half-baked product."

As Google vice president Marissa Mayer told students at Stanford: "The key is iteration. When you launch something, can you learn enough about the mistakes that you make and learn enough from your users that you ultimately iterate really quickly?"[30]

Use the feedback you receive from those surveys, conversations and user tests to prioritize the changes you need to make. Remember, you can "go public" with something less than final—a "minimum feature set," for example. It's just the beginning of the process anyway.

▶ Define a business model

Once you see how an audience responds to your project, you can form the first iteration of your business model. You can do this by making assumptions (maybe even projections) about what people will pay for, based on their activity. Or you can seek direct feedback from the early adopters who use your service or visit your site. Simply ask them what and how much they would pay for this service. If they don't want to pay for the service then ask them what would make it worth paying for.

If you plan to launch an advertising-based website, show it to potential advertisers and ask them the same questions. Advertising—the most common model—has been funding content operations for decades. It requires building an audience of quantity or quality—or, ideally, both. The key is providing an advertiser with the ability to reach an audience that is worth paying for. Thus, building that audience is the first step.

How to appeal to investors

Starting a new company would be so much easier with a few million dollars in the bank, right? This is the thinking that leads many entrepreneurs down the path of seeking investment from deep-pocketed angel investors or venture capitalists. While there are many benefits to having the kind of resources investors' money can buy, keep in mind that this is an extremely competitive arena.

What are investors looking for? Whether you're launching a news site, a Web portal or a mobile app, most investors will judge you on a few fundamental qualities:

How big is the opportunity? Investors are placing bets, and they hope to win big. Most of the time they lose, so the bets that win need to be large enough to cover the losing bets and give them new money to gamble with. The Huffington Post (acquired by AOL for $315 million) is an example of a BIG win (for the investors).

"It's kind of an old story: Investors are interested in where the money is," says Merrill Brown, who was the first editor-in-chief of MSNBC.com in the 1990s and is now involved as an investor or director in several digital journalism startups. "The most attractive startups have clear commercial missions and specific monetizable categories."

Traditionally, those categories have been limited to entertainment, employment and finance. "Everything else remains much harder," Brown says.

Ultimately, you need to find some way to make money off your idea. The method you choose will become your business model. In recent years, new media businesses have explored and experimented with numerous other forms of generating revenue, including professional services, premium reports, events and syndication.

It's possible, maybe preferable, to have more than one source of revenue funding your new media business. You can experiment with new sources

Who, what and where? Investors target startups that they believe have the right team producing the right product for the right market.

All three components are necessary. Investors tend to stick with markets they know, so those who have invested in media companies before are more likely to invest in them again. They also like investing in entrepreneurs whom they know or have invested with before, or who are referred by people they know.

What problem are you solving? As we discuss in this chapter, investors are interested in funding painkillers, not vitamins. In the world of news and journalism, the best way to prove that you're filling a need is to grow a relatively large audience relatively quickly. High audience numbers will validate your idea in the marketplace and demonstrate product-market fit, which investors love. SBNation, for example, is a network of more than 250 fan-run sports blogs that raised $13 million in 2008, five years after launch, once it grew its audience to a critical mass.

Brown says deals like AOL's acquisitions in 2011 have opened some investors' eyes to the potential of news websites. "People are paying more attention, meetings are easier to come by. But the market is still skeptical."

as your business evolves. In the early days, it's most important to be aware of your options, so that as you develop your product or service, you recognize where the potential to make money could be greatest.

▶▶ *Weigh your options*

With Internet-based services, you have a few primary options for revenue. You'll probably choose one or more to make up your business model. Following our exploration of possible revenue sources in Chapter 3, you should have started to identify the most viable possibilities for how your idea could make money. Let's take another walk through the more popular models as you try to identify which will be most applicable to your project.

- **Freemium:** Most of the content or service is free, but people pay for premium subscriptions. Titans like ESPN and the *Wall Street Journal* have used this successfully: Some of their content is freely available, but premium content is protected behind a "pay wall" and requires a subscription.

- **Advertising-supported:** Grow an audience of readers, and then sell ads to sponsors who want to reach that audience. If you choose the advertising route, the next decision is quality or quantity. If you hope to make ends meet with Google AdSense running automatically on your site, you'll need millions of page views each month. If you want to sell directly to businesses, you'll need a highly desirable and well-defined demographic to attract those ad dollars.

- **Nonprofit:** Use nonprofit status to seek grant money or member donations to cover operating expenses. Voice of San Diego, a local news website, uses the famous "NPR model" by soliciting funds from its audience. Grist, an environmental magazine based in Seattle, has a staff of more than two dozen, including a team to write grant proposals. These people are akin to an advertising sales force at a for-profit publication. Remember, nonprofit doesn't mean non-money. Nonprofits still need money coming in.

Secondary sources of revenue might help offset the costs of doing business if your primary sources can't do it alone. Some examples of secondary revenue sources:

- **Syndication:** Sell your content to other services for republishing. MedCity News developed a significant line of business supplying content to other publishers and healthcare organizations. Members of the Investigative News Network have made syndication a critical part of their revenue model. With more than 50 member outlets across the U.S., look for one in your area and learn where that content ends up.

- **Professional services:** Growing a new media audience requires proficiency in digital marketing techniques such as social media, Web design and search engine optimization. Once you've learned the techniques, you can get other businesses to pay for your help with these and other services they know little about. For example, Susan Mernit, who co-founded Oakland Local in 2009, relied on her media consulting business to support herself while the site began to grow.

- **Premium reports:** Take your knowledge and expertise and produce "one-off" reports that you can sell for varying amounts. One of the best examples comes from Marshall Kirkpatrick, senior editor of ReadWriteWeb, who says the site sold enough copies of his $299 special report on community management to pay his salary for a full year.

- **Events:** New media organizations such as New West, paidContent, St. Louis Beacon and others make money by hosting events. They use their credibility to attract speakers who can draw a crowd, then sell sponsorships. Events may not be something you can do right away, but it's an idea worth considering for the future.

When you're looking for new opportunities and options, don't be afraid to ask other entrepreneurs. People whose businesses don't directly compete with yours will usually be more than willing to help you understand what they've learned in trying to charge for different types of services. They may not offer exact financial figures, but they'll probably be happy to speak generally about their business model. You should also conduct thorough information searches online to learn everything you can. Numerous business publications, including Fast Company, Inc. and Openforum.com, publish profiles of companies and entrepreneurs that will help you gain an understanding of different business models.

▶ ▶ *Study the market and the competition*
Is your idea really unique? That's a question you'll want to answer sooner rather than later. Someone else may have already built your product or service, and you just don't know about it yet.

A thorough look at the landscape involves much more than a simple Google search. Talk to everyone you know who has some interest or insights into the market you hope to enter, either as a business person or potential customer or audience member. Then ask each of those contacts to list who else you should be talking to.

If you discover some direct competition, don't worry. That's actually a good thing. In the world of venture capital, it's called "market validation." VCs don't trust entrepreneurs who say they have no competition. In their minds, this means either that the entrepreneur doesn't know the market, or his/her idea isn't very good—because if it were, someone would already be doing something like it.

Competition should influence the development of your product or service, not discourage your pursuit of your original idea. Determine what your business can offer that the competition does not. Find the answer by asking these questions:

- Can you serve the audience faster, better or cheaper?
- Is there a technology that would help differentiate you from your competition?
- Can you beat your competition on price or service?

Be aware of the competition, but don't obsess. Chris Brogan, a popular social media and digital marketing expert, says focusing on what you're trying to do—and who you're trying to serve—is much more important.

"I think about my buyers and clients all the time. I think about my would-be customers all the time," Brogan says. "Do I think about my competitors? Not very often, no. Know why? Because what will that get me? Yes, I can see if any of their offerings are better than my offerings, but then, I create my offerings for my buyers, so why would I try to copy their offerings, which are for their buyers?"

This is the essence of business: Find a niche and attack it in a way that no one else can. Give your customers or audience real value in exchange for their time and money, and the competition will be worrying about you instead of the other way around.

Recognizing the competition is the first step to indentifying your target market. Without a target market—defined as the customers or audience most likely to buy your products or visit your website—you can't start a business.

Answer these questions (knowing full well that you're guessing right now at most of them) to start identifying your target market:

- Who are your ideal customers? If you know someone who would be your ideal customer, keep the image of that person in mind.
- Where do these ideal customers live? What are their online communities? Of all the many defining characteristics of people's lives (age, sex, education, income, geography, interests) which matter the most for your particular business?

- How will you get your product or service to them?

- How will they find you in the first place?

Once you get a sense of your original customer or audience base—the initial target market—the next step is to figure out how big that market could be. Obviously, bigger is better. Try to define your initial target market and the ensuing larger market opportunities in actual numbers: Is it dozens, hundreds or thousands?

These estimates will be very preliminary and will probably not hold up as your business evolves, but they're essential in the early stages to assist your product development process. You'll explore the competitive landscape and other important business concepts as you continue through the book.

BUILD YOUR BUSINESS **Stage 5**

Congratulations. You now have the basic elements of a business plan under way.

At this stage, it may not be worth your time to write a full business plan—unless you're planning to seek outside investment very soon. It is, however, a good exercise to build your business plan's executive summary. Because the executive summary hits the high points, drafting it will help you shape the idea in your head and give you something to share with others when you're seeking feedback.

Here are the basic elements of a business plan:

- Problem and opportunity: What are you trying to solve?

- Solution: What is your product or service?

- Competition and competitive advantage: Why are you better than the other guys?

- Revenue: How will you make money?

- Team: Who is going to do the work?

- Exit strategy (optional): Who would be willing to acquire the company?

An executive summary is essentially a digest version covering the same topics in less detail than the full business plan. The entire summary should span no more than three pages. Use the action items here to fill out your summary, with a few paragraphs under each heading.

?? THINK: What is the problem you are trying to solve?

✓ ACT: Clearly define the problem and explain why the opportunity to solve it is attractive from a business perspective.

?? THINK: How will you solve the problem you just outlined?

✓ ACT: Describe your product or service in enough detail to help someone "see" it.

?? THINK: Who else is trying to solve this problem? Size up the competition by looking online and talking to potential audience members and advertisers for your business.

✓ ACT: Describe what the competition is doing and then what you will offer customers or an audience that is unique. Will your startup stand apart through price, service, new technology or some other means?

?? THINK: How will you make money? Run through the list of possible revenue sources on page 165. Under each of those headings, what options might you have?

✓ ACT: Explain how money will come into your organization. It could be selling products, charging for advertising or receiving grants. Detailed financial projections are not necessary at this point.

?? THINK: Who is going to execute this plan?

✓ ACT: List the appropriate qualifications and experience for yourself and anyone else who will be working on the project.

Exit Strategy (optional): This applies only if you plan to seek angel investing or venture capital. Investors want their money back—and then some. Angel investors generally seek a return of three to five times their original investment, while venture capitalists look for a multiple of 10. To provide those returns on investment, you'll need to sell your company to someone much bigger or go public with an initial public offering (IPO). So the outline of your ultimate exit strategy should describe what will happen to the company that will bring that return to the investors.

Notes

1. Jessica Mayberry, "Creating Community Video Entrepreneurs in Brazil," from the MediaShift Idea Lab blog, Jan. 29, 2010. http://www.pbs.org/idealab/2010/01/creating-community-video-entrepreneurs-in-brazi1350.html

2. Mayberry, "Video Volunteers launches IndiaUnheard for rural issue," from the MediaShift Idea Lab blog, Dec. 7, 2010. http://www.pbs.org/idealab/2010/12/video-volunteers-launches-indiaunheard-for-rural-issues339.html

3. Mayberry.

4. Theodore Roosevelt, "Man in the Arena" Speech given April 23, 1910, Paris.

5. Steven Berlin Johnson, "Where Good Ideas Come From," from Johnson's TED talk, Sept. 21, 2010. http://www.youtube.com/watch?v=0af00UcTO

6. Carleen Hawn, "The F|R Interview: Y Combinator's Paul Graham," from the GigaOm network, May 3, 2008. http://gigaom.com/2008/05/03/the-fr-interview-y-combinators-paul-graham/

7. Marc Andreessen, "The Pmarca Guide to Career Planning, part 1: Opportunity," from his personal blog, Oct. 13, 2009. http://pmarca-archive.posterous.com/the-pmarca-guide-to-career-planning-part-1-op

8. Jessica Livingston, *Founders at Work: Stories of Startups Early Days* (Berkeley, CA: Apress, 2007) 17.

9. Livingston, 28.

10. Derek Sivers, as quoted in *Fast Company,* April 2010 issue.

11. Livingston, 28.

12. Chip and Dan Heath, *Made to Stick: Why Some Ideas Survive and Others Die* (New York: Random House, 2007).

13. Steve Blank, "Retooling Early Stage Development," Entrepreneurial Thought Leader Lecture, Oct. 1, 2008. http://ecorner.stanford.edu/authorMaterialInfo.html?mid=2048

14. Blank.

15. Blank.

16. Anthony W. Ulwick, *What Customers Want: using Outcome-Driven Innovation to Create Breakthrough Products and Services* (New York: McGraw-Hill, 2005) 25.

17. Ulwick, xiv.

18. Livingston, 124.

19. Chris Anderson, *Free: The Future of a Radical Price* (Hyperion, 2009).

20. Livingston, 221.

21. Audrey Watters, "Five Sources for Early Stage Funding," ReadWriteStart, May 14, 2010. http://www.readwriteweb.com/start/2010/05/five-sources-for-early-stage-f.php

22. Watters.

23. Watters.

24. Seth Godin, " 'Where to' might not be as important as 'how loud,' " from his personal blog, June 23, 2008.

25. Jeff Jarvis, *What Would Google Do?* (New York: HarperCollins, 2009) 114.

26. Livingston, 125.

27. Todd Bishop, "Geek Pride Day: Why it's OK to let your geek flag fly," GeekWire, May 25, 2011. http://www.geekwire.com/2011/geek-pride-day-geek-flag-fly-charts

28. Sean Ellis, "Free Customer Development Help—Survey.io," Startup Marketing Blog, May 18, 2009. http://startup-marketing.com/free-customer-development-help-surveyio/

29. Jarvis 91.

30. Marissa Mayer, "Nine Lessons Learned about Creativity at Google," Entrepreneurial Thought Leaders Lecture, May 17, 2006. http://ecorner.stanford.edu/authorMaterialInfo.html?mid=1554

CHAPTER 6

Build Your Business Know-How

E van Smith speaks like a Harvard MBA. He connects one purposeful sentence to another in a rapid-fire string with the self-assuredness of a successful businessman. His command of significant facts and figures would fare well on conference calls with Wall Street analysts.

But Smith is a journalist through and through. He spent nearly 18 years at *Texas Monthly* magazine and served as editor for nine of those years, leading the magazine to several national awards. He has a master's in journalism from the Medill School at Northwestern University, not an MBA from Harvard. Yet in 2009 he launched a multimillion-dollar company called the Texas Tribune, easily one of the most ambitious new startups in local journalism since the Internet disrupted mainstream media in the 1990s.

Smith's concept was audacious: He set out to raise millions of dollars to fund a nonprofit journalism startup and hire away the best political journalists from mainstream media in the state of Texas. The website covers public policy and government and nothing more. Because those topics have high societal importance and low attractiveness to advertisers, Smith knew a nonprofit model would be his only chance for success. He doesn't believe going nonprofit is the solution for everyone, however.

"If anyone tells you there's one model that will work, they are full of shit," Smith told a group at the Online News Association conference in 2010. "We are not a big box store of media. It's not just news; it's knowledge. It's not just journalism; it's information."

The tireless pursuit of his passion enabled Smith to raise $4 million in 2009; by the end of 2010 he had raised $2.4 million more. He has made his pitch to countless individuals and organizations, building a roster of more than 80 major donors (half have given at least $25,000) and 120 corporate

Figure 6.1 Texas Tribune

sponsors. More than 2,000 individual members have supported the Tribune with small-scale donations through the website as well.

"The challenge of sustainability requires that you have different buckets of revenue," Smith says. "It is possible—big, small or medium—to do this. The economics are not that crazy."

The Tribune's "revenue buckets" include running events, which Smith takes very seriously as both business and journalism. The company hired an events coordinator away from the *New Yorker* magazine and quickly grew an impressive line of business, earning more than $200,000 in 2010. To ensure that the events serve as journalism, too, Smith dons his journalist hat to interview newsmakers and public officials. Every event is professionally recorded and produced, and the videos are published on the Tribune website.

In addition to the events, the Tribune gives its content away to anyone who will publish it. That distribution helps spread awareness for the brand—and the cause—making it easier for Smith to drum up more financial support for the site. Sometimes, Smith says, the website seems like "the least important thing we do."

With an annual operating budget of more than $2.5 million, fundraising will continue to be a challenge. Smith is not about to cut corners, however. In 2011, the Texas Tribune had a staff of 26, including 13 reporters whom Smith calls some of the most experienced and talented in the state. The Tribune's staff accounted for one-third of the capitol press corps in Austin—but that says more about the mainstream press than the startup.

"We hired the best reporters away from for-profit journalism in Texas," Smith said. "We put together our fantasy football list, and we got everybody we wanted. And all of them had their minds open to a new model. We are not a teaching hospital. We swim in the deep end of the pool."

The audience noticed. In 2010, its first full year of operation, the Tribune counted 2.2 million unique visitors to its website and more than 23 million

> Figure 6.2 Texas Tribune <

page views. The site had more "likes" on Facebook than the newspapers from Dallas, Austin and San Antonio combined.

Smith knows that the momentum won't sustain itself. The staff will have to continue breaking new ground with comprehensive coverage, rich databases and compelling events. And Smith will continue to don his business hat and pound the pavement for more financial support.

"I feel like Indiana Jones outrunning the boulder," he says. "If I look away for a second, I'm gonna get run over."

Like many of the entrepreneurs you've met in this book, Smith proves you don't need a business degree to run a startup. All you need is an open mind, a creative approach to problem solving and some basic knowledge of the fundamentals. And a lot of energy for hard work.

Can you do it all by yourself? Probably not. Smith formed a team to help him get started and grew the team over time. To jump-start your startup, you need other people to help you build your idea and attend to the basic needs for starting and running a business.

So it's time to start thinking: Do you know talented people with the right skills? And, if so, will those talented people be willing to work for free, at least for a while? Maybe. You actually have many options for funding the work that's needed to get an idea off the ground, especially if you're building a digital product or service. In selecting your best option, you'll be considering many variables that we will look at next.

Then we'll discuss the more formal requirements of starting a business, from legal to accounting to developing a full business plan.

Here are the concepts in Chapter 6 that will help you get your business started:

- ▶ Assess your strengths and needs.

- ▶ Make a master list of tasks.

- ▶ Review business basics and lingo.

- ▶ Identify your human and financial capital.

- ▶ Find the right productivity tools and time-management skills.

ASSESS YOUR NEEDS

You have a great idea for a new website. You've spoken to enough people to be genuinely excited about its potential. The next challenge is turning that idea into a reality. That means actually creating something—often out of nothing.

You're excited, yet every time you to try to envision the day-to-day tasks involved in starting and running a business, your brain melts. You didn't go to business school, so how are you supposed to know how to raise the money, keep the books, hire and pay the staff, and perform the million other tasks you don't even know you have to worry about? How can you possibly do it all?

The answer is that you do it a little at a time. To get your business up and running, you'll probably need two forms of capital: human and financial. It's important to assess your needs for human capital before looking at the financial. Learn from the dot-com bust, when too many Silicon Valley startups made the mistake of hiring lots of people just because they could afford to, then ran out of money when the revenue didn't materialize as quickly as they had projected.

The human capital starts with you. The more of this resource that you can bring to the table, the easier it will be to get your new project off the ground. Start by assessing your skills and experience as if you were applying for a job. Make a list of those skills so you can refer to them as you move forward. You might be surprised to realize how many transferable skills you actually have to aid you in this new endeavor.

Regardless of what skills you already possess, you'll be doing plenty of on-the-job learning, so one of the most important qualities you can bring to the table right away is an open mind. Instead of thinking "I can't do that because I don't know how," try to turn your thinking around and tell yourself: "I haven't done that yet, but I'm sure I can learn how."

The Internet, of course, is there to help you get started with almost any question. Whether it's installing a new theme on a Wordpress blog or finding the right forms to help you register a new business, a simple Web search is usually the best place to begin. In this and many other ways, your reporting skills and journalistic curiosity are an asset. You know how to ask good questions, and you know where to look for answers. Don't discount those skills; plenty of people lack curiosity or are intimidated by the unknown. Plenty of people give up easily. But journalists don't.

No matter how resourceful you are, or become, you will likely need some help. Start by breaking down the work to be done and deciding which tasks should be taken care of first.

▶ Divide work into four areas

Fortunately, assessing your human capital needs to develop your idea is not rocket science. Start by simply drawing a pencil-and-paper dummy of the website, mobile service or other digital product you plan to create. If you have access to a dry erase whiteboard, find a couple of other people to help you brainstorm the sketch, the way startups and tech companies do every day. What you draw can be rough, even ugly. Just get the most important elements down somewhere.

Then think hard about what work will be needed to transform your rough drawing into an interactive and functioning reality. Remember, you probably won't be able to launch your whole vision at once. You may even want to do two drawings, the ultimate ideal and the more immediately possible version.

Make a list of the necessary tasks and arrange the list in priority order so you can quickly see which items must be done first. For many news-related startups, the work can be divided into four areas:

- Content.

- Design.

- Programming/development.

- Sales and marketing.

Even if you fancy yourself a jack-of-all-trades, it's probably not feasible for you to master all of these areas. These skills are quite different from one another, and each is important to building a successful Internet-based startup. If you know that you'll need the help of others, it's never too soon to start networking to find those future partners.

"Finding other people is foundational," says Tom Stites, the founder of the Banyan Project, a nonprofit news co-op that focuses on matters of interest to less-affluent Americans. "Advisors are crucial, partners even more important. Partners are way easier to find for a for-profit business than for a nonprofit that promises no stock payoff for the unpaid hard work of founders, but they're no less important. If I'd had partners, my project would have launched at least a year sooner."

Your master list of tasks, broken down into the four categories of work and prioritized in order of importance, is a valuable decision-making tool. For example, if you know that you have no programming/development resources on hand at the moment, you probably shouldn't plan to launch an iPhone/iPad app as the core feature of your new project. Instead, you can start with a Wordpress blog with a pre-made theme and try to build a proof of concept with the skills you have (content) and the skills that you can learn on-the-job (design, sales and marketing).

▶ Separate *now* from *later*

Everything cannot be done at once; most new businesses are launched in phases. If you could get just part of your site up and running, to introduce the idea to the audience, what might that part look like? Using your itemized and prioritized list of tasks, try to determine how many of them are critical to this first phase. This will become your "go-to-market feature set," or you might think of it as a "minimum feature set." It's the least amount of work that can be done to deliver a functioning product or service to an audience. That is your first goal.

Take your list of actions that need completing and input them into a project management or collaboration service to track progress, especially if other people are sharing in the work. (See the section on project management tools later in this chapter.) List all the items that need to be completed for launch in one section or under a heading such as "To Do before Launch." Anything that can wait until after launch should go in a different section or under a different heading like "Post-Launch To-Dos."

"Stay focused" is an oft-repeated mantra of successful entrepreneurs. It's easy to chase the next new idea that comes along and get distracted from the original mission. You need discipline to block out the new ideas and continue developing the core set of features or content that you need to launch. To make yourself feel better about not pursuing the rest of your ideas, start a list on paper or on your computer called "Not Right Now." You'll feel better knowing those thoughts won't vanish before you have time to return to them.

Using your list of tasks, assign each task to yourself or someone else, and, if possible, assign an agreed-upon deadline. This will give you a list of tasks that you have someone to complete and a list of tasks that you need completed but don't yet have anyone for. Look at the list of "person-less" tasks and think hard about whether they really need doing right away. Could that part of your business get going a little later? Move as many of those tasks as you can to your section called "Post-Launch To-Dos." This will keep your project moving forward instead of delaying it while you search for people.

▶ Consider staffing options

Eventually, you will probably need to find some skilled help for your project. Talented people are key assets to successful companies of all types and sizes. Unlike large, established companies, you don't have a great salary, full benefits and a 401k to offer the people you need. Not yet, anyway. That means you're likely looking for freelancers.

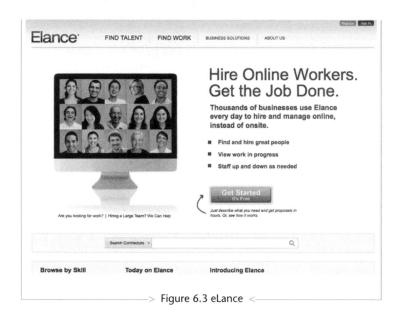

> Figure 6.3 eLance <

The freelance market is booming these days. Many talented professionals have chosen to work gigs instead of taking full-time jobs. In addition to spreading the word among everyone you know, you can tap into the global freelance market at websites like eLance.com, Odesk.com, 99designs.com, RentACoder, Freelancer.com and Guru.com. Most of these services allow you to post a job and receive bids from freelancers. You can see the quality of work from the people bidding on your job through examples and ratings. If you hire somebody, the money goes into an escrow account until both parties are satisfied, so it's safe, too.

"Although numerous online exchanges still act primarily as brokers between employers in rich countries and workers in poorer ones, the number of freelancers in industrialized nations is growing," the *Economist* observed in an overview of the digital freelancing market. "Gary Swart, the boss of oDesk, says the number of freelancers registered with his firm in the United States has risen from 28,000 at the end of 2008 to 247,000 at the end of April [2010]."[1]

If you prefer to work with someone locally, try posting your job on craigslist (under "gigs") or another local jobs board popular with programmers and designers. You should also look for local groups that meet around particular disciplines. For example, in most cities you can find regular meetups for Wordpress users, Drupal users, Ruby on Rails users, as well as local chapters of the Social Media Club. Plan to attend the next meeting and start networking.

Figure 6.4 Wordpress Meeting

Hiring freelancers entails a risk that the person won't deliver quality work or won't finish on time. Thankfully, this is rare, since a freelancer's reputation is essential to that freelancer getting more work. (And of course the freelancer is taking a risk too—that he or she will do the work and you won't pay.) Definitely check the freelancers' references; talk to someone for whom that person has done work.

Using a written contract will provide more structure and some legal protection. Find a sample freelance contract online that you can modify to suit your needs and have the freelancer sign it before starting a project. This is especially important if the freelancer is in another city and you're never going to meet. But understand the limitations: It's unlikely either party would sue the other over a few hundred dollars.

If you know someone in your city who is interested in your project, you should explore some creative options to give that person an incentive to work with you. For example, a small slice of the equity in the eventual company is often used to formalize a partnership. This allows the person to feel a sense of ownership in the project and can be structured to include deferred pay (once money starts coming in). You'd be surprised at how much work creative people will do for "free"—*if it's interesting to them.*

"Only the rare entrepreneur is an island," says Jane Briggs-Bunting, a professor at Michigan State. "You need the brain power, enthusiasm and skills of others to succeed. Thrashing out ideas, approaches, and identifying expertise and examples of efforts of others is critical to success. These folks can also give you a much needed morale boost when problems grow and issues seem insurmountable."

"Tell everyone what you want to do, and someone will want to help you do it," said W. Clement Stone, who parlayed $100 in savings into an insurance empire.[2]

Interns are another creative option for staffing. Most colleges have a jobs board or email list that you can use to find talented students looking for real-world experience. If you're not able to pay your interns, work with the school to see that the student earns credit for doing the internship. Federal law prohibits unpaid workers unless they're earning academic credit. Students need experience, and you need help to build a business that you hope will one day offer paying jobs. Keep in mind that an intern requires more training and supervision than an experienced professional. In exchange, you get fresh ideas (and probably some social media expertise) from someone who may be part of your target audience.

DETERMINE YOUR MONEY OPTIONS

If you can't do it alone and can't get the work done without paying people, how much money do you need? Quantifying how much work will need to be done is the first step in answering this question. Then you can begin to estimate how much it will cost to make it happen. Analyzing the costs in terms of time and money will help you prioritize the tasks and decide which to do first.

It's important to think in terms of project work, not full-time employment at first.

If you're starting from scratch, you probably can't pay salaries every week unless you've landed some serious funding. Take your list of the work that needs to be done for each phase of the project. Estimate how much each piece will cost to develop. If you don't have experience making such projections, solicit some estimates from freelance programmers or designers. Or you can post the jobs on one of the online freelance markets or craigslist to see how much people will bid for the work.

This should give you a baseline for how much money you will need. If the amount is a few hundred or thousand dollars, you can try to bootstrap your business and not worry about giving up any of your company to investors

DALLAS SOUTH NEWS

www.dallassouthnews.com

STARTUP SNAPSHOT

STARTED: 2009.

FOUNDER: Shawn Williams, blogger, columnist, formerly in pharmaceutical sales.

MISSION: To focus on an underserved portion of the Dallas area, target diverse populations, and train residents to produce their own stories. "Using news to make Dallas better" and target diverse populations.

STAFF: One full-time (editor), one intern, 30 volunteer contributors: writers, videographers, photographers and administrative help.

STARTUP CASH: $10,000.

WROTE A BUSINESS PLAN?: Yes.

MEASURE OF SUCCESS: Traffic nearly tripled in the first six months of 2011.

TOP BUSINESS TIP: Learn to love the business part of your business. Cash flow statements, balance sheets, sales pieces, advertising proposals are the things that will allow us to do what we want to do moving into the future. The longer you ignore them, the less effective your enterprise will be and the more likely you are to go out of business.

TOP CONTENT TIP: SEO is real and Google is King. The right title and tags can help bring people into your site and give them the opportunity to view content they may not have sought out otherwise.

or taking on loans that have to be paid back. If you need several thousand dollars and don't have a fat savings account, you will need to look for investment, a loan or a grant.

▶ Can you bootstrap your business?

There is a famous axiom in business that says all you need to know about bootstrapping: While everyone wants to build new products fast, good and cheap, you get to pick only two of those three. If it's good and fast, it won't be cheap to develop. If it's cheap and fast to develop, it won't be good. And if it's good and cheap—which is probably what you're looking for—it won't happen fast.

How much of the work can be done by you and your partners? That would be the cheapest way to develop your project, but how much time can you or your partners dedicate without pay? If you still have a day job and this is a side project, you can probably dedicate a few hours a night for as long as it takes. If you want to quit your day job, you'll be able to dedicate as much time as you want—as long as your savings account holds up.

This arrangement is called bootstrapping your business. Instead of taking money from investors or a bank loan, you build a product or service with sweat equity. It's not as sexy as venture capital, but it has proved successful for many entrepreneurs.

"Bootstrappers run billion-dollar companies, nonprofit organizations, and start-ups in their basements," Seth Godin wrote in the *The Bootstrapper's Bible*. "A bootstrapper is determined to build a business that pays for itself every day. At last count, there were several million bootstrappers in this country, with another few million wannabes, just waiting for the opportunity."

The best part about bootstrapping is that you get to start working on your idea immediately, instead of waiting for someone to give you the money to get going. The money to pay freelancers comes from the salary at your day job or the savings account you've built up. If you quit the day job to focus full-time on your startup, you need enough cash on reserve to pay the bills and buy food for you (and your family).

"You're not a true entrepreneur until you've made payroll out of your own pocket," is another common saying. You'll know you truly believe in your business when you use your own money to pay for it.

Bootstrapping means running on the cheap—at work and at home. You have to take pride in getting a great deal, in *not* spending money. If you can feel a sense of accomplishment every time you find a free meal or decide to forego a movie or nice dinner out, you have what it takes to be a bootstrapper. Of course, this means your family has to feel that sense of pride, too. Having the support of your immediate family and friends can be critical to your success; *not* having that support is a major stress factor.

Credit cards are another way to bootstrap, but be warned: It's dangerous to max out your available credit to fund a business. It's been done successfully many times, but probably attempted unsuccessfully many more. Declaring personal bankruptcy is no way to end a business.

That said, occasionally you might be able to rely on credit cards for one-time purchases of necessary goods or services (a new computer, for example). Just be careful not to overextend yourself.

▶ Pros and cons of loans, grants and investment

If you can't fund operations out of your own pocket, you'll need to look at other sources of funding. Given the amount you need to get started, what are the possible options for acquiring that money? If you need $5,000 to $50,000, then a grant, bank loan or friends-and-family funding is probably your best bet. If you need more than $50,000, then you're looking at either angel or venture capital investing.

Here are some pros and cons of each:

Grants: The Knight Foundation and McCormick Foundation give away millions every year to journalists. Dozens of other smaller entities dole out grants, too.

- Pro: This is free money; you don't have to pay it back. And just winning the grant gives your startup a credibility boost.

- Con: Grants usually involve a very competitive process that can take months — or longer.

Bank loan: This is the most traditional form of funding a new business. A line of credit is another option to explore with a local bank.

- Pro: Small Business Administration loans are guaranteed by the government, and aimed at helping entrepreneurs get started.

- Con: Loans usually involve reams of red tape to cut through. You have to offer collateral and make payments each month, including interest.

Friends-and-family funding: Even if you don't have a "rich uncle," you might be able to interest some friends and family in a small investment in your new company. Lots of new businesses start this way, usually with a few thousand dollars from a small group of investors. In return, you offer a percentage of the equity in your company or simply promise to pay the money back.

- Pro: Friends and family funding usually involves the least hassle. Usually the best terms.

- Con: You run the risk of damaging important personal relationships if the business doesn't succeed and money is lost. Also using this type of funding may influence you to continue pursuing a bad idea because you don't want to lose your friends' or family's money.

Angel investment: Angel investors, who invest their own money, are the fastest growing area of startup investment. You will likely give up 30 to 40 percent of your company in return for a round of investment of $100,000 to $500,000. (Most investment rounds are made up of several smaller investments, so raising $100,000 might mean securing $25,000 from four different angels.)

- Pro: Angel investment funding usually comes from successful entrepreneurs who provide expertise in addition to cash. Angels represent a large pool of money to tap into.

- Con: You need a business model that will aim to hit a home run, and an exit strategy. Investors want a return, which usually means selling the business to a bigger company or going public. Total investment will come from several individual investors, so acquiring the money is time-consuming.

Venture capital: Professional investors (managing the pooled money of others, not their own funds) who work on large deals only.

- Pro: Venture capital is big money.

- Con: Venture capital brings big stress. Even more than with angels, you'll need an ambitious plan to change the world in some significant way. Your idea had better be able to support a $100 million business if you want venture capital money. This is not a viable route for most journalism-based businesses.

SKIP BUSINESS SCHOOL, START HERE

First-time entrepreneurs often wonder whether they need formal education to start a business. It seems logical that a business degree would be a prerequisite, but that's not the case. You'll learn more by launching your own business than you would by going back to college and getting a business degree.

Consider the cash you'll save by not paying tuition. In fact, if you can, take the amount of money you would have paid for a business degree and apply it as an investment in your business. If you're planning an Internet-based business, it will probably cost less to launch a company than to go to business school.

A pretty smart guy named Albert Einstein once remarked: "All learning is experience. Everything else is just information." This chapter will give you the basic information you need to start getting the experience that Einstein was talking about.

▶ Do you need a lawyer?

(DISCLAIMER: The following information should not be mistaken for professional legal guidance. It is merely a broad overview of some of the terms and functions related to starting, owning and operating a business.)

Obviously, hiring an attorney can be helpful when starting a business. Attorneys can also be costly. You don't want to spend hundreds or thousands of dollars on legal help when you could be spending that money on website development, or programming, or design.

Fortunately, there are options other than hiring a lawyer to get the legal advice and documentation that you need. For starters, you'll find a wealth of information and resources online about all kinds of legal issues related to starting up a business.

When you're researching a legal question, start with a search engine like Google. You'll be surprised how much information you'll find this way, though you might need some expert help deciding which advice is worth heeding. You can also find sample documents that will work as starter drafts for some of the contracts you'll need. This is a frugal way to proceed. Simply search for the right kind of document—say, a contract to hire a freelancer—then download it, and, to the best of your ability, modify it to fit your needs.

Now you have a preliminary document to send to an attorney for review. Modifying the document will help you define exactly what you need, and it will save you money on legal fees because the lawyer won't be starting from scratch. Only after you've done all the work you possibly can yourself, including talking with others who've been through the startup process, should you consult with an attorney. You'll pay $200 to $500 per hour, so you want to do everything you can to limit the time that you'll need an attorney's services.

Plenty of websites, like avvo.com and lawyers.com, can help you research the background of local lawyers and find one who looks promising for your business. But you don't have to rely on the Internet alone. Look for free office hours by local attorneys; many lawyers occasionally donate their time to help entrepreneurs get started. Most cities have entrepreneurial organizations that will offer opportunities to network with experienced small-business lawyers willing to answer basic questions over coffee, a beer or glass of wine. Your fellow members of such groups will be great sources of ideas and recommendations as well. Basically, you're building a stable of trusted contacts, just as you would in reporting.

▶▶ *Business structures/entities*

Forming a business means first choosing what type of business you will be. To make it "official," you need to register with the state. There are several different types of business entities to choose from. Your choice will affect how much protection you have personally against debts your company may incur, and how much your company will pay in taxes (among other factors).

If you're launching something simple like a news website, your best bet is a sole proprietorship or general partnership. If you don't plan to take loans or outside investment, you won't likely have debt to worry about.

If you choose a corporation or LLC (limited liability company), you'll need an attorney to help you with an operating agreement and other documentation. Follow the advice in the previous section to minimize the cost of this process by doing as much work as you can on your operating agreement before you meet with an attorney about it.

Here is a brief look at the most popular business entities and the pros and cons for each:

Sole Proprietorship: An individual (or married couple) in business alone. Sole proprietorships are the most common form of business structure.

- Pro: These are simple to form and operate, because they are subject to less legal regulation and fewer taxes.

- Con: The business owner is personally liable for all debts incurred by the business.

General Partnership: Two or more people who agree to contribute money, labor, or skill to a business.

- Pro: Each partner shares the profits, losses and management of the business.

- Con: Each partner is personally and equally liable for all debts incurred by the business.

Limited Liability Partnership (LLP): A favorite of accountants and lawyers, it is similar to a general partnership.

- Pro: One partner does not have personal liability for the negligence of another partner.

- Con: Each partner is still personally and equally liable for all debts incurred by the business.

Corporation: A more complex business structure, it is commonly used when outside investment is necessary.

- Pro: A corporation has potential tax benefits, depending on whether it is a C corporation or S corporation.

- Con: You have less personal control in a corporation and you will need to assemble a board of directors.

Limited Liability Company (LLC): One or more individuals governed by a special agreement.

- Pro: The company, and not the individuals, is liable for debts of the company.

- Con: Operating agreements for limited liability companies can be complex and cumbersome.

Nonprofit Corporation: Another complex business entity, the nonprofit is typically run to further an ideal.

- Pro: A nonprofit will incur no taxes if you file and receive a tax-exempt status from the IRS.

- Con: Nonprofits are subject to strict donor substantiation and disclosure laws. The paperwork to attain tax-exempt status can be daunting and time-consuming.

▶ ▶ *Forms and licenses*

Starting a business is actually a surprisingly simple process. Once you determine which type of business entity your startup will be, you can make it official and create the basic infrastructure to get going.

- Register your business name with your state government. You will probably be required to fill out an application and then receive an ID number. Usually this takes place through the department of licensing or the secretary of state.

- Obtain a tax identification number from the IRS and your state revenue agency.

- Register for state and local taxes. No, it's not fun, but it's the law. Register with your state to obtain a tax identification number that you'll use for workers' compensation, unemployment and disability insurance.

- Obtain business licenses and permits. Consult federal, state and local agencies to figure out what licenses and permits are required for your business.

- Understand employer responsibilities. If you plan to have employees, get familiar with W-2, W-4 and I-9 forms. Businesses with employees are also required to carry workers' compensation insurance and may be required to pay unemployment insurance taxes or disability insurance under certain conditions or in certain states. Businesses are also required to verify the eligibility of employees to work in the United States.

For more details on each of these steps, visit **www.business.gov**.

In addition to the steps you are *required* to take, here are a few steps you'll *want* to take:

- Open a bank account. Sign up for a business account at your favorite local bank. It's important to keep your personal finances separate from your business. Ask other business owners and your banker if multiple accounts—operating, payroll and tax—would be beneficial, as well.

- Consider insurance. While you would never do anything to purposely put yourself in a situation of getting sued, we live in a litigious society. So imagine the worst-case scenario—your service goes down and your clients lose customers, or you libel someone in a news story—and then talk to an agent about a small business policy.

▶ ▶ *The legal responsibilities of publishing*

For decades, news organizations were mostly concerned with protecting themselves from being sued for libel and defamation. If you need more basic understanding of media law, visit the Citizen Media Law Project by the Berkman Center for Internet and Society at Harvard or the Media Law Resource Center.[3]

In recent years, new wrinkles in media law have appeared. In the era of Web 2.0, it's common to encourage your audience to participate by posting comments and their own stories, photographs and video. That brings additional legal questions regarding the liability of the publisher. Many publishers today are operating the social and interactive sections of their websites under a false assumption. They believe that if they edit any of the user content, they'll be responsible for publishing it and therefore liable for its veracity and potentially libelous statements.

Fortunately, that's not what the law states

David Ardia, the director of the Citizen Media Law Project, is an expert on the topic. He points to Section 230 of the Communications Decency Act passed by Congress in 1996 as the basis for how news organizations and other Internet publishers should handle comments, message boards and other controversial content submitted by users.

Figure 6.5 Citizen Media Law Project

The law states, "No provider or user of an interactive computer service shall be treated as the publisher or speaker of any information provided by another information content provider."[4] Court cases have done little to change the interpretation of the law since it was enacted in 1996.

"It hasn't changed in 15 years," Ardia said. "The law drew a very bright line between material you create yourself and material created by someone else and simply made available by you through an interactive online service."

This information allows Web publishers to open their sites to all manner of interactivity without having to worry about verifying every statement published by users. Many misconceptions have prevailed around this topic for years, but the law gives more power to the publishers than most people realize. The law is flexible enough to apply to all of the social media activity that now comes with any content website.

"On Twitter, if you retweet something and the original tweet is defamatory, as long as you don't materially change the meaning, you will not be liable," Ardia said. "In an offline world it's very different."

Ardia cautions online publishers, however, not to consider themselves untouchable because of this law. A publisher could still be subpoenaed to appear in court if there is litigation around a defamatory comment or one that invades someone's privacy.

You're still liable for anything on your site written by your staff, and you're liable if someone on your staff edits a reader's comment and makes it libelous when it wasn't before. Finally, of course, just because it's safe to have potentially libelous comments on your site doesn't necessarily mean you'll want them there. Vigorous audience debate is great. Just remember that every word on your site, no matter who wrote it, influences the way people perceive your operation and its standards.

Copyright is another legal issue you'll want to think about. You can protect yourself from some problems with copyright by designating a particular person to receive notices of copyright infringement claims against your business. This is an official process, per the Digital Millennium Copyright Act. Register a name and contact information with the U.S. Copyright Office in case someone has a complaint that you have published content in violation of his or her copyright. While registration costs $125, it could save you in the long run by keeping you out of court. The law also requires that you post the name of the designated person on your website. Registering and posting the name give you some protection from liability for copyright infringement.

As a publisher, you'll also need to be wary of any tort (wrongful act) that might happen in the course of someone reporting a story for your site—for example, trespass or intrusion on privacy. Most of all, though, you'll need to learn something about libel laws. The shortest definition of libel is three words: **injury to reputation**. And the surest way to prevent being sued is also three words: **Get facts right**. If someone is called a killer in a story or a post on your site, and he actually has been convicted of murder, you're fine. He can't sue you for libel. If he's only been *charged* with murder, however, the legal ground you're standing on is not so firm.

When it comes to protecting yourself against a defamation lawsuit, Ardia recommends common sense. "Ask yourself if what you're saying would upset you (if someone said it about you). Am I saying what I intend to say? Often people get in trouble by being sloppy with their language."

"It goes back to journalism basics," Ardia says. "Trace sources to ground; don't just rely on what you've heard. It all reduces the risk of being sued."

You can reduce the risk further, he says, by handling complaints well. If someone complains that you have published a damaging statement about him or her, listen carefully and be respectful of the person's concerns. People mostly just want to be heard; they want to feel they've been treated fairly. Be sure you have visible contact information on your site that says something like: "If you have a complaint or concern let me know."

"You can defuse the emotion that drives people to file lawsuits," Ardia says. "It goes hand in hand with good journalism." And of course it's wise to have professional liability insurance. Some companies now sell policies especially designed for Web-based businesses.

▶ Do you need an accountant?

Like attorneys, accountants are necessary to most businesses. How much or how little you spend on them depends greatly on how much you're willing to do yourself.

With accounting, software has greatly enhanced a small business owner's ability to handle most of the basic duties. QuickBooks, Mint and Freshbooks (among others) are intuitive bookkeeping services that make it easy to track expenses and revenues for your business. (If you prefer open-source solutions, check out SMB Ledger.) QuickBooks, the industry standard, offers online or standalone (installed from a CD) options and integrates with most bank accounts.

Figure 6.6 QuickBooks

Track your financial activity diligently, even if you are bootstrapping your project. You might not think the numbers are big enough to matter at first, but creating good habits of paying close attention to the bottom line will serve you well as your company grows.

You probably won't have to worry about talking to an accountant until it's time to pay taxes. And even then, software programs like TurboTax can alleviate the need to pay for personal accounting help. No matter how you get your taxes filed, the process will go much more smoothly if you were diligent with your books throughout the year. Some people find that if they hire an accountant for just one year and keep all the accountant records, the business owners can follow the same procedures the next year on their own.

▶ ▶ *Keeping the books*

Once your business starts moving, you will be sending invoices, writing checks, receiving and paying bills and other financial activities. Keeping track of these activities on a spreadsheet or in a bookkeeping notebook is important.

Make your bookkeeping a daily habit. It doesn't matter what system you use, just find one that works for you. Once you have a good system set up, accurate record-keeping will take just a few minutes a day.

"The keeping of accurate records is imperative if you are going to succeed at business," Linda Pinson wrote in *Keeping the Books,* a how-to guide for basic bookkeeping. "From time to time, I have had students in my small business classes who have wonderful ideas for products or services, but who do not want to be bothered with the details of recordkeeping. Their businesses are already doomed to failure."[5]

Most businesses use either cash-based or accrual-based accounting. The cash method is simpler: You count income when you receive it and expenses when you pay them. With the accrual method, you count income and expenses when they happen, not when you actually receive or pay them. For example, if you send an invoice to a customer in May but don't receive the payment until June, you would count the money as having been received in June with the cash method, but in May with the accrual method.

Your local library has a number of basic bookkeeping books that you can use for reference. At a minimum, you should be familiar with a few basic terms and functions that will make the bookkeeping process beneficial. Start with a beginning journal, which is a simple spreadsheet that tracks the following items (make these the column headings across the top):[6]

- Date.

- Check number or invoice number.

- Paid to or Received from.

- Explanation of Income or Expense.

- Income amount.

- Expense amount

Make sure to leave an audit trail so you can go back and reconstruct your company's finances quickly and easily. This means keeping your invoices and checks in numeric order, not skipping check or invoice numbers, and keeping separate bank accounts for your business and personal funds.

Software tools like Quickbooks will make this process easy and efficient.

▶ ▶ *Accepting payment from others*
One of the basic rules in business is to make it easy for customers to give you money.

You do want their money, right?

Consider *how* you will receive payments from customers, advertisers or vendors because it's unlikely that you'll be receiving cash, especially if you are starting an Internet-based business. That means you will need to be set up to receive checks and, possibly, credit card payments.

Checks are probably the form of currency you'll deal with most. Make sure you deposit any checks you receive promptly. This will increase the accuracy of your bookkeeping and avoid the situation where a check is forgotten and deposited too late (most banks will honor a check for only six months).

The only downside of checks is the possibility of insufficient funds in the check-writer's account. Your bank will generally try two or three times to deposit the check, but if it keeps coming back, you may have to consider going to small claims court or employing a collection agency to resolve the payment.

Accepting credit card payments will, at least initially, cost your business money and add extra processes in your daily operations. You'll need to set up a merchant account at your bank, which comes with a small fee each time you receive a payment. The convenience to the customer is usually worth the small percentage the bank will take, but it's still something to consider.

A convenient alternative for Internet-based businesses is online payment services like PayPal. It's quicker and easier to set up an account at an online payment service than to work with your bank to create a merchant account. The ease of use is similar to the end user—a credit card is entered on a secure website and the money goes into your account—but an online payment service will host that page on their site. With a merchant account you can integrate it into your existing website.

If you have a business-to-business (B2B) company, you will need to send an invoice to your customer to get paid. You can do this easily from software tools like Quickbooks and Freshbooks or find sample invoice forms to modify for your use with a simple Web search.

DOING IT EVERY DAY

Launching any kind of startup takes efficiency. Instead of time-sucking management meetings found throughout corporate America, you have the freedom as an entrepreneur to work on whatever you choose. You have to choose wisely, though, because while you can do *anything,* you can't do *everything.* Technology can help.

It's difficult, maybe impossible, to keep tabs on all the latest and greatest tools and services available online. Often you get the frustrating feeling that somewhere out there exists exactly the cool new thing you need to help you with your latest task—but it just doesn't seem worth the time and energy to try out new products from potentially fly-by-night companies.

In most cases, you'll find the return is worth the investment. With so many tools and applications available for free (or as a free trial), the barriers to testing new applications have largely been removed. Start exploring for the technology that can save you time, make you and your company more efficient, and streamline your processes.

▶ Manage your time

Time is the most valuable resource you have. Spending that precious resource correctly can mean the difference between getting your company off the ground and crashing and burning.

David Allen spawned a movement in 2002 with *Getting Things Done*. Allen's book has grown into a cult phenomenon, with "GTD freaks" launching and publishing blogs and websites tailored to the millions of people who have found Allen's lessons a perfect fit for their helter-skelter lives.

Allen does not rely heavily on technology, but his core principles— identify, capture, organize—can combine with digital technology to help streamline your professional and personal life.

▶ ▶ *Develop a strategy*

Forming a personal productivity strategy starts with a simple equation:

What you need to manage + the right tools to manage it = personal productivity.

What you need to manage (in a sample list):

- email.

- contacts.

- to-do lists.

- calendars.

- notes.

- word processing.

- spreadsheets.

- presentations.

Do not fear failure

Fear of failure is something every entrepreneur must deal with. A few are so passionate about their idea that all they can envision is wild success. They're the lucky ones. The rest of us must face the reality that, when starting a new business, the odds are stacked against us.

"Failure is inevitable; it happens all the time in a complex economy," says Tim Harford, columnist for *The Financial Times* and author of *Adapt: Why Success Always Starts with Failure.* "How did the economy produce all these amazing things that we have around us—computers and cellphones and so on? There were a bunch of ideas, and the good ones grew and prospered. And the bad ones were pretty ruthlessly weeded out."[7]

As startups have become a bigger part of U.S. business activity, the concept of taking a risk to follow your dream is much more part of the mainstream than it was 20, 40 or 60 years ago. Previous generations were mostly content to work for someone else their entire lives, as long as the paycheck and the pension and the benefits would be there. (My father worked for the forest service for almost 35 years. The longest I've stayed with a job is four years.) In today's world most people understand, and even admire, the person who has the guts to take that flying leap of faith.

If you have a startup dream but are having trouble overcoming your fear, it may mean you're not ready; you don't yet have enough faith

- images.
- databases.
- project management.
- Web or graphic design.
- collaboration with colleagues.

in your idea. That's where co-founders come in handy. If you can persuade at least one other person to commit to the project, your faith in the idea will grow and you will have someone to share the fear. If you don't have a co-founder, make sure you spend time around other entrepreneurs. The exchange of ideas will give you energy, and listening to others' fears and struggles will give you strength. Entrepreneur meetups can sometimes feel like support groups.

Realize, too, that you will gain exponentially from any startup venture, no matter how it turns out. The lessons you learn, the experience you gain and the people you meet will open doors and lead to opportunities you wouldn't otherwise have had. When my own startup stalled, I found a golden opportunity with the No. 1 TV station in Seattle. The position required someone with business development and other skills that I didn't acquire by working in a newsroom. So even if your startup doesn't take off, the process of launching a business may be what launches your career in some new, exciting direction.

It's only natural to feel some amount of fear before you jump. If starting a business were easy, everyone would do it. As hockey great Wayne Gretzky famously said: "You miss 100 percent of the shots you never take."

Some variables to consider in choosing tools:

- How much are you willing to pay? ("Nothing" is a viable answer, since many solutions are free.)

- Do you need to integrate with other systems for your job or with a particular mobile device? (Outlook for email and calendar, for example, or an iPhone.)

- Do you need an offline solution? (This is important if you regularly spend time working somewhere that does not have an Internet connection.)

▶ ▶ *Choose the right tools*

Once you know the answers to these questions, you can begin investigating possible solutions. Here is a list to get you started, with at least one option for each of the tasks listed above.

- Here are some options for office suites.

  - **Google**: contacts, email, documents, calendar, sharing.

  - **Office Live**: Word, Excel, PowerPoint.

  - **Zoho**: Full suite of "productivity and collaboration tools," most of them free. It includes tools for everything listed above, plus wikis, customer relationship management (CRM) and much more.

- Here are some options for specialized solutions and a quick overview of the more popular options:

  Accounting: Quickbooks is the industry standard. You can also use Mint for basic expense tracking when you're just getting started.

  Project management: Backpack and Basecamp are two excellent products from 37 Signals. If you need a free option, try Zoho, Open Workbench or Trac.

  Collaboration: Dropbox and Mozi are excellent for backing up files and sharing them with others. Google Docs can help you create documents and discuss them with others.

  Communication: Skype is great for video calls and chats. There are many free instant messaging clients available, from AOL to Google to Yahoo!. And check out Google Voice for free phone calls and SMS and some nifty text translations of voicemails.

  Customer Relationship Management (CRM): If you plan to contact people and ask them to buy your product or place ads on your site, you need a way to keep track of this activity. Salesforce is the market leader, but also check out Zoho, Batchbooks and Highrise.

  Marketing: GoToMeeting is a paid service that allows you to do live Web demos or webinars with potential customers. Yuuguu is one of many free options. To make screencasts of your product, try Jing.

  To-do lists: Evernote, Jott, Scribe and Vingo are some of the many to-do list services available for free. Many are also mobile applications that can record audio on your mobile phone and convert it to text.

Meeting scheduler: Try Doodle, Tungle, SetAMeeting, Meet-O-Matic or other services for scheduling a meeting with more than one person without a chain of emails.

As a bonus, here are a few more tools that may come in handy, too:

Oh Don't Forget: Quick reminder tool that sends SMS to anyone's mobile phone.

Socrata: Create dynamic databases from spreadsheets or from scratch.

MindMeister: Mind-mapping software for brainstorming, either as a group or by yourself.

In addition, visit Inc. Magazine's excellent resource library for starting a business and this search engine for free online apps.[8]

▶ ▶ *Organize your email*

Start with your email. While countless other tools and technologies have been developed in recent years, email is still largely how work gets done. Unfortunately, it is also how a lot of noise makes its way into our lives.

If you take some time to use organizational tools like filters and folders in your email program, you can bring order to chaos. Commit to following a few time-saving rules to manage an email account (or several) that receives dozens of messages each day.

The first is to limit the time your email program is up on your screen. Focus on other tasks for an hour—or two, or four—and then launch email again and address the new messages before closing it and getting back to your other duties. This will prevent you from being distracted by each new email that arrives in your inbox and will keep you focused when you do start working with your email.

One of Allen's best GTD suggestions is to spend no more than two minutes on every email. If you can reply in less than two minutes, do it. If you can't, file it. This system works only if you've set up an intuitive folder system so you can move emails without losing track of them. Allen suggests a "Waiting on" folder for storing emails that you can't reply to until you receive additional information, and a "Read this" folder for storing emails that contain attachments or more information than can't be read in two minutes. You can go back to those when you have time, or print them out and take them with you to read on a train or plane.

The goal is to look at each email message only once. This will save time and thought energy. This method is referred to as "Inbox Zero" by Merlin Mann, who created the popular personal productivity site 43 Folders. The goal is to have zero emails in your inbox after you finish an email session, much like clearing off your desk and putting everything away before you head out for lunch or home for the night.

▶▶ *Work smarter, not harder*

Email, of course, is just the beginning. All professionals, including journalists and freelance writers, have to manage contacts, to-do lists, calendars and notes. Depending on your profession, the list could also include spreadsheets, presentations, images, databases, project management, Web or graphic design and collaboration with colleagues.

Fortunately, there is a bevy of slick, simple-to-use tools for doing all this—and more. The key is to find as few solutions as possible that do as many of the things on your list as possible. That way you will streamline your productivity, visiting fewer websites as you get things done.

Manage your time by managing your inputs. For example, if you use a system like Backpack, you can add meetings and appointments to a calendar while simultaneously managing a to-do list. The system also stores any documents or images that are related to the meeting so you can keep

> Figure 6.7 Backpack ◁

all your stuff together. And you can access the material from anywhere, via the Web, and share it with others on your team.

An electronic system like this is better than paper because it's easy to edit and modify lists, changing the order or priority, and it also stores your calendar items and lists as an archive. Unlike paper, an electronic system can't be lost; your system is always waiting for you online. And it is easily shared by more than one person from more than one location.

These "virtual office" solutions range from Microsoft's Office Live Suite, which includes online versions of Word, Excel and PowerPoint, to free online solutions like Google Docs and Zoho, which integrates with Facebook, allowing users to find and share your documents while Facebooking.

Storing documents and conducting all your business online is a form of cloud computing. By saving your stuff "in the cloud" (on servers accessed through the Internet) you gain the advantages of always having access to your files, no matter where you are. But of course, that's true only if the place you're in has Internet access, an important consideration when planning your personal productivity strategy. Some online solutions feature an "offline" mode, which makes the system and your files available, even when an Internet connection is not.

Whatever system you use, remember to keep copies of your important files. This advice is worth following whether you store files in the cloud like millions of other people, or you store them in some system of your own. It's been said that there are two kinds of computer users: those who back up their data, and those who will. The first time your hard drive crashes and you lose important work, you'll know what I mean.

▶ ▶ *Manage your projects*
Because software developers often work collaboratively, they need effective ways to manage their projects. That's good news for the rest of us, because some of these developers have used their programming skills to create elegant, easy-to-use software that works for tracking all kinds of projects, including news stories—especially big projects or ongoing coverage.

"Project management, as an idea, goes back a very long way," Scott Berkun writes in *Making Things Happen*. "A dotted line can be drawn from the software developers of today back through time to the builders of the Egyptian pyramids or the architects of the Roman aqueducts."[9] All had the same goal: to accomplish a huge task by breaking it down and accomplishing a series of small tasks.

Project management programs allow you to assign tasks, share files, establish deadlines and include notes. This structure can bring order to an individual working on a big story with lots of moving parts, or an entire newsroom attempting to hit daily deadlines.

While Basecamp requires a subscription (30-day trials are free), other services like Zoho provide basic services free. Project management is more than just software; it's a skill that is acquired and honed over time. For some, it's even a career. You can take courses on project management at your local community college or online. Project management can help anyone manage his or her work, no matter what kind of work that is.

▶ Run a virtual company

Cloud computing has opened many opportunities for information companies. One of the most significant is the ability to work from anywhere at any time. That means a physical office is now a luxury instead of a necessity. If all of your email, documents and other data are stored somewhere on the "Interwebs," what's the point of paying rent on an office space so you and your colleagues can fight traffic and pay for parking?

"There's a lot of pressure to have an office, but if you can trust your employees and if you don't have a lot of physical stuff like prototypes, then it [a virtual office] is a great model," says Graham Hill, who founded TreeHugger in 2003 as a blog about the green movement and sold it to Discovery Communications in 2007 for $10 million. "You're going to save a bunch of money on real estate, and it's going to be good for the environment, because you're not commuting and you're not using an office.

"You can also live anywhere in the world. I conceived TreeHugger while I was living in New York, but I fell in love with this Spanish girl and ended up founding the company in her apartment in Barcelona. It was all contractors for the first two-and-a-half years. Writers were paid per post, with bonuses based on traffic."[10]

To be sure, many companies still find value in face-to-face communication and collaboration. Startups, however, are increasingly turning to virtual working as a way to save money on rent and as a perk for attracting excellent employees who don't happen to live nearby. Instant messaging, conference calls and video chats on Skype, as well as the project management and collaboration tools we've already discussed, make it possible for team members to be in constant contact without ever setting foot "in the office."

Figure 6.8 Treehugger

▶ Be agile, continuous and lean

No matter what type of company you may be starting or working on, from a one-person neighborhood blog to a corporate media operation, you can benefit from the principles practiced by startup software companies. The people running these companies, and the people working there, are fanatical about efficiency and making progress. As a result, several "movements" have gained critical mass in the software business, and you'd be wise to apply some of the principles to your own operation.

Among the most recent is a concept called "lean startup," a term coined by Eric Ries, who wanted to channel the lean manufacturing process, fine-tuned in Japanese factories decades ago to focus on eliminating any work or investment that doesn't produce value for customers.[11] This is efficiency on steroids.

"If it works, it will reduce failure rates for entrepreneurial ventures and boost innovation," says Thomas R. Eisenmann, a professor at the Harvard Business School. "That's a big deal for the economy."[12]

"The lean playbook advises quick development of a 'minimum viable product,' designed with the smallest set of features that will please some group of customers," Steve Lohr wrote in the *New York Times*. "Then, the start-up should continually experiment by tweaking its offering, seeing how the market responds and changing the product accordingly. Facebook, the giant social network, grew that way, starting with simple messaging services and then adding other features."[13]

Agile or continuous development is another trend that's been around longer (and was discussed in Chapter 4).

For example, Wordpress, the most popular blogging platform in the world, has updated its product more than 25,000 times in five years. That's an average of 16 product updates per day. Toni Schneider, the CEO of Automattic, the company that owns Wordpress, explained on his blog why this is a better approach.

"Launching products is one of the hardest things companies do," Schneider wrote. "Most companies pour months of work into making sure everything goes right at a launch—the features are right, the marketing is ready, the press is primed, the product is solid, etc. But a new breed of companies are doing things very differently. Instead of optimizing product launches to go as perfectly as possible, they optimize to have them go as quickly as possible."[14]

Understand that getting your company going is the hardest step. Once you begin publishing content or providing a service, every day will bring a new opportunity to change or improve your idea. There's nothing to stop you from doing that. But first you have to launch.

For anyone hoping to compete in the new digital landscape, speed matters. Make sure you create your company in a way that will allow you to stay as flexible and move as fast as possible.

BUILD YOUR BUSINESS **Stage 6**

In the last section, you were told not to write a full business plan yet. An executive summary of two or three pages is all you need in the early going to crystallize the idea. But as you move ahead, it's useful to flesh out your idea and try to define it more, in the form of a full-fledged business plan.

If you decide to seek outside funding, for example, you will need a well-written and thorough business plan, especially if you're looking for a bank loan. If you're applying for grants, a formal business plan may not be required, but the foundation will probably require an exhaustive application process that will be easier to complete if you have already completed a business plan.

Writing a business plan is a lot of work. The dirty little secret of startups is that much of what you write will, in all likelihood, be complete fiction. (See the Appendix for the Pegasus News business plan, annotated by founder Mike Orren.) If you are creating a new product or service, or entering a new market—which is what entrepreneurs do—you'll have few benchmarks and little history to draw on in making your projections. Be careful to protect yourself by not shifting too much of your time and energy away from *actually building your idea* to the arduous process of *writing about your idea*.

Still, thinking through all the various aspects of launching a business has benefits. Whether or not your forecasts (or guesses) prove accurate, taking those assumptions in your head and putting them down on paper can help. Investors, for example, know that business plans are built on guessing, but they gauge the value of the plan by how the entrepreneur determines the projections and supports them.

To write a full-fledged business plan, you'll need to address certain basic elements. For this chapter, these will be your Build Your Business questions:

6

Executive Summary: If you already created the executive summary as discussed in Chapter 5, you're off to a head start. It will be somewhat repetitive with information in the full business plan, which is where you will expand on the particular topics.

Problem and opportunity: Investors like to say they put their money in painkillers, not vitamins. The translation: Your idea should be essential for alleviating someone's pain.

✓ **ACT:** Describe the problem you are going to solve and the opportunity you have to solve it.

Product: This section will describe your product or service in more detail.

✓ **ACT:** Return to the drawing you did on page 178 and see if you can turn it into a full mockup or screenshot. Provide screenshots—or mockups—if possible. Detail the revenue streams and how money will be made and also discuss strategies for marketing and selling the product (customer acquisition) and customer retention.

Market and competition: If you plan to sell directly to other businesses (B2B), then include a section for industry confirmation to prove there is a track record of businesses paying for similar services. Remember, "there is no competition" is not an acceptable answer here. It shows that either you don't know enough about the market or you're trying to solve a problem that doesn't really exist.

 ACT: Describe the competition or comparables that you have identified. Assess their strengths and weaknesses and show how your business will do things better.

Operations: This section outlines how you will spend the money you're asking for. If you plan to hire, what are the positions, and how will each position contribute to the overall needs of the company?

 ACT: Detail the human resources you will need, plus infrastructure, from office space to hosting to other equipment like computers and cameras.

Company: Tie together the genesis of the idea with the strengths and talents of those working on the idea. For example, Chris Seper and Mary Vanac hatched the idea for MedCity News while working for the Cleveland newspaper in beats that involved business and medicine.

 ACT: Detail the qualifications of anyone who will be contributing and describe how the project came about.

Financials and projections: Financial projections are tedious and time-consuming and largely a guessing game. Don't agonize too long over the numbers. They probably won't hold up anyway. But do try talking to financial experts or other entrepreneurs to learn how to make realistic projections based on your specific idea.

 ACT: Start with a narrative explanation of how you will make and spend money and include a detailed spreadsheet with quarterly projections for three to five years.

Risk analysis and exit strategy: You need this section only if you are seeking angel or venture investment. This is how the investors will get their money back—plus some. In fact, you will have to project a return of three to five times the investment from an angel investor and 10 times the investment from a venture capital firm. (Hence the saying: "Go big or go home.")

 ACT: Describe how you will "exit," either by being acquired by a bigger company or by going public. To support your projections, include examples from similar startups that had successful exits.

As Cheryl Dell, publisher of the *Sacramento Bee*, likes to say: Think of a business plan as a compass instead of a map. It will get you going in the right direction, but until you arrive, you can't know all the turns and stops and starts you'll take.

Notes

1. "A clouded future: Online services that match freelancers with piecework are growing in hard times," *The Economist*, May 13, 2010. http://www.economist.com/business-finance/displaystory.cfm?story_id=16116919

2. Douglas Martin, "Clement Stone Dies at 100; Built Empire on Optimism," *New York Times*, September 5, 2002.

3. See: http://www.citmedialaw.org and http://www.medialaw.org/

4. U.S. Code Collection, "Protection for private blocking and screening of offensive material." http://www.law.cornell.edu/uscode/47/230.html

5. Linda Pinson and Jerry Jinnett, *Keeping the Books* (Chicago, IL: Upstart Publishing Co., 1998) 1.

6. Pinson and Jinnett, 4.

7. Renee Montagne, "'Adapt': Failure As an Option on the Way to Success," May 23, 2011. http://www.npr.org/2011/05/23/136503420/adapt-failure-as-an-option-on-the-way-to-success

8. See: http://www.inc.com/tools/ and http://searchfreeapps.com/Search_Engine.html

9. Scott Berkun, *Making Things Happen* (Cambridge, MA: O'Reilly, 2008) 1.

10. Graham Hill, "Why Virtual," *Inc. Magazine*, April 2010, 66.

11. Steve Lohr, "The Rise of the Fleet-Footed Startup," *New York Times*, April 23, 2010.

12. Lohr.

13. Lohr.

14. Toni Schneider, "In praise of continuous deployment: The WordPress.com story," from Schneider's personal blog, www.toni.org, May 19, 2010.

CHAPTER 7

Harness the Technology

A former concert pianist turned arts critic, Douglas McLennan is an unlikely Internet entrepreneur. If you think that being a 20-something tech geek is mandatory for starting and running a website, think again.

In 1999, when McLennan was writing for the *Seattle Post-Intelligencer,* he saw a story on *The Philadelphia Inquirer* website about an art collection in financial difficulty. Though the story was a couple of weeks old, he still found it interesting —which made him think the Internet must be full of stories that would interest people who cared about the arts.

"That was on a Tuesday," McLennan recalls. "On Wednesday I came up with the name, registered it, and bought some books on HTML. I got some yellow pads and sketched it out over the weekend and launched it that Monday."

The next week he upgraded his home Internet connection to broadband, and ArtsJournal.com was born.

About four weeks later, the *New York Times* published a story about McLennan's arts news website, and the word quickly spread. ArtsJournal has served as the go-to source for news and commentary about the world of the arts throughout the English-speaking world ever since. The site features links to other news sources, in addition to original content, mostly in blog form.

McLennan could easily have seen his lack of technology knowledge as a barrier to implementing his idea. After all, he had never published anything online when he started the site. "There were no content management systems" in 1999, McLennan said. "My big investment was I bought Front Page (website editing software), which was just a joke."

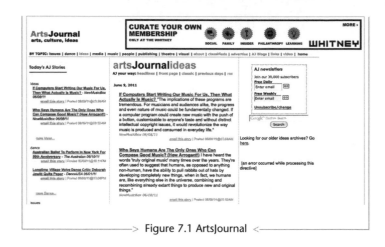

> Figure 7.1 ArtsJournal <

Realizing that the off-the-shelf software wasn't going to meet his needs, he took a different tack, using his journalist's curiosity to quickly learn the basics of Web publishing. It turns out that everything you need to know about publishing online . . . has been published online. He learned as he went, experimenting and trying new things.

"Things were constantly breaking," McLennan explained. "Once a month I would do these archives from particular topics. I never had the energy to input these flat pages into the system because there are thousands of stories." That's the way websites were built in the 1990s—individual pages linked together. Things have gotten much better. Now, through the advent of the content management system (CMS), content is stored in a database.

Today, in its fourth design, ArtsJournal attracts 250,000 readers each month. The site sells classified and display advertising to companies that want to reach this affluent niche audience, but ArtsJournal also makes money in other ways. Nearly 40,000 people have subscribed to the free email newsletters that the company produces, and 1,000 people pay $28 a year to subscribe to a paid newsletter. In fact, McLennan says, the website's 30,000 daily readers represent only half of the ArtsJournal audience.

"The reality is, a huge percentage of the people who use the site don't actually remember it's a website," McLennan says. "They're getting it through feeds or the newsletter, so I'm constantly running into people that are surprised it's a website, too."

Now that he realizes how many people access ArtsJournal content without visiting the website, he's changed his approach. Instead of spending so much time worrying about the placement of stories and the layout of the homepage, he focuses more on scouring the world's media to find good arts-related content.

Today McLennan is a Web publishing veteran, comfortable solving business and technology problems himself or finding help when he needs it. Once the site was set up, ArtsJournal became a matter of doing the journalism. With a network of 60 critics, the site offers plenty of original content. For the rest, he and his small staff sift through 2,000 stories every day to select the 30 they'll link to for this vibrant community.

"It's pretty much the same idea now as it was then," McLennan says. "We didn't do blogs back then because there weren't so-called blogs."

He has maintained consistency for his audience while changing the underlying technology that powers the website and newsletters three times in 10 years. Each revamping has been a massive undertaking for a small startup without an abundance of technical expertise. Making these improvements is important to continuing the business though, and thus, is all part of the challenge for McLennan.

"I'm always interested in doing things that are interesting to me," he says. "Usually that makes it a pretty easy call."

In this chapter, you'll be exposed to a plethora of choices for meeting your technology needs. The goal is not to make you an expert on the strengths and weaknesses of various Web publishing technologies. You need to learn enough about Web publishing so you can find the right tools to get your idea up and running as quickly as possible. First you need to form a clear vision of what you need from technology. Only then can it help you achieve your goals.

7

Here's a look at what we cover in this chapter:

- ▶ How to pick a platform for your website.
- ▶ Which social media tools will help you engage with your audience.
- ▶ How to track your audience.
- ▶ What the mobile revolution means for digital publishers.

PICK A PLATFORM

If you want to be a Web publisher, you're in luck: Today's technology makes it easy for anyone to produce a content website with a professional look and high performance.

You won't have to learn HTML or the "old-fashioned way" of building websites—namely designing static pages in a Web editor, such as Adobe Dreamweaver, and using FTP to publish your pages online. If you're planning to build a news or content site that will be updated frequently, you need dynamic Web technology, which means you create content in a database and then the site pulls from that database to update the pages. While this sounds complicated—and until a few years ago, it was—today a multitude of online publishing services and open-source technologies, such as the content management system (CMS) Wordpress, make the job relatively easy to accomplish for most people.[1]

When it comes to picking a CMS platform for your new site, you'll find both good and bad news. The good news is that you have plenty of options even if you don't have a budget and don't know code. Most of the services and technology detailed in this section are free, and the ones that aren't free are really cheap.

The bad news? With so many options, you could spend too much time evaluating each system. Don't fall prey to paralysis by analysis. Whichever solution you choose will probably work for you. It pays to ask around, though, and get feedback from anyone you know who is working with online content management systems.

"Decoding what CMS to use is when it is really important to use your network to find out what others are using and how or if they are happy with their choice," says Jane Briggs-Bunting, a Michigan State communications professor. "They can also fill you in on the upsides and downside of the CMS they are using."

Let's look at several promising CMS options for independent publishers, analyzing what they do and how they differ. Because each startup has a distinct mission, each will have unique needs. First, identify which of the four categories below most closely fits your situation. Then analyze the offerings explained in the sections that follow to find the best available solution for your site.

1. **Easy website construction:** If you need something simple and you don't plan to publish new content more than a few times a week, easy website builders can get you going quickly. These options work best for publishers who won't have more than two or three people working on the website and need to establish an Internet presence in a hurry at no cost.

2. **Powered by blog software:** Most appropriate for publishers who plan to post content several times a day, this solution will accommodate

a single person or a staff with dozens of writers and editors. The relevant section will tell you how to turn Wordpress into a CMS that will power a professionally designed news site.

3. **Open-source CMS solutions:** This option is most appropriate for an organization that plans to publish many times a day and grow in scale over time. This section takes a look at a few of the dozens of options out there and links to an in-depth look at Drupal, the most popular and powerful option for a free, open-source CMS.

4. **Ready to go, out of the box:** A quick look at three solutions—for beginner, intermediate and advanced publishers.

BONUS: No matter which solution you choose, consider using add-ons and other goodies as part of your Web publishing strategy. The section on add-ons and extras will help you find the right accessories to enhance your strategy.

▶ Build it simple and free

There are dozens of free Web site builders available today. Some have been around for years; others bring new, innovative approaches.

The biggest questions to answer before analyzing these services:

1. Do I want my own domain name?

2. Do I want a customized design? If so, do I have the skills to play with the code (or know someone who does)?

3. Are the pages optimized for search engines so I can increase traffic?

4. Am I hoping to sell ads or products to produce revenue?

Once you know the answers to those questions, you're prepared to enter the world of website builders. These are tailored to publishers who need a simple solution and don't plan to publish new content more than a few times each week. Here are some of the leading options:

Google Sites: Just what you'd expect from the Web titan—clean, simple and free. As you would expect, Google Sites plays nicely with other Google products, and if search engine optimization (SEO) is a concern, well, you would hope that a Google site would index well in Google.

Moonfruit: You may not have heard of Moonfruit, but the service has been around for 10 years and has been used to build more than 2 million websites. It's available at no cost, so it's worth a look. In a way, the

Moonfruit service is tailored to site owners who favor style over substance. If you want a highly designed site that will not be updated constantly, the SiteMaker tools are easy to use. But for a prolific site like a blog or local news site, the Moonfruit CMS is not going to be as efficient.

Yola: Formerly known as SynthaSite, Yola received $20 million in funding in 2009, has more than 2 million users, and has been around since 2003. The service is best for quickly building a simple website when you don't have a budget or technical knowledge. You can build a traditional site or a blog-style site very easily.

Bravenet: Claims to be the "number one provider of free Web tools in the world" and has been ranked among the top 50 most visited websites in the world. It has more than 7 million registered members; over 20 million unique visitors access a Bravenet product each month. The Bravenet tools will work for variety of needs, from small business hosting to blogging to simple site building. The free option comes with Bravenet's advertising and has a 10-page limit, however, so if a no-cost solution is a requirement, Bravenet is probably not the best solution for you.

Jimdo: A German company founded in 2007, Jimdo started as a group of three friends selling basic site-creation tools. The tools developed into a consumer version that now has more than 100,000 users and sites in seven languages (German, English, Chinese, French, Italian, Spanish and Russian). Jimdo is tailored to an intermediate user and provides the ability to build more advanced sites.

Weebly: A Y Combinator startup founded in 2007, Weebly offers what is arguably the easiest site-building tool to use, so even beginners will be able to publish in no time. Weebly also has developed a blog engine if you need blog capabilities for your site.

Finding the right Website-building solution should be easy. Use the free options from several of the services to compare one with another. You can test-drive them by creating an uncomplicated "test site" on each service. See which package works best for you before you "buy." Whether or not a particular user interface appeals to you is very subjective, so make sure you're comfortable with the system and how it works. With so many good options available, there's no reason to be stuck with a system you find confusing or frustrating.

▶ Blog systems good at any size

If you want to set up a simple blog-based site because you are a one- or two-person team, consider working with **Wordpress** or **Blogger.** These platforms make it easy to get started, and the blog format lends itself to the continual publishing of news and information.

"We were on Moveable Type which, when we moved over to it, I thought was the best at the time," McLennan said. "But Wordpress is just so far in advance of it now. That's going to enable us to do a lot more."

Wordpress has emerged as the leading force in CMS blogging solutions for news sites. In the last few years, many news sites of all sizes have switched from a traditional CMS to Wordpress. Since Wordpress is an open source solution, publishers save money by not licensing expensive enterprise software. They also benefit from the rapid development of the Wordpress community that has grown the back-end framework from a simple blog system to a powerful CMS. Because online news publishers need flexible, socially interactive sites—sites that go far beyond the static, digital representation of an old print model—Wordpress is a smart solution.

Wordpress offers the flexibility and functionality to build as big and as complex a news site as you can envision. For example, the websites for the *Cedar Rapids Gazette* in Iowa and the *Midland Express & Star* in the United Kingdom are both built entirely on Wordpress, but when you visit the sites, they look nothing like a blog. A good example of a news site using Wordpress can be seen at Harvard Gazette, and a good example of a neighborhood news blog is MyBallard.com.

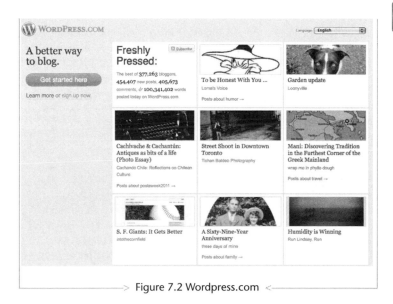

> Figure 7.2 Wordpress.com <

Dozens of college newspaper sites have switched to Wordpress in recent years, too. Most chose to use Wordpress instead of College Publisher, a CMS for college newspapers that is free, so the attraction of Wordpress goes beyond saving money. By allowing the publisher considerable flexibility and power, Wordpress can meet most needs.

The first decision point when choosing Wordpress is selecting which version you need. If you have no budget for hosting, then head over to Wordpress.com and sign up for a free Wordpress blog that has "wordpress.com" in the domain (e.g., mysite.wordpress.com). You can later upgrade to a Premium Wordpress.com account and have Wordpress host your blog with your own domain name when you have the budget. Remember, if you hope to customize your design, you'll need to add the custom cascading style sheets (CSS) feature.[2]

If you want the flexibility of hosting your own version—and a better domain name—then go to Wordpress.org. You can download and install the software yourself; Wordpress claims it takes only five minutes and offers a handy guide to walk you through the process.[3]

Or you can choose a hosting service that offers "one-click installation." Most Web hosting companies offer an option where they will install and set up popular Web services like Wordpress for you much as your own computer would install software. But a note of caution: Some hosts that offer one-click installs may limit your ability to add customized themes and widgets, so be sure to check out this potential limitation first.

A big advantage to Wordpress is that publishing content is so simple, even if you're not technically inclined. If you're new to Wordpress, visit their extensive library of video tutorials.[4]

Publishers control the look and layout of their Wordpress sites through Wordpress **themes**. Creating Wordpress themes has grown into its own global marketplace of ready-to-go options, all with different colors and layouts. More than 900 different themes are available for free[5] but you might also consider paying for a premium theme.

If you have access to the CSS files via Wordpress, you will be able to modify and customize color and style on any of the themes you download and install. So tweaking a free theme is one way to go. But if you're not comfortable with CSS design, spending $50 on a theme—if it's one you really like—is probably a good investment. Do a Web search for "cool Wordpress themes" and prepare to be overwhelmed by the choices.

▶ Get power, flexibility from a CMS

A CMS allows you to create, edit, manage and publish content in a consistently organized fashion. Publishers use a CMS for storing, controlling and publishing many different types of content, including news articles, operators' manuals, technical manuals, sales guides and marketing brochures. Each category of content may include assets such as text, photographs, audio files, video files and electronic documents, as well as user-generated Web content such as comments and ratings.

Fortunately for startup publishers, many excellent CMS options are available as free, open-source solutions. Web publishers favor an open-source solution for a multitude of reasons. Here are the most important for someone aiming to publish a news site:

- **Cost:** There are no license fees, but you'll probably still have to pay to host your site.

- **Growth:** If you choose the right CMS, you will have access to a community of developers building new and better technology for the system.

- **Flexibility:** While changing from a static HTML-based site to a robust CMS isn't painless, you are free to switch from one system to another if the system you're using isn't working for you.

The reason to choose a full-powered CMS over a blog platform or an easy website builder is power and flexibility. If you want to publish a professional-class website with multiple authors publishing frequently, a user registration system, and other advanced features, you may need the capabilities of a full CMS.

How do you choose among the many open-source content management systems available today? Here are some criteria to consider:

- Are you comfortable with the user interface for administering the site? Is it easy to use? If you are not a one-person operation, involve the people who help you run in selecting the CMS.

- How big is the development community? A big advantage of open source software is all of the volunteer developers who contribute to improving the system and fixing problems. If you choose an obscure CMS that only a few developers are working on, you won't have as much developer power as you will with a more popular framework.

As of 2011, Drupal and Joomla were the reigning kings of the open-source CMS world (Wordpress excluded). The two systems rank highly on freelance websites for jobs, have spawned a number of books, and receive far more traffic to their sites than any of the other popular solutions, which include Mambo, Plone and DotNetNuke.

The structure of every CMS is similar. Each consists of a core piece of software that runs the basic functionality, plus add-on modules or extensions that offer specialized features. Think of the system with the add-ons as a set of Lego blocks, or a "builder's kit" of pre-designed components that can be snapped together to build whatever you need. The goal of the CMS is to allow people who aren't programmers to make powerful websites. And if the Lego block you need isn't available as part of the basic installation, chances are pretty good that someone has created a custom version that you can download and install for free.

For example, if you want to offer users the ability to comment on stories or upload photos, simply "turn on" those modules. If you want to use Google Ad Manager to display and manage ads, find and download the custom module that others have created and install it on your site.

For whatever reason, Drupal is more popular than Joomla with news publishers. The *Florida Times-Union* and the *Seattle Times'* NWSource.com are two examples of large-scale newspaper sites using Drupal. Dozens more news organizations use Drupal as well, while just a handful of newspapers are using Joomla.

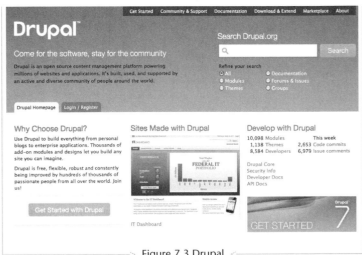

Figure 7.3 Drupal

▶ Ready to go, out of the box

If you're looking to take much of the guesswork out of launching a news website, a few out-of-the-box solutions aim to deliver a full news site experience immediately, without needing custom development.

You can choose a Wordpress option, either hosted by Wordpress.com—with additional features for your own domain and editing CSS—or a one-click installation on a professional hosting site. Then add a news-centric theme for a few dollars. Some theme options to consider that are tailored to news-style sites include:

- News.
- Live Wire.
- Gazette Edition.
- The New Yorker (A *New York Times* clone).
- Onyx Portal.
- Playmaker.
- Skyye News Theme.
- Magazine News Theme.
- NewsPress.
- WP Remix.

If you need a more robust solution similar to what Drupal offers for news sites, check out the Open Publish project or ProsePoint. Both of these products are bundles of modules and customizations tailored for online publishers. Their features support everything from basic news coverage needs to Web 2.0 trends, social media publishing and topic hubs.

ProsePoint is the more basic of the two products. A customization tool for Drupal made specifically for online publishers, ProsePoint features a newspaper- and magazine-centric data architecture that can aggregate stories into editions, which are versions of a publication series.[6]

Open Publish provides a starting kit of modules and configurations for the needs of publishers and integrates application programmer interfaces (APIs) from Reuters OpenCalais, Flickr and Yahoo!, so it's more advanced and robust than ProsePoint. Each component bundled in the distribution is well supported, documented and modularly designed according to Drupal architecture.[7]

If your plans are a little more ambitious, check out the Armstrong project.[8] Funding by the Knight Foundation helped the Texas Tribune and Bay Citizen package and make available the custom-built CMS that has powered those two startup news sites since 2009. The Armstrong project is open source with free base code, but you will need someone with Python code experience to manipulate and customize it for your use. With the right developer, this would be a great way to go.

▶ Find the right host

Once you choose a platform, your next step is deciding where to host your site. You shouldn't have to break the bank to do it. Many website hosts offer plans that start at less than $10 per month. There are too many options to list here, but you can start your search with these hosting companies that all feature one-click installation of Wordpress, Drupal and Joomla:

- DreamHost.

- Host Monster.

- Green Geeks.

- Media Temple.

- BlueHost.

But be careful. One-click installation often prevents you from having FTP access to the host's server. This means you won't be able to install additional modules and themes, so you'll be restricted to what the hosting service automatically installs for you.

▶ ▶ *Enhance your site with advanced features*

New technologies for online publishing specifically applicable to content websites abound. Below are some of the best options, most of which are free and easy to use, so you can take your site to the next level.

Event Calendars. A local news and information website generally needs a calendar of events. While some of the publishing platforms highlighted in the other sections feature their own calendar option, adding an external service such as Google Calendar has the advantage of allowing your users to add events, thus making your site more collaborative. As with most Google products, the price is right—it's free.

- Other free calendar options include Local Calendar or the Event Calendar Plugin for Wordpress users.

Liveblogging. The next generation of liveblogging can be seen though add-on services such as CoverItLive or ScribbleLive, which produce a module that embeds into any Web page and give a mobile journalist a blog-like interface. These services are great for liveblogging sports events, press conferences or breaking news, or scheduling online question-and-answer sessions from the office. Liveblogging services provides several feedback features not found in a traditional blog, such as allowing the audience to comment and ask questions or participate in polls in real time. And liveblogging sessions are all easily archived for later access online.

Live video. Streaming video on your site is a great way to attract more audience views. Free services like Ustream make it easy and keep the cost at the popular price point of free. All you need to stream video is a computer with a solid Internet connection and a video camera. Or, if you're doing a video blog entry, a microphone and a webcam will suffice. The Ustream software will automatically detect your camera and broadcast the video on Ustream's website. You can also record the video for publishing on your own site with services such as Justin.tv and Livestream.

- If you have a mobile phone that shoots video, several services—including Qik, Kyte and Flixwagon—make it easy to stream video live from anywhere even if you are without a computer or an Internet connection.

Mapping. You might want to add a customized map to your site. It's easy to build your own map mashup to identify content by location on a map, either with actual code or using a third-party service. If you are comfortable with HTML and want full control over your mashup, visit http://www.google.com/apis/maps and sign up for a free Google Maps API key. The Developer's Guide on Google.com walks you through the process for setting it up on your website.

- If you don't know HTML or want to work with it, try one of the free online services that will build the map for you. For example, Mapbuilder.net builds a map mashup as you enter locations with actual street addresses, one by one, and works with both Google and Yahoo! maps. If you want to turn a spreadsheet into a map mashup, try ZeeMaps, which allows you to build a map from a list of addresses in industry-standard .csv (comma separated value) format, or MapAlist.com, which allows you to convert a Google spreadsheet into a Google Earth mashup at no cost.

- Other mapping services include UMapper.com, which allows you to create a map on Google, Microsoft Virtual Earth or Yahoo! and set privacy settings or embed it on any site, and Google's own MyMaps. If you go to maps.google.com and click "My Maps," you can customize and save your own map to share with others. You can add photos and draw lines for routes and publish your "My Map" on other websites as well.

Social bookmarking. Link journalism is considered a form of Web "curating" or news work. Anyone can collect links, and algorithms can aggregate them. But only trained editors have the skills to select and collect the best information and use it to build a loyal audience.

- Link journalism also provides a method of collaboration for news organizations. Delicious, a link collection site, has been the dominant service for social bookmarking. If you plan to use links as a form of journalism or news gathering, a news startup called Publish 2 is an excellent option. Founded in 2007 and run by journalists, Publish 2 has developed innovative tools that make it an effective researching tool, as well as a powerful way to share links with your audience.

Databases. You can publish searchable databases on your site without knowing any code, thanks to services from a company called Caspio. Election returns, sports results and anything in an Excel spreadsheet can be published online in a usable interface using Caspio Bridge. It can also help you create Web forms. It's not a free service, but a 14-day free trial allows you to test it before spending any money.

Forums or bulletin boards. If you want to add message board–style forums to your site, both Wordpress (bbPress) and Drupal (Forum) feature modules that make it easy. If you're not using one of those platforms, then you have many options—so many, in fact, that an entire website (www.forum-software.org) keeps up with all the different possibilities and technologies. Among the most popular forums are vBulletin and PhpBB. Many of these solutions are free, but the top-rated vBulletin is not.

Email marketing. Creating, promoting and managing email lists for marketing or news can be an important piece of your overall business strategy. Publishing a regular email newsletter with links to your news stories or blog posts can significantly increase repeat visitors. A service like Feedburner automatically grabs an RSS feed and delivers it to users who subscribe on your site.

- If you publish an occasional, less frequent email (instead of a regular newsletter) and want to closely manage it, from the list to the look and feel, try MailChimp. It's free if you have fewer than

500 recipients and you don't mind the MailChimp badge on your emails. Newsberry is another email marketing service with a similar entry-level service at no cost. Also check out Constant Contact, which doesn't offer a free plan but is popular with nonprofits and other small businesses.

EXTEND YOUR REACH, TRACK YOUR PROGRESS

The platform or system that powers your publishing is only one piece of the overall technology strategy needed for running a new media business. You'll also need to leverage technology as you incorporate social media, track your audience, schedule and deliver advertising, and, of course, choose tools to run your business.

Here is a brief overview of tools to consider for social media engagement, audience analysis and mobile opportunities. See Chapter 3 for advertising technology options and Chapter 5 for an overview of tools to run your business.

▶ Leverage social media tools

You probably know that Twitter and Facebook should be part of what you do. But what exactly do you hope to gain from participating in these social networks?

"Figure out why you're getting on the social media bandwagon and what you want to accomplish with it," Sharlyn Lauby wrote at Mashable.com, the leading site for social media news and information.

While most social networks are "free" in the sense that you won't pay to join, they all require time and attention, care and feeding. For a bootstrapping startup, time is just as precious as money. If you plan to invest your time, you'll want a return on that investment (ROI).

The first assumption most journalists make when they see a microblogging platform like Twitter is that its primary use is for publishing breaking news alerts. True, it's an effective platform for that. But when it comes to breaking news, it's as important to be on Twitter to *receive* information about breaking news as it is to *send* it.

The last few years have brought countless examples of a news story breaking first on Twitter. In many cases, these news stories kept developing on Twitter before an established news organization could assemble even its quickest coverage. For example, on April 1, 2011, Shawna Redden used Twitter and the photo-sharing site Twitpic to share eyewitness accounts

Harnessing user-generated content

Incorporating material created by your audience into your digital media business is no longer a question of *whether* but *how.* Comments on blog posts or news stories; ideas for future stories; photos, sound and video; full-blown think pieces and regular blogs or columns are all forms of user-generated content that new media publishers bake into their business models. In fact, harnessing the power of the crowd is one of the prime advantages to setting up shop online; you have access to what your audience is thinking and caring about from day to day.

User-generated content may not strike you as part of a business model, but if your business is publishing, then finding and acquiring material to publish—and the costs associated with that acquisition— are critical elements. If you acquire content through licensing or by hiring people to create it, your expenses will increase and you'll have to bring in more revenue. If, on the other hand, you acquire content by marshaling users to produce it for you, the overall cost is lower, meaning less revenue is needed to cover costs.

The Huffington Post, with more than 1,000 unpaid writers, is the journalistic champion of user-generated content. Whether you agree with the model, the writers who contribute have done so by choice, either to increase their personal brand exposure or to push a particular idea in front of a larger audience. That HuffPo audience grew rapidly—to more than 14 million on the average weekday by early 2011—thanks to the deep content in a multitude of topics provided by these contributing writers.

Acquiring content at a lower cost sounds good on paper. But cheap does not mean free. When your site is new, simply getting people to submit material will take time and effort. When content does start coming in, someone will have to figure out whether it's any good and fits what you're trying to do for your audience. If some of it does, then someone still needs to prepare and present it. The Huffington Post pays editors, after all, to organize homepage sections and rank stories.

To see what extreme success with user-generated content looks like, check out icanhascheezburger.com or any of the 50 other sites in the Cheezburger Network, an ever-growing assembly of humor and entertainment that attracts more than 400 million page views per month. (The Cheezburger Network's CEO, Ben Huh, is a graduate of Northwestern's Medill School of Journalism.)

Scott Porad, chief technology officer at the Cheezburger Network, says crowdsourcing helps the company acquire content that is higher in quality and more relevant than what the staff could create on its own. Even so, he notes, "Only a fraction of the content submitted to us is of high enough quality to be used."

Sorting through submissions to identify the best ones is a "significant expense," Porad explains. So the company turns to its community to help. "Specifically, we employ a four-stage review process: Two phases leverage the user community to help us filter content, and two phases of review are done by moderators employed by our company."

Whether employees or users, all of Cheezburger's content moderation is done by humans, which is not cheap. The company has been profitable since it started in 2007, however, which means that it has done a good job of hiring staff as the need arose and finding revenue to offset those costs.

The secret to making user-generated content work is applying some of your limited resources to it, but only as part of an overall plan. Unless you work at cultivating community and defining your business's unique niche, you're likely to be underwhelmed by the response of the crowd. If you're worried about users providing too much content for you to handle—well, wouldn't that be a great problem to have?

BluestMuse Shawna MalviniRedden
@CBS13rightnow Happy to be alive. Still feel sick.6 foot hole in the skin of the plane five rows behind me. Unbelievable.
1 Apr

BluestMuse Shawna MalviniRedden
Sky! twitpic.com/4fv02d
1 Apr

BluestMuse Shawna MalviniRedden
@countupir mechanical. Hole ripped in the skin of the plane!
1 Apr

BluestMuse Shawna MalviniRedden
@KTXL_Kathy was calm. Pilot landed safely. Excellent crew!
1 Apr

BluestMuse Shawna MalviniRedden
@KTXL_Kathy terrifying but happy to be alive. Explosion sound, then a rush of air... masks dropped and a woman screamed. Everyone else was
1 Apr

BluestMuse Shawna MalviniRedden
Yikes! twitpic.com/4fuozb
1 Apr

BluestMuse Shawna MalviniRedden
Loss of cabin pressure, hands down the Scariest experience of my life.
1 Apr

BluestMuse Shawna MalviniRedden
@SouthwestAir Emergency landing in Yuma. SW pilots are amazing!

Figure 7.4 BluestMuse

from an emergency landing of a Southwest Airlines flight after a six-foot hole opened in the ceiling just five rows behind where Redden was sitting.

Redden (@BluestMuse on Twitter) communicated with news organizations in Sacramento on Twitter, relaying information from 35,000 feet after the cabin lost pressure and air masks dropped from the ceiling. "Happy to be alive," Redden tweeted to the CBS 13 news account, responding to a question. "Still feel sick. 6 foot hole in the skin of the plane five rows behind me. Unbelievable."

She also posted a handful of photos to Twitpic, including one of the hole that caused the emergency. News organizations around the world republished the photo, just as they did in 2009, when Janis Krums captured the iconic image of passengers loading into life rafts after the emergency landing of a commercial jet in the Hudson River. In the days afterward, Redden was interviewed by *Good Morning America,* Fox, MSNBC and The Associated Press, among others.

The primary goal of using social networks, however, is not publishing. It's connecting. Learning about breaking news is one benefit of listening to those in your network, but learning about what they're thinking, talking about, reading and doing is even more important. At no time in the history of journalism has a writer had this kind of access to his or her audience.

Sure, everyone is publishing these days, thanks to social media. As a news entrepreneur you have the opportunity to add a layer of journalism, on top of whatever the public is publishing, thus helping your audience filter and prioritize the information. In other words, your journalism knowledge allows you to add value to raw facts. And once you add value, you have the makings of a business model.

Tapping into your network of followers on Twitter or Facebook is similar to engaging readers of a blog. While the audience is probably smaller, the response and reaction is usually more immediate and more substantive. Even at 140 characters. That response and reaction is the whole point of social media.

Getting the most out of building a community on Twitter or Facebook takes a personal touch. There is power in finding new people to follow, thereby extending your network. There is social capital to be earned by actively participating in that network, where you give information and ask questions and expect your followers to do the same.

"Be a human presence on Facebook and Twitter; don't just attach your RSS feed to them and walk away," says Tracy Record, founder of the West Seattle Blog. "We have two main Twitter feeds. One is just RSS for those who only want links. The other one is all human, all the time, and if I send out a link

> Figure 7.5 Facebook WSB <

there, it's because I did it myself. Answer questions, post fragments, let people post to your wall/page. Be present."

Once a journalist has personally engaged in social media, new doors will open. Professional bloggers have discovered that Twitter can be particularly useful in providing real-time guidance and feedback on their journalism. By posting an item announcing an upcoming interview, then asking for suggestions on questions to ask, a journalist engages the audience to work with him or her to perform the journalism.

Posting also works when a journalist doesn't have someone to interview, but instead is looking for leads, background or other information on a particular subject. It's like interviewing or surveying the public, but much faster.

Remember, technology is a tool, not a strategy. Launching a Facebook page and a Twitter account are essential first steps, but you need to clarify what you hope to accomplish with these tools and services. Here are some quick pointers to help you execute a social media business strategy:

- Follow the 80/20 rule: 80 percent of your contributions to social media should be material that adds value to the "stream." Spend only 20 percent of your contributions on promoting yourself, your company or your service.

- Be relevant and timely.

- Be informative. Share others' information if needed, but contribute information, not clutter.

- Be instructive. Your audience will welcome tips and advice on a variety of topics.

- Include a link. More than 140 characters is often needed to fully convey meaning.

- Reflect your personality. Judiciously. If you're not funny in "real life," you're probably not funny online either.

- Build relationships. Ask and answer questions. Answer more than you ask.

Your goal should be to leverage social networks to build your brand. It's a concept conceived more than 50 years ago called "social capital," which is the advantage created by a person's location in a structure of relationships. Translation: Become the "trusted center" and/or become allied to the "trusted center" through digital communication, and you will gain trust, credibility and an audience.

Follow these basic steps to get going on Facebook and Twitter:

▶ ▶ *Use Facebook for engagement*

With 700 million registered users (and counting), Facebook is now the most visited site on the Web. It's even more popular than Google. Here is a quick-start guide to get you going with your business on Facebook.

1. Start by building a "page" for your website or product.

2. Add a Facebook widget for the fan page to your website. This will tell visitors to your site where they can join the community of other like-minded folks who also like your website or product.

3. Make sure your content can be shared with Facebook. Free tools like www.sharethis.com and www.addthis.com are two popular options that will put a Facebook logo and link on each of your news stories to make it easy for users to share them with their Facebook friends.

4. Add Facebook Connect to your site if you are hoping users will register. This will allow users to sign in with their Facebook account instead of creating a new one. It will also prevent anonymity, since you are who you are on Facebook.

"Similar to a company blog or website, your Facebook page can be used to share useful information with your fans," says Adam Ostrow, editor in chief of Mashable. "The idea here, though, is to not be overly self-promotional, using the 'Write Something' feature to broadcast not just news and promotions for your business, but also links and information that your fans might find useful. Remember, these updates show up on your fans' homepages. Like any form of marketing, if you create too much noise without providing value, they'll opt out."[9]

▶ ▶ *Build community with Twitter*

Each month, Twitter publishes more than 1 billion tweets into the world. It's an essential tool for businesses, especially if you are hoping to grow a community. Here's how to get started.

1. Register the best available username you can find at twitter.com, meaning the one most similar to your business or product name. If you need to add an underscore "_" to make it happen, do so.

2. Find Twitter users who are likely to be your initial target market. Go to search.twitter.com and enter keywords that represent the content you are interested in and find people who are publishing that content. Follow them. Most will follow you back. Then read

their Twitter streams and look at who else they're following to see who you should follow as well.

3. Add a Twitter widget to your website and blog so users will see your most recent tweets. Go to twitter.com/goodies for a selection of widgets and buttons to add to your site.

4. Start using a third-party application to manage your Twitter. Try Twhrl, Hootsuite or Tweetdeck.

5. Use a URL shortener that offers tracking so you can see how many clicks each link you tweet is getting. Bit.ly is a popular option. Hootsuite offers this as an integrated service; others may as well.

Facebook and Twitter are very different communities with very different operating norms. Think of Facebook as the social graph, connecting people who have actually met or know one another. Think of Twitter as the interest graph, connecting people who have a shared interest but, more often than not, haven't actually met.

When it comes to news sites, Facebook appears to work better as an engagement platform where the audience offers feedback to a publisher. Twitter is better suited for the publishing of news headlines and links around a particular area of focus. It's a way to build credibility in a specific topic area.

▶ Go beyond social networking

Twitter and Facebook are great tools, but often you'll need a way to communicate directly with your audience in messages longer than 140 characters or a Facebook status update. Blogging, audio and video are tried and true methods to reach and cultivate a community. You might already be planning to use these technologies to publish the new content that will be essential to your business, but you should also explore using them for marketing purposes.

As with social networking, the goal should be authenticity and collaboration with your audience. Too much of a "look at me" approach will turn off prospective audience and customers.

This is your outlet to speak directly to your audience. If there is benefit in taking your readers "behind the story," this is the place to do it. Blogging, audio and video are simple tools that are easy to incorporate into your regular workflow. Once you form the habit of updating them, it will become just part of what you do.

▶ ▶ *Use a blog to personalize your business*

Once you have a clear idea of the business you want to build, launch a blog on your own publishing platform or set up a separate Wordpress blog. Include photos of you and your staff, if possible, to personalize your business and give readers a peek behind the scenes. Then update the blog with insights and observations about your company or project's progress, including links to other sources for context.

As a new media entrepreneur, you are probably following other new media startups or other news sites in your particular topic area. You can post links to news stories or other blog posts that discuss these other sites, even if they are "competitors." Be open with your audience and let them see just how complicated and exciting this new area of media can be.

The "company blog" is also where potential funders, advertisers or other customers will turn to research your operation. That makes it doubly important to put your best foot forward and make as many positive announcements as possible without appearing too boastful.

If writing lengthy, analytical blog posts seems too arduous, try one of the short-blogging services that are growing in popularity. Tumblr and Posterous make it easy to update a blog-style Web page with short updates, links to other content or photos and videos. Tumblr relies on a toolbar that you can install on your Web browser, while Posterous allows you to post directly from email, which is pretty slick.

Yes, apparently some Web workers feel the need for a platform that is shorter than a blog but longer than Twitter. The primary motivation is to save time and make it easy to regularly post content.

▶ ▶ *Reach an audio audience with podcasting*

Podcasting is the distribution of audio files over the Internet using RSS subscription. The files can be downloaded to mobile devices such as MP3 players or played on personal computers. The term *podcast* (iPod + broadcast) can mean both the content and the method of delivery. Podcasters' websites also may offer direct download of their files, but the subscription feed of automatically delivered new content is what distinguishes a podcast from a simple download. Usually, the podcast features one type of "show" with new episodes available either sporadically or at planned intervals such as daily or weekly.

Podcasting with video files is often referred to as vodcasting (video + podcasting). It works the same way, but includes video. If you download a vodcast on an MP3 player that doesn't have a video screen, you will still be able to hear the audio.

In format, podcasts are similar to conventional radio programming, with a host or hosts interviewing a subject, playing music or introducing recorded audio stories. You can use podcasts to host informal conversations with newsmakers or regular contributors to your site. A podcast could be a weekly news roundup or a series of interviews that you are doing anyway that are recorded and published.

Reporting and publishing news involves a natural collaboration, so recording some of that collaboration and publishing it makes for an effective podcast. Todd Bishop, a former *Seattle Post-Intelligencer* business reporter who is now managing editor of Geekwire.com, says that is exactly how he and partner John Cook recently started their podcast.

"We're doing the podcast primarily for ourselves," Bishop said. "We've worked together for years, and it's part of our routine to get together when we can to catch up on things in person, talk about the past week and, ideally, think ahead to what we should be thinking about next on the site."

Podcasts can generate revenue through advertising or underwriting, too. A number of news-based websites consistently produce sponsored podcasts. For example, journalist Leo Laporte reportedly brings in $1.5 million a year in advertising revenue through his tech news podcasts.[10] Similar to a radio ad, a 10- or 30-second message at the beginning of a show can be another "product" for sale to support your operations.

Figure 7.6 Leo Laporte

Setting up a podcast will allow a reader to subscribe and automatically receive new files as they become available. Creating a podcast that others can subscribe to is easy and free—if you have an RSS feed set up. Go to iTunes and click on the "Submit a podcast" logo or use another service like Podcast Alley. For technical details on how to set up a feed, go to http://www.apple.com/itunes/podcasts/specs.html.

If you have a smartphone, you can publish directly from your device with an app like Cinch or AudioBoo. Simply record your thoughts or interview and publish it directly from the phone. It's easy to connect the podcast material to your Twitter or Facebook account, too, so you can alert your audience to the latest installment.

▶ ▶ *Make video simple*

Video cameras are everywhere, especially on mobile phones. Video content viewing is still growing online, and new devices like tablet computers and better smartphones and faster networks will only lead to more growth.

The best practices of shooting and editing video can span an entire chapter or even entire books. Here's a quick look at some of the technology needs for producing video.

Most computers have a video-editing program like Windows Movie Maker or iMovie already installed. (Windows 7 shipped without Movie Maker, but you can download Windows Live Movie Maker for free.) There are also a host of powerful programs for $100 to $200 that will feel like professional editing suites to amateur video editors.

Publishing video is a bandwidth-intensive. Today the best approach is a Content Delivery Network (CDN) like Brightcove or Akamai or a free video sharing service like YouTube, Vimeo, Blip.tv and MetaCafe. These services take your video files, in several different formats, and convert them to Flash while compressing them so they are smaller in size and transfer faster over the Internet, meaning less wait time for your audience.

The services also offer embed codes so that you can publish the videos on your website—and other people can publish them on their site—meaning no one's users will have to leave a site to view the video content. Most services even handle high-definition (HD) video files and serve them in their native 16:9 aspect ratio (think of the shape of a flat-screen TV).

Each of these services makes it drop-dead simple to publish video. In addition to providing a simple means for publishing your video online, websites like YouTube and Vimeo can also help you gain a bigger audience for your video than if you were to post it only on your own website. These sites have much larger audiences and much more search engine visibility than your site, greatly improving the chances for more viewers. And the embed codes that allow others to publish the videos on their blogs and websites make it easy for others to help distribute your video, too.

"It's great to host videos on your own site, but you can greatly expand your audience if you seek out viewers at their own watering holes," says Angela Grant, a video journalist who publishes the website NewsVideographer.com. "Distributing your videos on the popular video sharing sites can only help you, especially if you brand your video with a logo in the corner and you include a note at the end telling people to find more coverage on your URL."

Grant recommends a Web service called Tubemogul, which automatically uploads your video to as many as 20 different video-sharing sites, including YouTube.

▶ Track your traffic

Knowing your audience is a critical component to publishing any type of website, but especially a news site. Learning how many people are viewing your site, what pages on your site they are viewing most often, and how they found your site is essential for a digital publisher, both for making content decisions and for attracting advertisers.

Web-based tracking services are the most common practice for measuring your online traffic. You simply copy and paste a small piece of JavaScript code provided by the service into the HTML footer of every page on your site (hopefully you have a universal footer file that replicates the code across all pages automatically). The code keeps track of everyone who visits the page and sends the data it records over the Web to another website, where those results are tallied and displayed.

Just sign up for an account, paste the code on your pages, and visit the tracking service's website anytime you want to check on your traffic. There is one catch: Any service that relies on JavaScript code won't work if the visitor's browser blocks JavaScript.

Google Analytics is a free Google tool that thousands of websites use to track their visitors. It's easy to get started and the administration screen is fairly intuitive and powerful, although it is tailored to Google Adwords customers with emphasis on conversion rates and other customer metrics. The drawback of Google Analytics is the lack of real-time tracking. If you want to know how many visitors are on your site today, you have to wait until tomorrow for GA to update.

BARISTANET

www.baristanet.com

STARTUP SNAPSHOT

STARTED: 2004.

FOUNDER: Debbie Galant.

MISSION: To bring a bright sassy voice to local news, and make money.

STAFF: 18 part-time.

STARTUP CASH: $6,000.

DID YOU WRITE A BUSINESS PLAN? No.

MEASURE OF SUCCESS: 9,000 visits per day in 2011. 50 advertisers at any one time. The staff appears in the Montclair Fourth of July parade each year with a float.

TOP BUSINESS TIP: We thought we were a tech business, but now we realize that we're a people-based business. We're more like a local indie bookstore than we are like Google.

TOP CONTENT TIP: Good journalism and quality content is a very expensive proposition in this world. Journalism doesn't happen out of any business sense. It happens because someone wants to work hard and is not worried about the business side.

Also, keep the tone conversational. Use polls, maps, video and graphics to involve the reader.

Alternatives to Google to consider include Clicky, Chartbeat, Woopra, Reinvigorate and Piwik. Some may cost $5 to $10 per month, but they give you real-time reporting and emergency notification via email or text message if your site goes down.

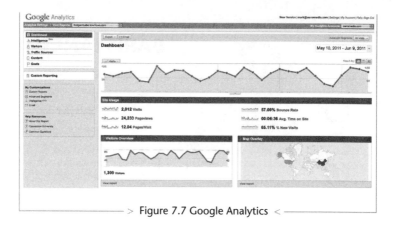

> Figure 7.7 Google Analytics <

Once you have data, you have to do something with it—namely, analyze it for insight into your audience and opportunities to pursue. Start by benchmarking the basic statistics for unique users, visits and page views and tracking them on a daily, weekly and monthly basis. Then start digging deeper by asking your data additional questions:

- What search terms are readers using to find your site?

- What's the return frequency of your local audience? (If you are a local website.)

- Which content sections have the highest percentage of visits from local readers? (If you are a local website.)

- What's the bounce rate among visitors who enter at articles? What about the homepage? (The bounce rate measures visitors who leave the site after viewing only one page.)

- What social media sources send you the most visitors? (Who are the referrers?)

DEVELOP A MOBILE-FIRST STRATEGY

We live in a mobile, global world. Increasingly, mobile means money.

"In our lifetimes there will be no better opportunity to make money than mobile is today," says Tomi T. Ahonen, author of *Mobile as the 7th of Mass Media.* "Mobile is what we call an inherent threat mass medium because it can technically and commercially replicate all previous existing mass media."[11]

Ahonen says no technology has grown as swiftly as mobile, and none has impacted so many other businesses. He believes the "next barons of industry" will be the innovators who master the eight "unique benefits of mobile":[12]

- Mobile is the only personal mass medium.

- Mobile is permanently carried.

- Mobile is always connected.

- Only mobile has a built-in payment channel.

- Mobile is available at the creative point of inspiration.

- Mobile has the best audience information.

- Only mobile captures the social context of consumption.

- Mobile enables Augmented Reality to reach mass markets.

Talking about a strategy for mobile users no longer refers to the future. Now, it's the present. Smartphones began outselling personal computers in the fourth quarter of 2010. Earlier that year, Google CEO Eric Schmidt declared his company would be operating with a "mobile-first" strategy. If that's where Internet searching is heading, shouldn't news be turning in that direction, too?

"News organizations are belatedly, reluctantly and often awkwardly pursuing 'Web-first' strategies," says Steve Buttry, a veteran newspaper editor and new media trainer. "As we fight these web battles, I am increasingly coming to believe that 'Web-first' is what the military would call fighting the last war. News organizations need a mobile-first strategy."

Even as most industries stumbled through the global economic crisis at the end of the decade, mobile was booming. Most news and media companies, however, were still focused too tightly on their legacy operations and, maybe, the traditional web. This created a huge opportunity for other companies and entrepreneurs to enter markets that traditional media once dominated, as the audience increasingly moves to mobile.

The mobile media sector has too many variables and is moving too fast to capture in this brief overview. Because of this, the mobile delivery of your content, or the extension of your service to mobile platforms, should absolutely be part of the roadmap for your new business.

▶ Not just apps: Mobile websites work, too

Connecting with mobile readers and consumers is generally done in one of two ways: through a mobile website accessed with a Web browser on the mobile device, or with an application ("app") specifically developed for a particular platform. There are hundreds of thousands of apps for the iPhone, for example, while mobile devices that run on the Android or BlackBerry operating system have thousands of apps.

Many of these apps cost money, and some publishers have developed apps that successfully create an additional revenue stream. The *Miami Herald,* for example, developed an app for Miami Dolphins fans in 2009 and sold 25,000 of them at $1.99. The paper built a new Dolphins app in 2010 with additional content and features and was able to re-sell the app at $3.99, thereby creating a repeat revenue stream.

The alternative, of course, is to offer an app at no charge in order to shoot for a larger audience, and then either sell advertising sponsorships into the app, or offer premium features within the app that users must pay to access.

The vast majority of app downloads are for free apps. As of 2010, only 5 percent to 15 percent of app downloads were paid. Development can be expensive, especially when you need to build an app to run on several different platforms, which is the strategy most experts advise.

> Figure 7.8 iTunes apps <

"If the mobile industry wishes to introduce a model based on applications, then it must ensure that those applications are accessible by a wide range of handsets ranging from smartphones to mass market devices," said Windsor Holden, an analyst at Juniper Research.[13]

You can find custom app developers through the same methods we discussed in Chapter 6 for finding other freelancers (eLance, Odesk, craigslist, etc.). Some companies also offer cheaper options based on RSS feeds from your website. These apps are not as sophisticated but will get you into the game for a lot less money and give you a sense of how popular your content will be as an app.

The alternative to apps is for your audience to access content through a mobile website. It is relatively easy to optimize an existing site to display differently on a mobile device. (A "user agent" installed in the code of the website will determine whether to display the mobile version to a user or not.) The growing popularity of HTML 5 means developers and publishers can create powerful, sophisticated mobile sites that look and feel like apps but are built once and run on any platform.

Indeed, analysts are already predicting the decline of app downloads, possibly as early as 2013.[14] Oversaturation of available apps may contribute to a peak in the app marketplace. The evolution of mobile websites is likely to have an impact, too, as it becomes more cost-effective to develop one mobile site instead of many different apps that will work on each mobile phone's platform, plus the iPad and other tablet computer devices.

▶ Location, location, location

If it's mobile, it's local. The "killer app" in mobile media is the ability for the device to know exactly where in the world the user with the device happens to be at any given moment.

GPS, or the Global Positioning System, has emerged as a game-changing technology. The ability for a person's mobile device to know where that person is changes the way that person expects to receive information. News, information, and even advertising can be automatically served to you based on where you are right now.

This technology also changes the way people contribute information. As it becomes standard for a mobile device to attach latitude and longitude information to a photo, video or text, people will be able to quickly and easily publish to sophisticated websites that organize content geographically. For example, a news website might use this technology to publish neighborhood-level content sections and invite readers to share news, photos and video capture by mobile phone.

To deliver content and advertising based on location, your platform must recognize geography. If you use an open-source CMS like Wordpress, Drupal or Joomla, there are several modules or plug-ins that will help make this happen. A freelance developer can also use a service like SimpleGeo to add location to your content.

"*Where* has always been a journalism fundamental, the fourth of the five W's," Buttry says. "Well, in the mobile-first world, it might become the first W. In gathering content of any kind, we need to provide specific location metadata wherever location is relevant."

As an entrepreneur, you should be aware of the potential advertising and local business opportunities that location-based services (LBS) represent on mobile devices. We explored this, and other mobile advertising considerations, in Chapter 3.

The time for technology is now. It has never been easier, cheaper or faster to launch a publishing business.

BUILD YOUR BUSINESS Stage 7

Swimming in a sea of technology choices might make some people less likely to move forward with building their idea. Understand that everything mentioned in this chapter is an *option*, not mandatory. Pick one option to get moving, then add additional options when the time feels right.

?? THINK: Of all the technology options and strategies examined in this chapter, which seem most essential to launching your particular business? Why? Research your priorities by looking at sites with a mission similar to yours and talking to tech people and entrepreneurs.

☑ ACT: Write yourself a "Now and Later" note. What technology needs must you deal with *right now,* in order to get your site up and running? Once you're set with those, what will be your next priority, and then your next after that? Include a quick *why* note with each option, to remind yourself of your goals. Keep this note in some easily accessible place and refer to it—and change it—at least once a quarter.

?? THINK: If you plan to publish a news site, you need a dynamic publishing platform. Determine which type is right for you, from a blog platform to a full-powered CMS.

✓ ACT: List your essential needs in a publishing platform. Then take a tour of several websites using the options you're interested in (Wordpress, Drupal, Joomla, etc.). Make a note of which options seem most prevalent in each platform. Then talk to at least one person who has published a site using each platform and ask if that particular platform will do everything you are hoping to do.

?? THINK: Every website needs hosting, so your next step will be to choose an appropriate hosting provider, based on your platform selection. Evaluate the options listed in this chapter—or other options you know about—and select a "top 2."

✓ ACT: Write up a comparison of these two providers. Look at cost. Assess their quality by researching them online and talking to current customers. Based on all of this data, which one will best support the platform you chose?

?? THINK: Social media will be an essential tool in your operation. Take some time to think about how you will use Facebook, Twitter and other options.

✓ ACT: Sign up for accounts on any of the social media platforms you plan to use, taking care to choose the best names possible. Look at the Facebook pages for the startups mentioned in previous chapters to see how you might design your business page on Facebook. Based on what you've seen on sites similar to yours, and on your wildest brainstorming, what uses of Twitter and Facebook might you be able to implement right away, as soon as your site goes live? What would be cool to do but not immediately essential? Add those items to the "Later" section of your "Now and Later" list.

?? THINK: Mobile opportunities will continue to increase for digital publishers. How will you leverage mobile technology for your business?

✓ ACT: List three ways that your business can use mobile phones and tablet computers for distribution, customer acquisition or brand promotion.

Notes
1. To learn more about the difference between static and dynamic websites, visit the Wikipedia entry on websites: http://en.wikipedia.org/wiki/Websites.

2. CSS is the code that controls the design of the site. CSS seems complex at first but is fairly easy to learn. See: http://en.wordpress.com/products/

3. See: http://codex.wordpress.org/Installing_WordPress for information on installing WordPress

4. See: http://wordpress.tv/category/how-to/

5. See: http://wordpress.org/extend/themes/

6. See: http://www.prosepoint.org/

7. See: http://drupal.org/project/openpublish

8. See: http://www.armstrongcms.org

9. Adam Ostrow, "Why your business should be on Facebook," American Express Open Forum, June 22, 2009. http://www.openforum.com/idea-hub/topics/technology/article/why-your-business-needs-to-be-on-facebook-adam-ostrow

10. Andrew Ran Wong, "Leo Laporte's Podcasts Pull in $1.5 Million in Annual Revenue," WebStudi013.com, Oct. 4, 2009. http://webstudi013.com/2009/10/04/leo-laportes-podcasts-pull-in-1-5-million-in-annual-revenue/

11. Tomi Ahonen, "Everything you ever wanted to know about mobile, but were afraid to ask," from the blog "Communities Dominate Brands," May 28, 2010. http://communities-dominate.blogs.com/brands/2010/05/everything-you-ever-wanted-to-know-about-mobile-but-were-afraid-to-ask.html

12. Ahonen

13. John Levett, "Mobile Apps Revenues to Exceed $30 billion by 2015, Juniper's Latest Mobile Apps Research finds," June 9, 2010. http://www.juniperresearch.com/viewpressrelease.php?id=232&pr=189

14. Electronista Staff, "Mobile app downloads seen declining by 2013," June 17, 2010. http://www.electronista.com/articles/10/06/17/research.shows.mobile.app.stores.near.height/

CHAPTER 🎱

Go to Market

To launch a successful product or business, you must identify your market. Who will your audience or customers be? Without them, you don't stand a chance at creating a sustainable project.

In 2003, Ben Ilfeld and Geoff Samek were finishing college and thinking about what to do next. Starting a news website seemed unlikely for Ilfeld, an economics and political science major, and Samek, a computer science major. But the friends were frustrated with the quality and quantity of local news available in their city of Sacramento.

Ilfeld and Samek started talking to people about how to launch a local news site, and in 2005 they formed a limited liability corporation. Ilfeld and Samek identified their customers (readers and advertisers) before they ever wrote a single line of code or a single news story. They used that insight to shape their business model, and they continued to make adjustments and listen to the market during the formative years of the project. They spent about a year and a half building the site and then launched in a very small, almost private beta phase.

The site, SacramentoPress.com, covered a small area at first—only about 16 square blocks. The project developed slowly because Ilfeld and Samek took time to talk to people in the community about the kind of news they wanted and the kind of site that would attract them and keep them coming back. They built relationships with future readers, writers and advertisers before they ever launched a single Web page.

Based on what they learned from the community, they custom-built the site from the ground up, making sure every detail added value to their mission of providing both news and real community engagement. They

Figure 8.1 Sacramento Press

hired developers on a part-time basis, trading equity in the company for computer programming services. The platform they built enabled people to share information about their neighborhoods and interact with one another. Sacramento Press editors then promote the best contributor content to the front page and other section pages to highlight great work.

"We hired developers at a fraction of what they would normally cost," Ilfeld says. "They were already invested because they thought it was an amazing project. So we made an exchange in ownership for something they thought was really big and helpful for their community."

The market needed something new. One of the nation's largest news publishing companies, McClatchy, has its corporate headquarters there and publishes the *Sacramento Bee* and SacBee.com. But Ilfeld and Samek saw gaps in McClatchy's news coverage and segments of audience not being served by the mainstream press. Those gaps created an opportunity not just to serve those people but to build a business in a different way.

The company developed a number of innovative ways to spread the word about the site. Staffers rode custom-branded bicycles called "shuckers" to distribute coupons and fliers at events. They used direct mail and went to dozens of meetings to recruit writers. They hosted three or four workshops a month to help writers understand exactly the approach the company was looking for in news coverage.

They also used social media extensively, and the market took notice. Readers engaged with Sacramento Press on Facebook, Twitter and other channels. Advertisers saw how quickly and effectively this young startup built an audience and created awareness for a new brand. When companies began to inquire about the Sacramento Press team's strategies, wanting to get more social media-savvy, Ilfeld and Samek saw another opportunity.

Social media consulting became the top revenue driver for the company in 2010. It's a testament to a business identifying a market need and adjusting its model to serve the recognized need.

"You're probably the expert at something in your community. You can sell that skill," Ilfeld says. "Consult with local businesses. If you're out there pitching strategy, ask them how they feel about Yelp. About Facebook. About Twitter. Listen to what they tell you and look for opportunities."

Ilfeld and his team found their place in the value chain for local news and information and met the needs of potential customers. In addition to their consulting services, Sacramento Press found a more traditional revenue stream by selling advertising on the news site. Then, listening to the market again, the company formed the Sacramento Local Online Advertising Network (SLOAN), partnering with more than 40 other independent publishers in Sacramento and selling ads on those sites, too. "SLOAN was a need. Publishers came to us," Ilfeld says. "We are really good at ads on our site. We have ridiculously high retention rates."

The entrepreneurs behind the Sacramento Press achieved success by first studying their market, then tailoring their model to fit that market and using those earlier connections to spread the word. It's a tested formula for startup success. This chapter will feature some best practices on how new media startups have put that formula to work through these steps:

- ▶ Build an audience from scratch.
- ▶ Identify the market and find a product-market fit.
- ▶ Make your site visible.
- ▶ Understand the competitive landscape and assess competitors.

DEVELOP A STRATEGY

You can build a fantastic website, write engaging articles, shoot amazing photographs and make great video. But you have to build an audience—a market—if you are going to make a business.

"Your marketing strategy starts, ends, lives, and dies with your customer," Michael Gerber wrote in *The E-Myth Revisited*. "So in the development of your Marketing Strategy, it is absolutely imperative that you forget about your dreams, forget about your visions, forget about your interests, forget about what you want—*forget about everything but your customer.*"[1]

Entrepreneurs and investors have a number of catchy phrases for this test of where the rubber meets the road. "Will the dog eat the dog food?" is probably my favorite. Another good one is "Just because you can make a dog jump doesn't mean people want a jumping dog." (Investors seem to really like dogs.)

Having a business—even a nonprofit business—means people have to want your product, your jumping dog. Whether it's a subscriber, an advertiser or a foundation doling out grants, *someone* has to believe in your product enough to give you money for it.

Gerber identifies two pillars of a successful marketing strategy: demographics and psychographics. Demographics, the science of marketplace reality, tells you about *who* buys. Psychographics tells you *why* those people buy, or why they visit a particular website.

According to Gerber, the famous dictum "Find a customer need and fill it" should actually be "Find a *perceived* need and fill it"—because "if your customer doesn't perceive he needs something, he doesn't, even if he actually does."[2]

While entrepreneurship requires a certain leap of faith, it shouldn't be a blind leap. You should have learned all that you can about the potential target market while formulating your business plan. Now it's time to test your assumptions about whether your offering will resonate with real people.

▶ Identify the market

The first step in developing a go-to-market strategy is identifying the market. Then you can test to get the word out and measure response. It may be necessary to assess the potential of adjacent markets if your original target market isn't developing fast enough.

Keep this process as simple as you can. Based on your assumptions thus far, construct a profile of your ideal audience. What is their age, gender, background and profession? Where do they live? How you learn this information is simple: You ask for it.

In Chapter 5, we discussed several options for using surveys to solicit feedback on your early working prototype. If you included some basic demographic questions in those surveys, you now have some information to draw on. If not, refer back to Chapter 5 and construct a new survey to discover this information.

The next step is to find some people who fit this profile. Start with people you know. Who among your network of contacts fits the demographic profile you've constructed? In terms of geography or background, who among your acquaintances is the kind of person likely to buy your product or visit your site? Make a list that includes any contact information you have for these people.

Now examine the list to identify the extended networks of those contacts. For example, if one of the contacts is a small business owner in town, perhaps he or she is a member of the chamber of commerce. If so, you have a link to that network. Leverage your connections on LinkedIn. For example, if you have 80 connections, you have something like 12,000 second-degree connections, meaning people connected to your connections. Tapping your own network for business purposes can sound silly until you realize how very many people you're actually connected to.

The challenge is always determining the size of the target market. Don't fall prey to the 1 percent fallacy that has mesmerized many entrepreneurs. Sure, if you got just 1 percent of everyone in the United States to buy your $1 product, you'd make $2.8 million. But how are you going to reach those 2.8 million people?

Instead of a top-down estimate, go from the bottom up. Think about how many people you can reach directly (look at the list you compiled). That is your initial target market for now. This stage of thinking is the reason the Sacramento Press founders chose to focus only on 16 square blocks at first.

To make some projections for the future, consider the technology adoption life cycle described in *Crossing the Chasm*, a hugely influential technology marketing book.[3] Author Geoffrey Moore's ideas on moving from the Early Market to the Mainstream Market can also apply to other product-market scenarios, including a startup news company.

Your first two groups of customers or audience are known as the Innovators and the Early Adopters. Together, they make up the left side of the bell curve. The fat middle consists of the Early Majority and Late Majority. If you can reach these two groups, you have a sustainable business. If not, you don't. (The Laggards are the final group, but they're simply icing on the cake.)

Figure 8.2 **CHASM**

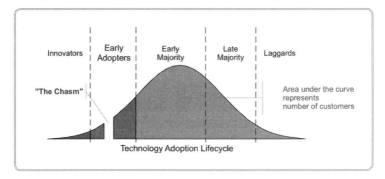

Between The Early Adopters and The Early Majority, according to Moore, lies The Chasm. Many technology companies fall into The Chasm and die because they mistake early adoption for market acceptance. Innovators and early adopters buy into new product concepts very early in their life cycle; they don't need well-established references, meaning they don't need to hear about this great new product or website from people they trust. The Early Majority, meanwhile, is pragmatic and waits for those well-established references before investing their time and/or money in something new. The Late Majority waits even longer, until a product or service becomes an established standard.

To understand how this model applies to a startup news site, consider the West Seattle Blog. It started in 2005 when a winter storm knocked out power around the community of about 60,000 people in—you guessed it—the western part of Seattle. Founder Tracy Record, with 20 years of local TV news experience as a writer, editor and producer, began posting power outage information to the blog. Thanks to the magic of the Internet search, Innovators (from the Chasm model) were able to find the site while searching for terms like "West Seattle power outage."

This initial traffic gave the West Seattle Blog its start. As Record continued posting news even after the storm blew over and power returned, Early Adopters discovered the site and began to visit. News of the blog spread by word of mouth around the community, and after several months of continuous publishing, The Early Majority started visiting the site. Once that happened, local businesses started hearing about the site and started calling Record, asking to advertise.

> Figure 8.3 West Seattle Blog <

Having recognizable local businesses appear on the site offered one version of the well-established reference that The Early Majority needed. The other version was word-of-mouth recommendations, and the combination of the two began to draw in The Late Majority. (These audience developments also contribute to the Influence Model discussed in Chapter 1.)

The result is a startup news site covering a neighborhood of 60,000 people that will serve 11 million page views in 2011 and brought in more than $100,000 in advertising.

While Record didn't originally plan to create a sustainable business when she started covering the power outage in 2005, she and her husband Patrick Sand identified their target market early and have remained focused on it ever since. The 60,000 people who live in West Seattle make up the total market, but the West Seattle Blog is only viable for those people who want to know what's going on in their community. Fortunately for Record and Sand, that means most of the community.

▶ ▶ Get the word out, test and measure
Let's hope you've been talking up your idea with your friends and colleagues and anyone else who's asked what you're up to. It's rarely a good idea to operate in "stealth mode" unless you have trade secrets or legitimate competitive fears because you plan to directly challenge an

existing business. Even then, you're likely to benefit less from secrecy than you would from spreading the word.

The first step when you go to market is to define the stages. Will you go public in one fell swoop? Or do you think it would be wiser to "soft launch" your new site or product with a small test group? (You can put a "Beta" tag on the banner to feel like one of the cool tech kids.) If you plan to rely on community contributions such as user-generated content, you're probably better off starting small. This will give you time to build your content before asking people to come check it out. It's important to have a "there" there, because if people don't like their experience the first time they visit, they aren't likely to come back.

You can contact this initial group of customer/testers—the ones on the list you put together—with messages via email, Facebook, Twitter, LinkedIn or other platforms. Be sure the recipients are made to feel a little special for being included so soon. Call it a "private Beta" or a "sneak preview" if you want, and take care to create the expectation that you hope to receive feedback and suggestions. Give them a specific date when you'll follow up to see what they think. This will create a deadline for the recipients, which will help motivate them to visit the new site.

When you do follow up, ask a few specific questions. Don't send your testers a 100-question survey; no one will take the time to complete it. You want to know specifically what they liked and disliked about the product or service, what other content or features they would like to see, and what other products or services they currently use that are similar. (See Chapter 5 for suggestions on survey tools to use and specific questions to ask.)

Next, analyze your Web traffic (and, if applicable, product sales) on a daily basis and ask these questions of your data:

- Are users coming back, or do they visit once and never return?

- How are users finding your site?

- What areas of the site are proving to be the most popular?

- Which social networks are sending the most traffic your way?

Answering these questions will help you decide which content areas to focus on (those that are most popular) and which social networks have the best return on investment (ROI). Answers to these questions will also give you a relative sense of the health and momentum of your new operation, and whether it is growing or not.

▶ ▶ *Respond to the market*

Launching something new is not a pass/fail test. It's nearly impossible for your assumptions to be entirely accurate. Based on the information you receive and analyze, you'll want to adapt your original plan to meet the needs of your audience. This is where iteration becomes critical. Since most business plans don't work as originally envisioned, the key to launching a successful startup is adapting to meet your market.

Silicon Valley entrepreneur and investor Randy Komisar cowrote the book *Getting to Plan B* because this stage of company development is so important. Komisar is a partner in Kleiner Perkins Caufield Byers, one of the Valley's most prominent venture capital firms. He told an audience at Stanford about the type of entrepreneurs his company looks for:

"Finding people who are flexible, who will, in fact, respond to metrics. Finding people who have the tenacity and dedication to course correct in the near term against a bigger idea. And who can separate the big idea from the immediacy of the reactions they're getting from the marketplace. Finding a group of people with a curiosity, that's going to keep them thinking about their big idea—not just keep them wedded to something that is based upon assumption upon assumption upon assumption, without any good metrics."

What he looks for, in short, is "the team that can actually respond to the market."[4]

Keep this in mind as you go through the process of targeting and attacking a market. If you don't hit a perfect product-market fit right away, don't give up on the market until you've considered adapting your product.

Remember the story of Rafat Ali from Chapter 2? When Ali started paidContent.org, he was hoping it would help him land a new job, not become a multi-million-dollar business. In 2002, the "nuclear winter" for software startups and online advertising meant a technology journalist like Ali had few job opportunities to pursue.

Instead he quickly built a following for his new blog, all through word of mouth. One key lesson here: If you publish quality content that people are interested in, word of mouth—or "word of link," in the age of social media—will work. For Ali, the collapse of the online ad market meant a flurry of interest in whether an audience would pay for content online; hence the name, paidContent. No one else was covering the developments on this topic, so Ali's "interactive resume" grew quickly by tracking this new trend.

> Figure 8.4 paidContent jobs

Turning a popular blog into a business, of course, is a challenge for someone with no sales experience. Ali learned about creating a business on the job.

"I had no idea, zero idea," he says. Because he was covering the online advertising industry, he knew what CPMs were and he knew some of the terminology. "But I really did not know how to price it and all that stuff."

Ali did, however, know how to "read" the market and respond. As the online ad industry rebounded, he expanded the focus of the site to include any way that content was getting paid for—advertising, subscriptions and other methods. PaidContent became the go-to source for media executives hoping to discover who (if anyone) had figured out how to make money publishing content online.

"It really did spread by word of mouth," Ali says. "There was no other way. I mean, word of link online. Being at conferences, covering conferences, meeting people. It really was one subscriber at a time that we built this over six years."

▶ Audience: How much is enough?

Responding to what your audience wants is an essential skill. But how do you know how *much* audience you'll need to make your business work? It's difficult to define how many users/customers/viewers/readers are enough. Start by determining how much it will cost to operate the business on a monthly or annual basis. Then estimate how much each user or customer will be worth. For example, if you can sell $10,000 of advertising each month and have 100,000 visits per month, your average customer worth is 10 cents per visit.

This basic equation may apply if you're planning a news site that covers a specific local geography and you have only a few people you need to pay. For a news site, you'll pay for web hosting and the occasional technology development project (a new Wordpress theme or an iPhone app, for instance), but the bulk of your expenses will be paying your employees and yourself.

Once you have a grasp of your annual expense budget and some early data on how much revenue can be generated from your current market size, you can extrapolate the numbers to define your target market size for your business to work. Set ambitious but reasonable goals for audience or customer growth. Having a specific number to shoot for each month will help you focus on that all-important task.

Understand, too, that this exercise serves as an important reality check. While you may be passionate about your project and think you've found an untapped market to serve with journalism or other content, the cold, hard numbers will tell you whether your idea is a sustainable business or not. If your background is in journalism, you may find it easy to focus on that aspect and avoid grappling with the elements of entrepreneurship you feel less comfortable with.

"After talking to one enterprising journalist after another, I have found almost uniformly that they are making the mistake that has proven to be the downfall of many an entrepreneur: Instead of trying to build a business, they are trying to give themselves the job they always wanted," Alan Mutter wrote on his influential blog Reflections of a Newsosaur. "The passion for the product they are creating causes entrepreneurs to work so hard on their journalism that it distracts them from the real job of building an enterprise that not only sustains itself for the good of the community but also provides a sustainable lifestyle for the journalist himself."[5]

Finding the time and willpower to remove the journalist hat for the marketing hat will be one of your more difficult challenges. Most journalists who spent years in a traditional newsroom never had to worry about marketing, advertising or revenue. But by this point in the book, you should appreciate the importance of these operations.

A commitment to business and numbers can maintain the issue of sustainability front and center. You don't want to be one of the failed journalism entrepreneurs that Mutter describes as: "so busy being journalists—and, frankly, too confident that the quality of their coverage will be sufficiently compelling to attract an ever-growing audience—that they put scant effort into marketing, promoting and monetizing their sites."[6]

Don't worry that you feel like you're guessing when you make the financial projections and set the marketing goals that will sustain your business. Forecasting numbers is an uncertain task for all entrepreneurs, not just journalists.

"At this point you come face-to-face with the first dilemma encountered by everyone going into business," Gerber wrote in *The E-Myth Revisited*. "How can you possibly know now what your business is going to produce in sales that far in the future?"

And Gerber's response? "The answer is, you can't! But it doesn't matter. At the beginning of your business, any standards are better than no standards."[7] So put aside your uncertainties and excuses and get going.

▶▶ *Find a product-market fit*

If you ask seasoned entrepreneurs and investors to agree on a recipe for startup success, you will likely hear a common refrain: *product, market, team*. To grow a company out of nothing into a success takes the right team to develop the right product and deliver it to the right market.

Marc Andreessen, who founded Netscape and Ning and has invested in many successful Silicon Valley technology companies, says the market is the most important factor in a startup's success or failure.

"In a great market—a market with lots of real potential customers—the market pulls the product out of the startup," Andreessen says. "The market needs to be fulfilled and the market will be fulfilled, by the first viable product that comes along.

"Conversely, in a terrible market, you can have the best product in the world and an absolutely killer team, and it doesn't matter—you're going to fail. You'll break your pick for years trying to find customers who don't exist for your marvelous product, and your wonderful team will eventually get demoralized and quit, and your startup will die."[8]

Andreessen calls product-market fit "the only thing that matters." When it isn't happening, he writes, you can feel it: Word of mouth isn't spreading, page views aren't growing fast, press reviews are kind of "blah," and the sales cycle—the amount of time it takes you to make a sale—is too long.

Conversely, you can feel a product-market fit when it *is* happening. Usage is growing fast. Checks arrive in the mailbox faster than you can deposit them. You want to hire help but don't have time. Reporters are calling because they've heard about your hot new thing and want to talk to you about it.

Obviously, you can't find a product-market fit until you actually launch the product. That's why so many entrepreneurs, investors, advisers and educators highly recommend getting a product to the market as fast as possible. "Launch early, launch often" is a well-known phrase in tech startup circles. It means get the product out the door and in front of actual users. And if it doesn't "fit," start iterating until it does.

"The reason to launch fast is not so much that it's critical to get your product to market early, but that you haven't really started working on it till you've launched," says Paul Graham, a serial entrepreneur who founded Y Combinator, the startup incubator that has launched hundreds of companies. "Launching teaches you what you should have been building. Till you know that, you're wasting your time. So the main value of whatever you launch with is as a pretext for engaging users."[9]

You need to be brutally honest with yourself when gauging your product-market fit. The numbers don't lie. If the market isn't "pulling" your product to it, you need to change the product—or find a different market.

▶ ▶ **Explore adjacent markets**
When Plan A is not working as well as you'd hoped, it's time to consider adjacent markets. In business terms, "adjacent" refers not to physical location but to taking your product and tweaking it enough to find new uses or new customers—or to appeal more to the customers who you were aiming toward in the first place.

This new offering is not a complete overhaul of your original product or service. Hopefully it's a fairly minor shift in strategy or content that can be done quickly. It's all part of the ongoing experiment that is growing a company from scratch.

The roster of companies that started with one idea and found success with an adjacent market is too long to list here. A few famous examples:

- Flickr started as a service to connect gamers with one another. But when the photo-sharing feature proved a hit, the company shifted its focus from gamers to photographers and retooled the service. (Yahoo! acquired Flickr in 2005.)

- Craigslist: Craig Newmark started a basic email newsletter for event listings in San Francisco in 1995. The newsletter morphed into a bulletin board website after people started posting jobs and other non-event listings. Newmark formed a private, for-profit corporation in 1999, and in 2010 the combined craigslist sites drew 20 billion pageviews per month.

- MediaBistro: Laurel Touby wanted to host social gatherings for people in journalism and media in New York City, so in 1993 she started MediaBistro. It grew into a multidimensional online network with jobs, training courses, events, forums and even a premium subscription service. WebMediaBrands acquired the site for $20 million in 2007.

The ability to shift focus and attack a new opportunity is a form of agile development, or running a so-called "lean startup," which we explored in Chapter 6. This concept of altering the aim of your business is also known as a "pivot." While maintaining focus is critical to startup success, the focus at the go-to-market phase in any startup needs to be laser-like and pointed specifically in the direction of customer development. If you're not finding the right fit, you need to pivot by changing your product, your positioning or your marketing.

"Startups are inherently chaotic," Steve Blank, author of *Four Steps to the Epiphany,* wrote on his blog. "The rapid shifts in the business model are what differentiate a startup from an established company. Pivots are the essence of entrepreneurship and the key to startup success. If you can't pivot or pivot quickly, chances are you will fail."[10]

The Sacramento Press performed this kind of pivot when it started selling consulting services around social media. Instead of clinging only to the traditional revenue model of selling advertising, company leaders saw an opportunity to leverage valuable skills to bring in a supplemental stream of revenue that eventually became the company's top money-maker.

UNDERSTAND THE COMPETITIVE LANDSCAPE

As you take your product or service into the marketplace, you will inevitably run into competition. Some of this competition may be direct: companies or websites that are targeting the same audience with similar products and services. Other competition may be indirect. For example, if the people in your target audience spend much of their online time tweeting and Facebooking about local news and events, they may not feel a need to visit your local news site.

EVERYBLOCK

www.everyblock.com

STARTED: 2007.

FOUNDER(S): Adrian Holovaty, previously a Web developer/journalist at washingtonpost.com, ljworld.com/lawrence.com, ajc.com.

MISSION: An automated news feed for your block and a forum for community conversation.

STAFF: Three developers, one designer, one "people person."

STARTUP CASH: $1.1 million Knight Foundation News Challenge grant.

WROTE A BUSINESS PLAN?: Yes.

MEASURE OF SUCCESS: Won the Knight News Challenge grant. Acquired by MSNBC.com in 2010.

TOP BUSINESS TIP: Stay focused and just do it!

TOP CONTENT TIP: As valuable as automated updates of crime, media mentions, and other EveryBlock news are, contributions from your fellow neighbors are significantly more meaningful and useful.

Although both forms of competition are important to understand, it's also important to maintain perspective. Don't spend too much time obsessing about your competition. As a startup, you only have a limited amount of time and energy each day, so stay focused on your own operation. Worry, fear, angst—these feelings will not help you grow a business.

"What is entrepreneurialism, really, besides not being stopped by the fear that everyone naturally feels?" Lynda Resnick, who created POM Wonderful juices and other products, asked at an entrepreneurial journalism workshop at the University of Southern California in 2009.

▶ Assess competitors and comparables

It's possible to learn from others' successes and failures without becoming preoccupied by the fear that they will steal your business. An analytical review of the strengths and weaknesses of your competition will help you chart your course.

First, try to figure out how big your competitors' audiences are. Use a Web tracking service to get a sense of how many visitors competing websites receive. Big companies pay big money for data from Comscore, but you can get a rough idea from free services like Compete, Quantcast and Alexa. Google Ad Planner is another excellent tool that can give you interesting insights.

Comparative data is not an exact science, unfortunately, since these tools can't actually measure the traffic on every site online. Each uses a different methodology with varying success. But the services are extremely easy to use (just enter a URL) and will give you a basic understanding of the landscape. You should be able to get a sense of how your site compares with the competition by analyzing numbers from these services and matching them with your own Web traffic reporting. At least you know your own numbers are right.

Next, look at how your competitors are doing accumulating Facebook fans, Twitter followers and comments on news stories or blog posts. This will give you a sense of how much engagement your competition has with its audience.

Then reach out and contact your competition. Yes, you can actually do this! In most cases, your competition will gladly exchange emails or set up a phone call to trade information. Don't try to be sneaky about it. Simply position yourself as someone with a like mind who would like to "talk shop." If you ask too sensitive a question, your competitor may decline to answer, but that's OK. Knowing the competition personally could open up the potential for partnerships down the road. In the short term, it will probably give you more knowledge about your market and what has worked and not worked so far.

You should also set up a news alert on Google, Yahoo! or Bing based on keywords that will bring you news any time someone writes about your competition. (For extra productivity points, route those alerts to an RSS reader like Google Reader instead of delivering them to your inbox. You don't need more email, do you?)

If you're competing against publicly traded companies, you can find all the financial information you'd ever want through public disclosures and 10-K forms. It can be difficult to separate a specific business segment from a large corporation, but reading through the reports will give you details that may help paint the picture.

Finding information on privately held companies can be more challenging. But you're a journalist, right? So you should know how to investigate, dig and research a topic. If not, start learning how to do this at businessjournalism.org.

▶ Identify your value proposition

As we've cautioned, spending too much time focusing on your competition can be bad for your health. If you're competing for news coverage, you may be tempted to "match" every article pertaining to your area that is being covered by the daily newspaper or local TV station. This is a strategy for failure.

While you should be aware of what the competition is doing, your job is to focus on the strengths of *your* operation and the value proposition that you offer to your audience or customers and to your advertisers. "Value proposition," a key term in business, refers to what your business offers that no one else does. You need to define your value proposition and measure your competition against it. If your competitor is targeting the same market, but with a different value proposition, you may be in a position to partner instead of compete.

"Before you can drive your competition crazy, you have to understand what your own company stands for. Otherwise, you'll only succeed in driving yourself crazy," says Guy Kawasaki, author of *Reality Check* and *Art of the Start*. "The second step is to truly understand what your customer wants from you—and for that matter, what it doesn't want from you."[11]

Defining a value proposition, fortunately, requires an analysis that will be very familiar to journalists. Remember the "Five W's" in reporting? Use them to formulate the value proposition for your new journalism business.

1. **Who:** Whom are you serving with your product or service (in other words, who's the market)? *Who* also includes *you*—what makes you the best person to provide this product or service?

2. **What**: What is your company about? Describe exactly the product or service that you're offering.

3. **Why:** What are the benefits to your offering? Why will people use your service or product?

4. **When:** Is timing one of your advantages? Do you publish news faster or more frequently than the competition?

5. **Where:** Is location one of your advantages? Do you focus more closely on a particular area than anyone else? Is your target market underserved?

The value proposition is really a marketing statement, one that is critical to the overall mission of the business. Drafting a value proposition forces you to summarize why a consumer should visit your site, use your service or buy your product. It should convince potential consumers that your product or service is worth the money or the time that you are asking from them.

BUILD AN AUDIENCE FROM SCRATCH

How many websites are online today? Billions. How will anyone find yours among the clutter and noise on the global Internet? It's not easy, but there are a few tried and true practices you can use to build an audience from scratch, even for a brand new site.

Stragetic use of search engine capabilities and social media are the best methods to make your site findable. Instead of an expensive marketing campaign with big budget advertising and a public relations firm, many online entrepreneurs have quietly—and often quickly—built an audience with free techniques like search engine optimization (SEO) and free tools like Facebook and Twitter.

While these techniques don't cost money to purchase, they are not totally "free." Using them to attract new audience takes skill and dedication. You'll need to be consistent with your attempts to improve your search-engine-friendly headlines and grow your social media connections. Growth won't happen overnight, and there is no magic involved. Unless you have a six-figure budget for a major marketing push, these free techniques are the best option available for building an audience from scratch.

▶ Make your site findable through search

How do you drive more audience to those good ideas everyone is excited about? Because traditional marketing can take you only so far, SEO and viral distribution through social media have grown increasingly important.

To understand how to optimize your Web content to be more easily found in search engines, you must first understand how search engines work. Search engines perform three main functions:

1. **Crawling with spiders and robots:** These terms refer to small computer programs that are sent out by search engines like Google and Yahoo! to crawl through the Internet and track and record the information found on websites. Spiders and robots are programmed to look for new pages or new information on existing pages and send back reports to their respective search engines for indexing.

2. **Indexing:** Larger, more powerful computer programs on the search engines' servers take the information sent from the spiders and robots and build large database files with references to all the content, connected to the right links. This is the catalog of the Web that a search engine refers to when you perform a search.

3. **Queries:** When you type a keyword search into the homepage of Google or Yahoo!, you are making a query of that search engine's database. Additional computer programming takes your keywords and looks in the index for the most relevant results, then returns and presents those results as links to websites for you to explore.

Search engines rank the results and present them on a series of pages, usually displaying 10 results per page. What has made Google the dominant search engine during the past decade are the algorithms it uses to establish relevance. Based on the peer-reviewed journal method found throughout academia, Google gives more importance to a website that other sites are linking to.

In Internet terms, a link is an endorsement. The more credible (endorsed) a site is, the more credibility or authority it can give to another site by linking to it. Pages with lots of links, which therefore rank high on searches, are said to have "Google juice."

The vast majority of Internet searchers do not venture past the first page, so having your website show up in the first 10 results is a huge advantage if you're hoping to grow your audience. Many news sites receive as much as a third of their Internet traffic from search engines. Thus, improving the ranking of your pages in search engines is a smart strategy. That's the goal behind search engine optimization, or SEO.

"What you need to understand is that the search engine has done all the hard work of collecting and analyzing web pages," Ken McGaffin wrote

Partnering with big media

Will new media replace old media? That's a sexy topic for journalism conferences, but for entrepreneurs, a better question is how new media and old can collaborate.

Some startups, especially the ones that define themselves by their differences from traditional media, are skeptical about partnership. You certainly don't want to team up with any company whose goals you don't share. But with a partner you respect, consider the advantages. The big media partner can jumpstart your startup with instant traffic referrals. It might also share advertising revenues in exchange for placement on your site. If you don't have a sales staff or sales experience, this perk is huge.

Ana Acle-Menendez, for example, has partnered with *The Miami Herald,* her former employer, to develop West Kendall Today, a hyperlocal site focusing on one of the most populous sections of the Miami metropolitan area. She gets more readers for her journalism by publishing on a subsection of the *Herald*'s website, and the *Herald* gets deeper coverage into West Kendall. The goal, of course, is to grow readership and revenue with the content that Acle-Menendez produces.

"On a personal level, I want my community covered and I've always wanted to be an entrepreneur," she said. "In my case, I trust the two executives who approached me because I had worked with them for

on Wordtracker.com. "BUT it only makes that information available when someone does a search by entering words in the search box and hitting return."[13]

The goal of SEO is to leverage all of that work the search engine has already performed. Let's say you publish a story on organic broccoli farming that's so good that dozens of other sites link to it. All of those links mean that when someone enters the keywords "organic broccoli farming" into Google, years. I knew their character. They also didn't sugarcoat it, described it as 'jumping off the cliff.' I appreciated that honesty."

Local TV stations are also partnering up. KNSD's relationship with the nonprofit news site Voice of San Diego has gone so well since 2006 that the president of NBC Local Media urged other NBC stations to seek partnerships in their markets in 2011. "We've collaborated on everything from investigative reporting to news production, and we've been able to deliver some great stories through both our broadcast, and voiceof-sandiego.org's news site," said KSND's news director, Greg Dawson.

John Wallace, president of NBC Local Media, said the company was looking for "top-notch, nonprofit news organizations" that represent a range of diverse communities and viewpoints in the markets they serve.[12] That's generally what big media want in partnerships: access to the markets they can't reach as well on their own. In return, the startup gets credibility and exposure.

While the NBC plan focuses on nonprofits, many partnerships between old media and new media involve for-profit companies. In 2010, I helped KING 5 Television partner with *The Seattle Times* to form a local advertising network called BeLocal Seattle that included more than a dozen hyperlocal and online-only publishers in the region. The newspaper and TV station sales reps sell the ads, and the new media sites run the ads and share the revenue.

8

the search engine will display your story at or near the top of the first results page, driving more traffic to your site than any other.

▶ ▶ *Use SEO to grow your audience*
The importance of SEO, and its more commercial cousin SEM (search engine marketing), has led to a multi-million dollar industry. You can hire a company to help you engineer your Web pages, and some companies even "guarantee" your site top placement in the big search engines. But

with so much information available on the Internet, most Web publishers can do their own SEO—at least on a basic level.

At its core, the practice of SEO is simply a matter of making sure that your Web pages include the words that a prospective reader would type into a search engine if he or she were looking for a particular article. Some keywords are static, like the title of your website and the description you create for your site. Other keywords are new to your site every time you publish a new piece of content.

Entire books have been written about the practice of SEO. Assuming you don't have the time or inclination to take a deep dive into the topic, here's a quick guide to get you started.

Content is king: Fortunately, journalists have a big advantage in the SEO game. E-commerce and marketing websites struggle to publish quality content on a regular basis to impress the search engines. But journalists? Hey, this is what we do for a living.

Linking is queen: Tap into good web karma by linking out to as many sites as makes sense. This will increase your authority in many search engines and could lead to more Google juice if the sites that you are linking to recognize it and return the favor.

- Make sure you link between your own pages, too. This is an easy way to increase the number of links to your pages and will also increase the usability of your site for your audience.

- The most important links should appear on the homepage. Search engines give greater value to those links.

- Make sure your links make sense. Instead of the generic "click here to read more," your links should include specific information about what a user will find on the page that they are about to click. "Top 10 grossing organic farms in the United States" is an example of a good link.

Title tags: The title tag appears at the top of a user's Web browser. Many content management system and blog platforms have the ability to display the headline from the story or blog post in the title tag. This is helpful, as search engines give more prominence to the headline and the title tag on a Web page. So headline writing is especially important for good SEO and will be covered in a separate section.

HTML meta tags: If you right click and select View Source on a Web page, you will see the computer code that is behind the page. Near the top are some HTML meta tags that provide information about the Web page, even though this information doesn't actually display for the user. Web designers used to "stuff" this area with as many keywords as they could dream up in the hopes that a search engine would give their pages credit for those words as content. Google and other search engines have changed their algorithms to account for this scheme, but including a few relevant keywords in the meta description is still a good idea.

More information on SEO and keywords can be found here:

- SEO introduction: http://searchenginewatch.com/2167921

- Keywords: http://freekeywords.wordtracker.com/

- SEO for journalists: http://www.journerdism.com/seo-tools-for-journalists/

▶ ▶ *Better headlines increase visibility*

Almost everyone writes headlines today, but not everyone writes them well. Twitter, Facebook, videos and other multimedia content all need to have headlines, and headlines are crucial to attracting audience. On average, eight in 10 people will read a headline, but only two in 10 will read what follows. That's the secret to the power of headlines, and why they matter so much in determining the effectiveness of an entire piece.[14]

Headlines relate to SEO because both connect content and audience. Mac Slocum, a contributing writer to Poynter.org, points out, "You don't need to know the intricacies of indexing, but basic SEO is the conduit between an audience and content. It's not just a business initiative."[15]

Appreciating the importance of headlines is even more important for independent journalists who don't have the power of a big news brand and all that Google juice behind their stories. Given how important headlines are for search engines and audience, you can see that it's critical for every news site to put considerable thought and strategy into headline writing.

Remember, you have two audiences online: **readers** and **robots**.

For readers: Often in search results or even on the main page of your own site, Web headlines have no friends. They sit alone—without the deck heads, photos or graphics that may accompany them on their own page— so the headline has to carry the entire load. Make headlines simple, literal and direct. Clever is cool in print, but for online search purposes, clever has to include keywords, too. A good headline must motivate readers to move the mouse and click.

For robots: SEO means that if a headline contains search keywords that are also repeated in the text of the story and elsewhere on the page, the story will acquire more Google juice and be returned with a higher placement on search pages.

You may not realize how often you write headlines for your site: one for each new article, blog post, video, photo gallery, etc. Each instance is an opportunity, so take a few extra minutes to make your headlines better. Here's how:

Keywords, Keywords, Keywords. Think about Journalism 101: who, what, where. The answers to these questions attract readers *and* robots. Sports headlines must mention the team name. Headlines for local stories must contain the city name. Write for readers with Google in mind: If you were Googling for information on this news story, what words would you use? If someone's looking for information on immigration reform and you have a great piece about immigration reform on your site, the headline needs to contain the terms "immigration" and "reform" if you want that person to know it's there.

Use conversational language. Write headlines in a way that makes the reader want to know more. Be direct, and focus on the unique. Instead of "Springfield council votes to raise taxes," try "Get ready to pay more property taxes in Springfield" or "Springfield property owners: You'll be paying higher taxes."

Don't be afraid to inject a little attitude. You must be fair and accurate, of course, but that's no reason to be boring. On the other hand, if you're pressed for time and have to choose between direct and cute, go for direct. Search engines will reward you.

Look at your headlines the way searchers will see them on a search page: standing alone, without the context of the story. Make sure they contain not just the keywords the searcher is looking for, but also something to engage that potential reader and draw him or her to your site.

Think about readers and robots when writing headlines. Come up with a handful of keywords you would use to search for this story, blog post or video. Then use sound judgment to see how many of those keywords you can work into the headline without sacrificing its potential interest to readers.

▶ Develop a social media strategy

The strong growth in social media applications like Facebook and Twitter offers opportunities to connect with more audience in a personal way.

These applications are just tools, however. To use them effectively, you need to develop goals and objectives for your site; otherwise, you're just wasting your time.

"Don't confuse tactics with goals," says Ellyn Angelotti, interactivity editor and faculty member at The Poynter Institute. "Getting more followers on Twitter or more fans on Facebook is not a goal, it's a tactic."

Defining a goal means knowing *why* you want those followers and fans. Maybe you hope to convert them into loyal readers of your website, thereby increasing your audience size. Or maybe you want to increase collaboration with your audience and learn from them as you develop the content on your site. Either way, be clear about why you are using social media. Don't do it just because everyone else does.

You don't *need* to be on Facebook. You don't *need* to Tweet. You don't *need* to blog. But you do need to talk to your audience in an open and honest way. And more important, you need to listen.

Angelotti recommends the audience funnel concept to understand how a news site can pursue a goal of expanding an existing audience in an engaging way. The objective is to convert a fraction of your total audience into a smaller, but more loyal audience segment. You can use a range of tactics to pursue this goal:

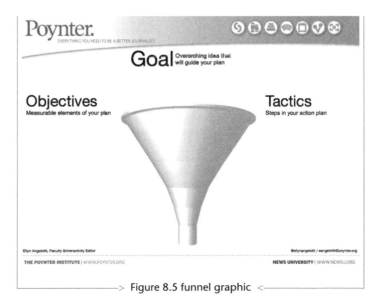

> Figure 8.5 funnel graphic <

- Use SEO to draw people to your website.

- Use RSS feeds to deliver your content.

- Use Facebook postings to draw more fans.

- Use Twitter postings to draw more followers.

- Use an email newsletter to attract subscribers.

- Use website registration to know your audience.

- Use comments and forums on the website to get feedback.

- Use link-sharing tools to get your content out there.

- Use the opportunity to create content on your site to keep people coming.

Establish your own goals, objectives and tactics. But don't make the task more complicated than it needs to be.

Define your goal:

- Who are you trying to reach?

- What do you want consumers to know about you?

- What do you want to know from consumers?

Once you know what you are trying to achieve, choose a tactic to pursue it. Measure your effectiveness by determining whether your goals are being reached. Having 1,000 fans on your Facebook page doesn't matter if they're not the people you aimed for, or if your fans aren't telling you what you hoped to learn.

If you are not getting what you need, adjust your tactics. Either try a new platform or change how you are using your current ones. Find others who have succeeded in developing a social media channel like the one you want and ask how they did it.

▶ ▶ *Authenticity, collaboration and transparency*
While social media has been around for only a few years, you can explain why they work with a sociological theory that is 50 years old. *Social capital* is the advantage created by a person's location in a structure of relationships. It's the value a person gains from becoming the "trusted center" (or becoming allied to the "trusted center"). If you have become a voice of influence in your community, one that your audience really trusts, you can become a trusted center.

Social capital can be gained by working for a brand with built-in credibility, like the *New York Times* or NPR. Because a startup doesn't yet have that brand recognition, it must earn social capital another way. Participating in a real, honest exchange of information with others is a good place to start.

"Be unbelievably open and inclusive with your audience," says Ben Ilfeld, one of the founders of Sacramento Press. "Let your audience be a community and drive your brand and your coverage. Sell the community as such when dealing with advertisers or sponsors."

To build a community that will further your mission and be seen as valuable to advertisers or sponsors or funders, you need the true two-way communication and completely user-controlled environment of social media. If you're not used to "mixing it up" with a community, you're in for a new experience. You are asking to fit into *their* world. Users will act, they will share, and they will build a wave of support, approval or protest related to your content.

You won't always like what you see or hear, and that's OK. As long as it's authentic, collaborative and transparent, you will build social capital and enhance your brand, whether it's dealing with problems or praise.

Collaboration, transparency and authenticity are the first rules of new media. Make this your marketing plan. Invest in social capital, and create networks of benefit. News efforts that are successful participate in a symbiotic relationship with readers to create a community around the journalism.

Mobilizing an audience for news tips and other crowdsourcing efforts does more than lend a hand to newsgathering. It provides a deep connection with an audience that manifests itself in word-of-mouth and viral marketing. The influential book *The Cluetrain Manifesto* proclaimed that "Markets are conversations."[16] News should be a conversation, too. Building a collaborative community around content is a winning strategy, both for ensuring good news coverage and for marketing your site and your brand.

▶ ▶ *Make it essential, not extra*
It's easy to think about social media as something you'll do with your spare time. Guard against this assumption for two reasons: Social media is too important to be relegated to your spare time, and as an entrepreneur you won't *have* any spare time.

Attracting users, earning social capital and collaborating with an audience are all essential and all easier to accomplish through social media. If your target audience already has the habit of starting their day with Facebook, then that's where you want to meet them and connect. If they are heavy users—and influencers—on Twitter, then you need to become part of their "circle."

"Forget about your platform and use social media platforms wherever your audience spends time," Ilfeld says. "Be platform agnostic about building your community. We do not care if you engage with us on our site or Facebook or Flickr."

Even mainstream news organizations know this. When Peter Horrocks took over operations for BBC News, he stressed the importance of social media to all employees. "This isn't just a kind of fad from someone who's an enthusiast of technology," Horrocks was quoted as saying in the BBC in-house weekly. "I'm afraid you're not doing your job if you can't do those things. It's not discretionary."[17]

If social media is that important for a globally recognized news brand like the BBC, think how important it is for a news startup. "Social media cannot be isolated in the marketing department!" Ilfeld says. "The position in our organization is in operations. In addition, everyone is encouraged to use social media tools, and we train our staff and even hold workshops for our community."

▶ News is a conversation

News used to be a one-way lecture. Now it's a multi-directional conversation. One of the greatest challenges facing journalists is how to manage and leverage that conversation. MSNBC.com editors call it the sixth "W" of journalism (who, what, where, when, why and *we*). That *we* brings the benefit of new channels for distributing content, in addition to cultivating a community for source development, transparency and credibility.

"Online social networks are essential tools for journalists," Roland Legrand wrote at MediaShift.org. "They make it possible to build extended networks, search for story ideas, build contacts and dig up information. But even more important, they help to shake up the relationship between the individual journalist and the people formerly known as the audience."[18]

Collaboration makes for more effective engagement. Whether it's a message-board forum on your site or someone else's, or a status update on Facebook or Twitter, or a comment on a blog post, try to create an encouraging tone rather than adversarial tone. Let people know that you welcome their expertise because they're the ones you'll need to help build a community.

The benefits to news as a conversation are many, including:

- Discovering new story tips and reporting angles.
- Providing transparency on the reporting process.

- Enabling an immediate feedback loop.

- Spreading awareness of news coverage through word-of-mouth marketing.

With all its positive outcomes, news as a conversation also poses challenges. Trolls, flame wars and spam comments have soured many website operators on the notion of open, Web 2.0 features. Don't let the rants of a few bad apples in the comments section crush your spirit. Stay connected to the users who are loyal, and stay on top of all the discussion and content created on your site. Reach out to people who are playing the game correctly to thank them and encourage them. (You might find great new columnists and bloggers this way, to feature on your site.) Hopefully this model behavior will be repeated by newcomers.

Write a terms and conditions page on your website, in plain English, to help users know what you are expecting or requiring from the audience that is contributing content. Be real. Be nice. Don't lie. Attack ideas, not people. Don't take credit for something that is not yours. Basic rules like that. You know, the stuff we all learned in kindergarten.

▶ ▶ *Alternate forms of distribution*

"If the news is important enough, it will find me." This aphorism illustrates the power of social networking, where breaking news often makes its way to the status updates of Facebook users and has crashed the servers at Twitter on many occasions. (The statement itself is an example of "word of link," since searching the Web for its origin yields more than 10,000 references, most of which attribute the quote to an anonymous college student in a focus group.)

If you want the masses to distribute your content and become trusted sources for news tips, you must become part of their conversation. This means following the 80/20 rule: Add value to the community 80 percent of the time and promote your own content the other 20 percent. You can't develop loyalty if you do nothing but post links and explicitly ask people to share your content. You have to be more subtle.

Web publishers can leverage social networks to distribute content in multiple ways:

- Judiciously posting links to your content through generic, large-scale social networks like Facebook or LinkedIn.

- Finding sources through niche social networks, like CaféMom.com or Gather.com, and creating a community that will distribute your content for you.

- Building a niche social network for your sources and stakeholders with a tool like Ning or Google Groups. Create loyalty among this new community and they will promote your brand for you.

Becoming an authentic member of a community is the best way to use social networks for distribution. Remember, the most valuable marketing ever done for your brand will be done by your audience or customers. The trick is getting them to endorse your brand without directly asking them to do it.

Here is a starter list of social media marketing channels that most—if not all—news websites should be watching and participating in. Commenting and linking, when appropriate, is an effective way to get others to view, link and comment on your content and become part of your community.

- Blogs: Read blogs that write about the same subjects you do. Contribute to the conversations found on them, too.

- Flickr, YouTube, etc.: Follow the channels and streams of people who post content that is related to what you cover. Link to interesting content on these sites from blogs or other pages on your site.

- Twitter, Facebook, LinkedIn, etc.: More and more people get their news from a social network every day. Make sure they can get *your* news through these popular platforms, too. Create Facebook pages for specific sections or topics you cover. See Chapter 4 for information on using Twitter and other microblogging services.

- Digg, Reddit, Fark, StumbleUpon, etc.: Social news and bookmarking sites can provide a significant short-term boost in traffic. Converting those new audiences into one that is loyal is the challenge. "Digging" your own stories used to be ethically questionable for journalists. Not anymore. Promote your stories on any—or as many—websites as you can.

It's customary for a news organization to appoint one person or a small team to manage the social media distribution efforts. For independent journalists or bloggers, this will have to be one more task. You can develop automated solutions that help, like Facebook applications to display your headlines. Providing "quick click" solutions on your Web pages will make it easy for your audience to help distribute your news, too.

According to the traffic measuring company Hitwise, Facebook referrals are more loyal than any other. This makes sense when you realize that a link from a Facebook friend comes with a recommendation that is more powerful than finding a link with your own search.

Figure 8.6 HITWISE GRAPH

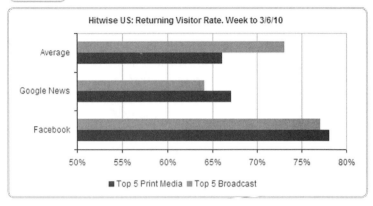

Hitwise US: Returning Visitor Rate. Week to 3/6/10

■ Top 5 Print Media ■ Top 5 Broadcast

Also take advantage of RSS feeds and email newsletters to distribute your content. While they feel a bit "old school" these days, both techniques are effective ways to increase loyalty and repeat visits among casual users.

For example, Julia Scott, who left her job as a reporter at the *Los Angeles Daily News* to start Bargainbabe.com, has used contest giveaways to increase the number of subscribers to her email newsletter. A $25 gift card can generate a few hundred new subscribers, well worth the marketing expense.

Building your audience and your value proposition will take all the energy and creativity you can summon. Going to market is an exciting time for any entrepreneur. It's also nerve-wracking. What if your product doesn't fit the market? What if the first potential customers you talk to seem clueless about your concept? Don't stress. You're about to join a large community of entrepreneurs who have taken that bold step from idea to reality and will be there to support you along the way.

The lessons you learn as you start your business will help you grow personally and professionally, possibly more than anything else you will ever do in your life. As a journalism entrepreneur, you'll be using your unique vision to help create what's next for news. What could be cooler than that?

BUILD YOUR BUSINESS Stage 8

Going to market means finding real people to talk to about your business and real people to use your great new website, product or service. Salespeople recite the mantra ABC, Always Be Closing, to stress the importance of constantly making sales. For entrepreneurs, it's ABS: Always Be Selling (your idea, your product, yourself). While you'd like to focus on the content or the next new feature, that work could come to nothing unless you're always selling your idea to real people and using their feedback to help you to refine it.

?? THINK: Given what you know so far, what are the demographic characteristics of the ideal audience for your site? Who do you know who fits that profile? Check your Facebook friends or LinkedIn connections for likely prospects.

✓ ACT: Make a list of those people, on a spreadsheet that includes contact and demographic information. Now look at each of them and think about who else those people are connected to, and what other networks they link with. All of these names are real people whom you can contact, present your idea to, and get feedback.

✓ ACT AGAIN: Of the people you know on that list, which do you think might be innovators? Early adopters? Talk to those people about how they find news and decide which new websites are worth a visit.

?? THINK: Now develop an initial list of people to test your idea. Hopefully you have a working prototype at this point to show. If not, you'll have to illustrate your idea with mockups or similar sites. Either way, it's important to get specific feedback.

✓ ACT: Create a message in which you give this test group an intriguing "sneak peek." Write something direct but enticing. Ask for feedback on a few specific questions (Do you understand what the site is about? Do you like the look and feel?), then put those responses into a spreadsheet so they're easy to analyze.

?? THINK: Who are the competitors, either perceived or real, for your new business? What do they do that will make it more difficult for you to find your audience? How big are their audiences?

✓ ACT: Taking each of the main competitors you've identified, define your value proposition, the unique thing that your business can offer that this other cannot. Form this as a response to potential customers who hear your pitch and ask, "What about brand X?"

?? THINK: Social media has made it easier to spread the word about something new, like your product or business. What objectives do you have for using social media for your business?

☑ **ACT:** Develop a social media strategy. What platform will you use and what's the first move you'll make on social media to build awareness for your new brand and engage with customers? Once you have that one platform going, what's next?

⁇ **THINK:** Go back through all your responses to the Build Your Business Questions throughout this book. Reflect on how much your idea of a business, and your understanding of what's involved, has changed from the first questions you answered in Chapter 1.

☑ **ACT:** Assemble and organize your responses in a way that will make them a helpful reference for you. Get rid of the ones that don't apply anymore. Consolidate the key responses into a single document if you prefer.

☑ **ACT AGAIN:** Look at the sample business plan in this book's appendix and compare it to the information that you've generated on your own startup idea. If you were to write a business plan right now which areas would be your strongest? Which would still need work? Write a to-do list to remind yourself of important next steps.

Take a moment to celebrate your hard work. Share a toast with a friend to the progress you've made in developing your idea, and get ready for this journey you've already begun.

Entrepreneurship is a journey, not a destination. Once you embark, get as much as you can from the experience. Starting your own business is hard work, for sure. But no matter what eventually happens, the experience will be worthwhile. You will learn so much about so many different things— and so much about yourself—that it may change how you define success.

Ideas are cheap. Execution is everything. The future is now.

Notes

1. Michael E. Gerber, *The E-Myth Revisited: Why Most Small Businesses Don't Work and What to Do About It* (New York: Harper Collins, 1995) 218.

2. Gerber, 225.

3. Geoffrey A. Moore, *Crossing the Chasm: Marketing and Selling High-Tech Products to Mainstream Customers* (New York: Harper Business Essentials, 1991).

4. Randy Komisar, from talk given as part of Stanford's Entrepreneurial Thought Leader series, April 8, 2010. http://ecorner.stanford.edu/authorMaterialInfo .html?author=27

5. Alan Mutter, "Journalists running start-ups face tall odds," Reflections of a Newsosaur blog, June 7, 2010. http://newsosaur.blogspot.com/2010/06/journalists-running-start-ups-face-tall.html

6. Mutter.

7. Gerber, 151.

8. Marc Andreessen, "The Pmarca Guide to Startups, part 4: The only thing that matters," June 25, 2007. http://web.archive.org/web/20070701074943/http://blog .pmarca.com/2007/06/the-pmarca-gu-2.html

9. Paul Graham, "Startups in 13 Sentences" from his series of essays, Feb. 2009. http://www.paulgraham.com/13sentences.html

10. Steve Blank, "Why Startups Are Agile and Opportunistic—Pivoting the Business Model," from his blog www.steveblank.com, April 12, 2010. http:// steveblank.com/2010/04/12/why-startups-are-agile-and-opportunistic-%E2%80%93-pivoting-the-business-model/

11. Guy Kawaksai, *Reality Check: The Irreverent Guide to Outsmarting, Outmanaging, and Outmarketing Your Competition* (New York: Penguin Group, 2008) 297.

12. Chris Ariens, "NBC's Local Stations Look to Partner with Non-Profit News Organizations," TVSpy, May 23, 2011. http://www.mediabistro.com/tvspy/nbcs-local-stations-look-to-partner-with-non-profit-news-organizations_b10613

13. Ken McGaffin, "Keyword Basics Part 1: How Search Engines Work," Wordtracker. com, Nov. 24, 2006. http://www.wordtracker.com/academy/keyword-basics-part-1-how-search-engines-work

14. Brian Clark, "How to Write Magnetic Headlines," http://www.copyblogger .com/magnetic-headlines/

15. Amy Gahran, "How Much Should Journalists Know about SEO?" Poynter's E-Media Tidbits, March 13, 2009. http://www.poynter.org/column. asp?id=31&aid=160037

16. David Weinberger, Rick Levine, Christopher Locke, Doc Searls, *The Cluetrain Manifesto* New York: (Basic Books, 1999).

17. Mercedes Bunz, "BBC tells news staff to embrace social media," from PDA: The Digital Content Blog, Feb. 10, 2010. http://www.guardian.co.uk/media/ pda/2010/feb/10/bbc-news-social-media

18. Roland Legrand, "Journalists Should Customize Social Networks to Maximize Experience," June 2009. http://www.pbs.org/mediashift/2009/06/journalists-should-customize-social-networks-to-maximize-experience152.html

APPENDIX A

> **Pegasus News Business Plan—Annotated
> by Founder Mike Orren**

Mike Orren, founder of Pegasus News, *explains what you see on
these pages:*

This document was used as our primary collateral material for
potential investors and acquirers. Early on, we worked on a
longer-form, 50-page business plan complete with risk factors
and an excruciatingly detailed description of everything we did.
We abandoned that for two reasons. One was that we were too
busy actually running a rapidly changing business to take time
to continually update a long, complex document. The second
and more important reason was that no one—angel investors,
venture capitalists or media companies—actually wanted to read
a 50-page business plan. We distilled the key information into
this summary and updated it about once a month.

Bear in mind that this was written in 2006 and extensively
edited with one goal in mind—attracting capital.

OVERVIEW

Pegasus News is a digital media service that delivers individually customized local, niche and neighborhood-level news, data and advertising. Its proprietary behavioral profiling of local users, fueled by a unique low-cost content-acquisition model allows *Pegasus News* to bring the precision and efficiency of direct marketing into a market previously dominated by unwieldy and expensive mass media.

> *We slaved over every word of this intro graf, massaging it into something that we thought covered every base and every possible knowledge level of our industry space. Perhaps that's why it neither flows, nor gives the best idea of what we did. We tried not to give this document to anyone who had not seen a demo, but in some cases, it was our first volley.*

With individually customized local offerings that include a robust website, email newsletters, content feeds, custom user-printed editions, and wireless messaging, *Pegasus News* bridges the worlds of mainstream media, citizen journalism, city guides and local search.

> *We were really trying to cover every base and every buzzword of the day, hoping that one of these angles would catch the eye.*

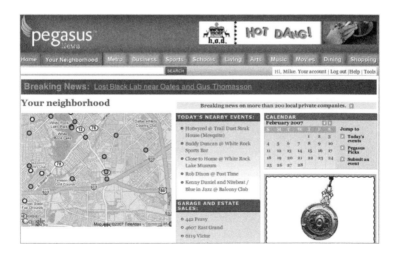

We selected our Neighborhood hub to illustrate the business rather than the homepage, which is a more traditional choice. We felt that the Neighborhood hub most readily showed what was different about our offering, from the breaking lost pet alert to the map of news, events and garage sales.

Pegasus News delivers a deeply personalized experience via its proprietary user-tracking system.

Investors always want to know that there is technology you have that no one else does. Sometimes, even when it is clear your business isn't a tech play, they'll look for it. By now, we knew to highlight our technology.

Without having to provide any explicit data or fill out any forms, each user automatically receives a customized homepage with news and event information of particular interest to him or her, along with ads narrowly targeted to these interests. For example, a given user's homepage might contain content and ads concerning his or her neighborhood crimewatch, child's school, favorite local college team, favorite genre of music and/or line of business. This customized information also appears in other selected areas of the site.

This was our biggest innovation and value proposition; it's how the site worked at its best. The problem was that many of the advertisers willing to spend more money just wanted run-of-site (ROS) advertising, which made it hard for us to show off examples of this capability.

After successfully testing its model with the launch of an award-winning local music and entertainment site, *Pegasus News* launched in its Dallas/Fort Worth test market in December 2006.

Early on, we spent more time pitching investors than building and were frustrated at not having a product to show. We knew that if we released the full Pegasus News *product without enough depth, it would be ill-received. So we picked a vertical (music) and launched a beta site.*

The site is already drawing a large local audience and substantial advertising without any investment in marketing.

In retrospect, I wonder why we didn't quantify that. Like any good writing, a pitch should "show, not tell."

The company intends to launch in other major U.S. metropolitan areas strategically identified as possessing the characteristics best suited for its business model. Within each additional market *Pegasus News* will have substantial depth of coverage, strategically building deeper into fewer markets rather than "planting a flag" in many cities with shallow coverage.

> *This was a big differentiator at the time, as most players in the space were launching in multiple markets, but receiving less traffic across their network than we were in Dallas/Fort Worth alone.*

KEY DIFFERENTIATORS

> *Proof this document is geared towards investors—we've barely painted a picture of what we do and now we're differentiating.*

1. *The Daily You™. Pegasus News'* proprietary tagging system and content-delivery algorithm provides each reader with a customized homepage containing relevant links to both professionally-written and user-contributed stories about events

in the reader's particular neighborhood. The company also delivers stories concerning topics of unique interest to that reader based upon his or her usage. *Pegasus News* has defined more than 130 neighborhoods in the DFW area and uses geo-coding technology to assure the right reader receives the right article.

> *An example of how you find yourself running a business for investors rather than users. We constantly debated making our neighborhood distinctions larger to ensure a wealth of content, but agreed that the more we could claim to cover, the more impressive it sounded.*

For readers who want to read in print, there is an automated user-print edition that includes the stories and advertisements that are most relevant to that reader. Content is updated continuously and is archived for long-term access. In addition to those items available on their customized pages, readers can easily access all content on the site.

> *This is the sort of writing you get when trying to succinctly address the objections you've heard in a hundred pitch meetings.*

2. *Evergreen informational content. Pegasus News* has collected and continuously refines a wealth of evergreen data, which is housed in numerous interconnecting, easily searchable databases that link to its news content. For example, when a reader views a listing for an art exhibit, listings for restaurants and other amenities in the same area are automatically displayed. The site currently has comprehensive data on nearly 8,000 entertainment venues, bars and restaurants; 750 civic organizations; 1,300 local bands; all public and private schools in the area; and a local events calendar tracks deep data on more than 2,000 events weekly.

{ *Again, big numbers are impressive. Flaunting them.* }

Because of the efficiency of this system and the involvement of readers in the update process, these databases require minimal labor to maintain. For instance, the local events calendar requires fewer than 40 manhours per week to update.

{ *The sort of detail you wouldn't tout to customers—you talk to users about how the database is lovingly hand-curated. Many investors cringe at such talk, wanting to know how cheaply it can be done.* }

3. *Unique content acquisition process. Pegasus News* is delivering a greater volume of local news and information than the daily newspapers or the websites of any television station with approximately ten full-time equivalent staffers on the content team. At the same time, the company is providing engaging content that drives traffic far in excess of that attracted by do-it-yourself "citizen journalism" sites. This is achieved by starting with aggregation technologies to gather a wealth of content that is quickly geo-tagged and then edited for relevance and to add a human voice. Additional items are added from local content partners ranging from bloggers to suburban newspaper chains to broadcasters. This content is all supplemented with user-contributed text, photos, audio and video. Finally, the small staff reports on news that no one else in the market is covering, carefully "picking shots" so as not to duplicate the efforts of other outlets. Editors carefully monitor the user conversation on the site to maintain civility and to pick up news tips that other outlets miss. All of this is woven together with a light and homespun tone that is somewhere between *The Daily Show* and a neighborhood

meeting. As the only news outlet offering professional news content and user-generated content in the same environment and without segregation, and by providing summaries and links to outside sources, *Pegasus News* achieves a breadth and depth of coverage unavailable elsewhere, becoming a true news and information hub for the city.

Remember that we started doing this in 2005, when it was much less common than today.

4. *"Panlocal" breadth. Pegasus News* is the only local news service in the country to successfully integrate broad local news with neighborhood and suburban news in the same product and environment. This is a tremendous advantage in that it provides readers with niche content that they cannot find in their daily paper or TV newscast while supplying enough widely interesting content to reach an audience that is not willing to seek out a secondary news source to find that kind of information. By running submitted, but edited, content from any local individual or organization and then targeting it to the most likely readers along with more mainstream content, *Pegasus News* is able to attract readers to the site by providing the widest possible array of news and information.

This is an attempt to separate us from the "hyperlocal" businesses that had failed during our gestation period. We were never really hyperlocal, but that was a label often applied to the business.

5. *Multiple Distribution Media.* Each reader can choose the methods by which he or she receives news and information. Choices at the outset include the robust online service, customized user-printed editions, email, wireless text messaging, a "lite" version of the website for wireless internet access and automated RSS (Really Simple Syndication) feeds that allow subscribers to view content via Yahoo!, Google and other aggregators.

It's shocking how many pitches we made that were utterly derailed because a tech-challenged prospective investor wanted me to explain to them how RSS works.

That cell phone really looks quaint now.

6. *Highly-Targeted Advertising. Pegasus News* offers neighborhood-level advertising targeting, so that an ad for a Realtor or dry cleaner can be delivered primarily to those subscribers who live or shop in its immediate vicinity. Once the Daily You™ reaches a critical mass of data in Q2 2007, the company will be able to provide highly-targeted advertising based upon user behavior. For instance, an ad for a theater group would be delivered primarily to subscribers who have read theater reviews or bought theater tickets from one of the company's advertisers. Each advertiser will therefore know that its ads will be viewed by the readers most likely to patronize them. Advertising can be targeted by day of week and time of day, enabling "just in time" advertising that moves perishable inventory. In light of these capabilities, the company will be able to charge premium advertising rates while remaining affordable for even the smallest business.

> *I am proud that this vision stayed consistent from the very first draft of our plan in 2004,*

7. *Local search optimization. Pegasus News'* continually updated databases keep its results high in all major search engines. Further, a process has been developed for writing search-friendly headlines that fare exceptionally well in news searches. This drives a substantial amount of daily traffic and has helped charge growth without marketing investment.

REVENUE SOURCES

Advertising Revenue:

Pegasus News' revenue is derived primarily from advertising, most of which is currently sold on a cost-per-pageview basis. While there are a limited number of pay-per-click text ads, on the local level a click is generally the wrong metric to measure effectiveness of an ad. As more user preference information is gathered from the Daily You™ data, the company will experiment with pay-for-performance mechanisms that measure in-store sales as a means of reaching even more small merchants. The company also intends to add pay-per-call advertising for service-related businesses.

> *Early on, we wanted to do a model that was logistically similar to the daily deal businesses like Groupon, in that we would take a piece of a discounted transaction instead of selling ad space. An idea before its time.*

Despite only one advertising salesperson on staff since October, the company has already signed on nearly 50 local advertisers. These are primarily small businesses and, based on the strength of the site's entertainment databases, consist primarily of restaurants and nightclubs. However, small retailers and realtors are beginning to sign on, expanding the company's revenue base.

> *The omitted phrase was "at rock-bottom introductory rates."*

Ancillary Revenue:

Over time, *Pegasus News* will use its platform and market position to create ancillary revenue opportunities. For a negotiated fee, the company will provide more sophisticated business intelligence data to advertisers than the basic data provided as part of the standard advertising package. In addition, the company will offer unique syndicated content to local TV and radio partners for a subscription fee or in exchange for broadcast marketing. The company's current financial projections do not include revenue from any of these sources.

> *None of these were ever realized, but at the time it seemed important to highlight every possible way we could make money.*

COMPETITORS AND COMPETITIVE ADVANTAGES

> *This is the section where you build and destroy strawmen to show that you've thought through competition.*

For both readers and advertisers, *Pegasus News'* primary competitors are large incumbent daily newspapers, such as *The Dallas Morning News,* and alternative weekly newspapers, such as *The Dallas Observer.* The company also competes to a lesser extent with limited circulation neighborhood and niche newspapers, regional magazines, city network sites like *Citysearch,* Craigslist and local broadcast media, as well as for advertisers with the Yellow Pages, direct mail, couponers, and billboards.

Operationally, *Pegasus News'* emphasis on hyperlocal content enables lower cost of production compared to less focused mainstream competitors. In addition, as a small, privately-held company using a wide range of dynamic media, *Pegasus News* is able to be exceptionally nimble and responsive to the rapidly changing media environment.

> *As a disruptive business seeking capital, one inevitably falls back on the argument that the incumbents are so slow and entrenched in their methods that they won't be able to do what you do. That's usually a good and valid argument that no one believes.*

Readers distinguish *Pegasus News* from competitors based on the site's customized content and advertising; unique hyperlocal content; conversational, open-source method of reporting; and multimedia approach to distribution. The coverage of niches that other local media ignore combined with the site's data-driven content management system has made the site exceptionally "sticky," which not only drives readership, but helps place the site's search rankings above the mainstream local outlets on almost every major story and event. Additionally, by providing "panlocal" content that can't be found elsewhere alongside a more user-friendly version of the commoditized broad news, the site is able to engage an audience that has largely disconnected from local media.

> *In early 2007 local media outlets seemed largely ignorant of good search engine optimization practices, creating an unexpected advantage for us.*

Merchants distinguish *Pegasus News* from competitors by the ability to place targeted hyperlocal advertising so that ads can be sent only to those consumers most likely to respond. This mechanism enables merchants to spend their advertising dollars more efficiently and provides opportunities for small businesses that cannot afford to advertise in most traditional outlets. As a unique value-added service, the aggregate data from readers' page views and click-throughs will allow the company to gather business intelligence that can be shared with advertisers.

> *These were points that were very attractive to investors. However, it was a rare small business that was fully equipped to take advantage of these offerings.*

Furthermore, although the company has only been in the market for a short time, advertisers have noted the following additional advantages:

- The ability to only charge advertisers for actual pageviews
- Realtime reporting of statistics

- The ability to change messaging by day of week and time of day

- The ability to initiate "just-in-time" campaigns on short notice

- The sharing of traffic data above and beyond ad clicks

> *All of these except the last are now de rigeur in the industry. The last was and is an interesting way to demonstrate the hidden relationship between advertising and content consumption.*

Upon rollout to additional markets, *Pegasus News* will face potential competition from new companies such as Backfence, YourHub and the like. These types of companies rely solely on user-generated content and focus primarily on small suburban markets. Therefore, they are having difficulty gaining enough regular readership to draw substantial advertising revenue. In addition, these companies have a strategy of entering many markets with little depth of coverage, as opposed to *Pegasus News*' strategy of building deeper in fewer, larger markets.

> *We couldn't have been more different from Backfence and YourHub. But they were getting a lot of coverage and we often found ourselves being asked to distinguish ourselves as an investment proposition.*

ASSETS

> *Here, we explain what you're actually buying.*

At this time, *Pegasus News* has the following key assets:

- The *Pegasus News* brand.

- A rapidly growing website currently more than 25,000 pages deep; with more than 185,000 unique monthly visitors; and more than one million pageviews per month as of March 1, 2007.

> *We eventually got over 450,000 monthly uniques, but we had a hiccup here because our early analytics seemed to have been overcounting by not filtering well enough for bots. Earlier versions of this document claimed more in the 250,000 range.*

An agreement with *Lawrence Journal-World* for:

(i) an exclusive license to their award-winning World Online site management technology, widely regarded as the best in the local news industry, for the Dallas/Fort Worth consolidated metropolitan statistical area;

(ii) the right to purchase on attractive terms similar exclusive licenses to use the World Online technology in the following additional pre-selected markets:

Atlanta	Houston	Portland, OR
Austin	Indianapolis	Raleigh-Durham
Charlotte	Las Vegas	San Diego
Columbus	Minneapolis/St. Paul	Washington, DC
Nashville		

(iii) a first right of refusal in those thirteen markets; and

(iv) the right to purchase nonexclusive licenses in other markets.

- Substantial improvements to the World Online technology, which the company has made and to which the company owns the rights.

- A proprietary algorithm that parses the metatag data gathered from user clicks into individual profiles for the purpose of delivering customized content and advertising to each reader's *The Daily You*™.

- A proprietary taxonomy of more than 2,000 hierarchical metatags for classifying news content and advertising into categories of interest for individual readers.

- Partnerships with several niche publishers and broadcasters to provide the site with content, promote *Pegasus News* to their readers, and in some cases share advertising revenue generated by their content. These partners include:

{ *There was only one partner with a revenue share, and it was nominal.* }

  - *Today Newspapers* (covering Lancaster, Duncanville, Cedar Hill, DeSoto and Grand Prairie)

  - KERA (North Texas Public Broadcasting)

  - *The Voice* (gay & lesbian newspaper)

  - Andrew's Star's Page (popular subscription-based Dallas Stars site)

  - Ed Bark (former TV columnist for *The Dallas Morning News*)

  - The Column (local theater news and reviews)

  - Dallas South Blog (south Dallas politics)

  - Dallas Progress (politics)

  - Keller City Limits (suburban politics)

  - The UnObserver (music)

  - *Urban South Magazine* (music)

  - Slacker Country (music)

  - Adopt a Dallas Pet (pets)

  - Repairing Texas' Healthcare System (local doctor's blog)

  - Larry James' Urban Daily (social issues)

  - The Law Reviewers (dining)

{ *This list of partners eventually grew to nearly 150, and was one of our biggest assets.* }

- Comprehensive informational databases for the Dallas/Fort Worth market that include more than two million discreet pieces of data (and growing). These databases currently include restaurants, bars, nightclubs, coffee shops, museums and galleries, amusement parks, arcades, auto dealers, batting cages, botanic gardens, bowling alleys, comedy clubs, dog parks, ice rinks, laser tag courses, malls and major shopping destinations, miniature golf courses, movie theaters and showtimes, planetariums, pool halls, paintball courses, race tracks, rock climbing walls, roller rinks, stadiums, tea houses, water parks, wineries, elected officials and campaign contributors.

> *In retrospect, the depth of this list strikes me as silly in the context of an investor document. We were trying to illustrate how our database was much deeper than what others provided.*

- A proprietary feed of more than 800 local news sources germane to the Dallas/Fort Worth market, many of which do not have published RSS feeds.

LEADERSHIP

> *This section is always very important to investors—do you have a team that can pull off an ambitious plan? While our team was generally considered a strength, we were often dinged for lack of a pure sales leader.*

Mike Orren, 34, *President and Publisher.* Mike has more than ten years of profit-driving experience in all aspects of media management, with special expertise in launches and relaunches. Mike most recently served for three and a half years as the Publisher for the Texas Division of American Lawyer Media, where he produced record EBITDA and growth for *Texas Lawyer* and its affiliated products during years in which the economy as a whole performed poorly. Mike was a key leader of the team that relaunched Law.com and Texaslawyer.com as profitable websites with both paid subscriptions and advertising. Mike launched a targeted direct email marketing program that dramatically increased margins on books and seminars and became a model for all divisions of American Lawyer Media.

Mike served from 1995 to 1998 as a business-side relaunch leader of *D Magazine* (Dallas), which he helped lead to profitability in two years on the heels of a two-year hiatus preceded by eight years of losses. Simultaneously, he launched Dmagazine.com as one of the first city magazine websites in the country. In 2000, Mike won $15,000 in the inaugural business plan competition held by Duke's Fuqua School of Business in a field of more than 50 entries. The next year, he won the North Carolina Press Association's award for Best Special Interest Publication for his work as publisher and editor of *For Charlotte's Future.* He has served as an online strategy consultant for Cox Communications and several niche magazine publishers.

The *Dallas Business Journal* named Mike as a Top Executive Under 40. Mike is a member of the Young Presidents' Organization. He received a BA in Political Science from Duke University after graduating in three years while lettering on the varsity swim team and turning around the university's financially troubled student publishing operation.

Gary Cohen, 37, *Vice President, Chief Operating Officer, and Secretary.* Gary worked for eight years as a large-firm corporate, securities, and tax attorney prior to forming State Street Ventures, LP, a self-owned investment firm. Gary worked for Ernst & Young LLP from 1995–1997; Liddell, Sapp, Zivley, Hill & LaBoon, LLP from 1997–1998; and Carrington, Coleman, Sloman and Blumenthal, LLP from 1998–2003, specializing in venture capital finance, mergers and acquisitions, initial public offerings, and financial restructurings. Gary received his JD from the Duke University School of Law and a BA in Psychology from Duke University after graduating in three and a half years. Gary grew up in Dallas and is a graduate of St. Mark's School of Texas.

Jeremy Dunck, 30, *Chief Technology Officer.* Jeremy is an expert software developer with 12 years of experience in both corporate and startup environments. Jeremy has worked for MCI, Ernst & Young LLP, Micrografx and Interstate Batteries, developing web, handheld and desktop applications. He is one of the two maintainers of Greasemonkey, an innovative Firefox extension for web personalization, and he is a contributor to Django, the software framework underlying *Pegasus News.* Jeremy has lived in Dallas for 16 years and has an avid interest in journalism and access to knowledge.

Strategic advisors and investors:

{ *Investors hate risk, so this section reassures them that smart people with more domain expertise than they have are involved. This list only represents about half of our group, omitting some really key engaged people, but highlights the ones who had industry cred in our space.* }

Christopher Bancroft

As a director and major shareholder of Dow Jones Inc., Chris has been involved with *The Wall Street Journal*'s pioneering online media business since its inception. He is President of Bancroft Operations, a private investment firm, and is a partner in the Beta Capital Group, LLC, a Dallas, Texas, investment partnership. Chris currently serves on the boards of Ignite Technologies Inc. and Vistas Unlimited, Inc. He previously served on the boards of Jobs.com, EInstruction, Inc., North Texas Public Broadcasting, Inc. and the Dallas Museum of Art.

Christopher Harte

Chris is a director of Harte-Hanks, Inc. He is a private investor and served as President of the *Portland Press Herald* and *Maine Sunday Telegram.* Prior to becoming President of these newspapers, Chris spent nine years with Knight-Ridder Newspapers, during which time he served as President and Publisher of two newspapers. He also serves as a director of Geokinetics, Inc., a provider of services to U.S. oil and gas businesses, and Crown Resources, Inc., a minerals mining company.

Jeremy Halbreich

Jeremy is Chairman of the Board, President and Chief Executive Officer of American Consolidated Media, which owns and operates 34 community newspapers in Texas and Oklahoma. Previously, Jeremy worked at *The Dallas Morning News* for 24 years where he served as President and General Manager his last ten years. He serves on the board of Newsstand, Inc. and is President of the Texas Daily Newspaper Association.

Wick Allison

Wick is the founder, publisher, editor and owner of *D Magazine,* one of the country's most successful city and regional magazines. He also owns and operates several other local business and lifestyle magazines, including People Newspapers in the Dallas area. Wick is the former publisher of *The National Review* and *Sport,* and founded *Art and Antiques.*

Kerry North

Kerry, a senior investment banker with extensive financial and legal experience, is a managing director with Bluffview Capital. Previously, he served as the head of Dresdner Kleinwort Wasserstein's Dallas office. He is a former partner at Baker Botts LLP. Kerry started his professional career as a reporter at the Corpus-Christi Caller-Times, where he was Texas Reporter of the Year in 1975.

FINANCIAL SUMMARY

> *For any startup, this section always makes me hearken to the Scott Miller song, "The Lie I Believe." The numbers are, almost without exception, overoptimistic, and driven by what the investor wants to see. We found that VCs wanted really aggressive numbers; media companies more conservative numbers.*

Financial Information:

The following is projected financial information for *Pegasus News* in the Dallas market only, with launch taking place at the end of 2006:

DFW Financials ($M)	2007	2008	2009	2010	2011
Revenue	$0.6	$4.4	$11.0	$19.1	$26.3
Operating Expenses	$1.8	$4.0	$6.8	$9.7	$12.3
Operating Income	-$1.2	$0.6	$4.2	$9.4	$14.0
Operating Margin		13%	38%	49%	53%
Cumulative Operating Income*	-$1.7	-$1.1	$3.1	$12.5	$26.4
Net Income (35% tax rate)	-$1.2	$0.6	$3.2	$6.1	$9.1
Cumulative Net Income*	-$1.7	-$1.1	$2.1	$8.2	$17.3

* Cumulative Operating Income and Cumulative Net Income include $0.5M of expenses incurred prior to launch.

> *Suffice to say that while we did well, these were not the numbers achieved, in either expense or revenue. We never, in any year, spent near the operating expense indicated for 2007. Nor did we ever get to the 2008 revenue number.*

The company's complete financial model is available to prospective investors upon request.

> *This was the mother of all spreadsheets, spanning a dozen tabs and with hundreds of assumptions and calculations. This is something that anyone who got serious picked at with a fine-toothed comb. Even the smallest error would yield really tough questions and expressions of doubt.*

Preliminary Rollout Schedule:

The following table shows a preliminary timetable to enter an additional 13 metropolitan markets:

YEAR OF ANTICIPATED MARKET ENTRY				
2006	2007	2008	2009	2010
Dallas	Austin	San Diego	Las Vegas	Portland
		Atlanta	Raleigh-Durham	Washington, DC
		Charlotte	Nashville	Minneapolis/St. Paul
		Houston	Indianapolis	Denver

CURRENT STATUS

Traffic:

Pegasus News launched in December 2006. In February 2007, the site had more than 212,000 unique visitors, reflecting a growth of approximately 18% over the prior month. The following compares *Pegasus News'* February 2007 recorded traffic to other DFW-area news and entertainment sites based on data obtained from Quantcast:

> *There can be plenty of debate about the validity of outside traffic measurements and estimates. At the time (and still now), we felt Quantcast provided the best information available for local sites. Still, this always came with a verbal disclaimer that we couldn't know precise traffic stats for another site.*

SITE	MONTHLY VISITORS
DallasNews.com	652,000
DFW.com	402,000
Dallas Craigslist	387,000
PegasusNews.com	**212,000**
Dallas.citysearch.com	210,000
GuideLive.com	102,000
DallasObserver.com	73,000
Quickdfw.com	11,000
DallasBlog.com	8,500

The following table compares *Pegasus News'* February 2007 recorded traffic to the most well-known hyperlocal and citizen journalist websites in the country:

SITE	MONTHLY VISITORS
PegasusNews.com	**212,000**
YourHub.com[1]	109,000
NewWest.net	37,000
Backfence.com[2]	8,400
Outside.in[3]	2,181

Financial status:

> *This shows what we'd raised and what we were looking to raise. We wound up selling the company instead of completing another raise.*

The company received $135,000 of convertible debt financing in June 2005. In March 2006, the company completed a second seed round of $155,000 in convertible debt financing upon the same terms as the June 2005 financing. These convertible notes currently have junior status.

---

1. Includes traffic from more than 50 sites.
2. Includes traffic from three metro areas.
3. Includes nationwide traffic.

In September and November 2006, the company raised a total of $400,000 of senior secured convertible debt financing at a pre-money valuation of $750,000. An additional $100,000 was raised under the same terms in February of 2007 at a pre-money valuation of $1,150,000.

An additional $2 million in capital would allow the company to reach quarterly positive cash flow in Dallas. Management estimates that it will require approximately $1–1.5 million in capital to launch and become cashflow-positive in each additional metropolitan market.

Advertisers To Date:

As of February 28, 2007, *Pegasus News* had the following advertisers:

- White Rock Coffee
- Nokia Theater DFW
- Spune Productions
- Rock Steady
- The Hungry Musician
- Americana Roots
- Travis Hopper
- Absinthe Lounge
- Deep Ellum Arts Festival
- The Jones Thing
- Club Dada
- Carmichael Arts
- Lone Star Music
- Glamour Shots
- Wildflower Arts & Music Festival
- The Green Elephant
- KHYI 95.3
- Bandsite Live
- Good Records
- Eisemann Center for Performing Arts
- Pearl Nightclub
- Cindy's Deli
- Lakewood Bar and Grill
- Stampede Beer
- House of Dang
- Dolly Python
- Twisted Root Burgers
- Godard Gallery
- Savor Dallas
- Chef's Gallery
- Marco's Pizza
- Scott Carlson Real Estate
- The Double Wide
- City Tavern
- Exposition Cafe
- Tacoda

Honors To Date:

The following awards were won by *Pegasus News'* beta predecessor site, TexasGigs.com, which was focused on local music and currently exists as the *Pegasus News* music section:

- *Editor and Publisher:* 2006 EPpy award for Best Entertainment Website with fewer than 1 million unique visitors. Other competition winners included Movies.com, *New York Times, Washington Post* and CBS News.

- *Dallas Observer:* Best Music Website 2006; Readers Choice Best Music Website 2006

PEGASUS NEWS IS ALREADY ATTRACTING ATTENTION

Like the investor page, the point here is to reassure that industry people believe in what we were doing. We also used these in a slideshow while people gathered for investor presentations.

"A new local news company called *Pegasus News* is aiming to reinvent local market content and advertising . . . Their model has tremendous potential . . . it's worth watching."

–CyberJournalist.net

"I'm intrigued, to say the least. *Pegasus News* is looking to do *the* local newspaper a one-up, but with a pay-for-play model that, at least based on their hopes, will be fair to everyone involved, from the readers to the advertisers."

–TheMediaDrop.com

I think what Pegasus is doing really is different from some of the other hyperlocals. Their reluctance to rely on users (i.e. unpaid and possibly partisan) is smart, as they make good use of all the resources that the Net has made available.

–Frank Banarko, Dow Jones Marketwatch

"I'm willing to call it the best of the local news site so far, where a lot is done right. You could do a lot worse than modeling a local news site after *Pegasus,* both as a new voice and as competition for existing media. It's that good."

–Mark Hamilton, Notes from a Journalism Teacher

"Extensive and ambitious."

—Online News Squared

"One of my favorites."

—Terry Heaton, AR&D

"*Pegasus News* personalization exists within a controlled environment that makes monetizing and 'behaviorally targeting' the content somewhat easier than in RSS . . . That's smart."

—Greg Sterling, Screenwerk

"If I were running a traditional news outlet I would be looking very closely at . . . *Pegasus News* and other innovators."

—Robert Cox (President, Media Bloggers Association)
Project for Excellence in Journalism Roundtable

"I do think we can watch an important part of the new media develop courtesy of the *Pegasus News* blog. . . . If you have a professional or merely speculative interest in where the journalism profession is headed, you need to bookmark this blog . . . Are you intrigued yet? If you aren't, better check your heartbeat because this is like getting an email from your as-yet-unborn child. This one definitely bears watching."

—Mark Tapscott (Director of The Heritage Foundation's
Center for Media and Public Policy)

". . . The newspaper website of the future hasn't been produced by a major newspaper company but by an upstart Dallas start-up called *Pegasus News.*

"Pegasus News performs the traditional commercial function of a newspaper in a non-traditional way. Instead of being a one-to-many medium, *Pegasus News* creates dozens of virtual communities that make it possible for advertisers to target their messages to users based on their preferences and behaviors. And that, folks, is the future of the media business."

—Alan Mutter, Reflections of a Newsosaur

APPENDIX B

> ## Resources for Journalism Entrepreneurs

▶ Books

You could fill a library with the books that an entrepreneur would be wise to read. Here's one man's view of the best of the best, the books that helped to shape the lessons in this book.

Anderson, Chris. *The Long Tail: Why the Future of Business Is Selling Less of More.* New York: Hyperion 2006.

Berkun, Scott. *The Myths of Innovation.* Cambridge, MA: O'Reilly Media, 2007.

Blank, Steven. *The Four Steps to the Epiphany: Successful Strategies for Products That Win.* Cafepress.com, 2010.

Burlingame, Bo. *Small Giants: Companies That Choose to Be Great Instead of Big.* New York: Portfolio Hardcover, 2005.

Doctor, Ken. *Newsonomics: Twelve New Trends That Will Shape the News You Get.* St. Martin's Press, 2010.

Gerber, Michael. *The E-Myth Revisited: Why Most Small Businesses Don't Work and What to Do About It.*

Godin, Seth. *The Dip: A Little Book That Teaches You When to Quit (and When to Stick).* New York: Portfolio Hardcover. 2007.

Heath, Chip, and Dan Heath. *Made to Stick: Why Some Ideas Survive and Others Die.* New York: Random House, 2007.

Kawasaki, Guy. Art of the Start: *The Time-Tested, Battle-Hardened Guide for Anyone Starting Anything.* New York: Porfolio Hardcover, 2004.

Kramer, Larry. *The C-Scape: Conquer the Forces Changing Business Today.* New York: Harper Business, 2010.

Moore, Geoffrey A. *Crossing the Chasm: Marketing and Selling High-Tech Products to Mainstream Customers.* New York: Harper Business, 1999.

Mullins, John and Randy Komisar. *Getting to Plan B: Breaking Through to a Better Business Model.* Cambridge MA: Harvard Business Press, 2009.

Livingston, Jessica. *Founders at Work: Stories of Startups' Early Days.* New York: Apress, 2007.

Locke, Chris, Doc Searls, David Weinberger, and Rick Levine. *The Cluetrain Manifesto.* http://www.cluetrain.com/ (1999).

Tapscott, Don, and Anthony Williams. *Wikinomics: How Mass Collaboration Changes Everything.* New York: Portfolio Hardcover, 2006.

Ulwick, Anthony *What Customers Want: Using Outcome-Driven Innovation to Create Breakthrough Products and Services.* New York: McGraw Hill, 2005.

Vaynerchuk, Gary. *Crush It!: Why NOW Is the Time to Cash In on Your Passion.* New York: Harper Studio, 2009.

▶ Online

There is no limit to the amount of online information available for entrepreneurs. Here's a short list of some of the best resources, blogs and ongoing coverage of new media to help you quickly build a solid foundation of knowledge and also keep tabs on the latest developments in the rapidly changing landscape of the digital media business.

▶ ▶ *Resources*

Inc. magazine tools for entrepreneurs ▶ www.inc.com/tools

Answers for startups ▶ answers.onstartups.com

Y Combinator Library ▶ ycombinator.com/lib.html

Mixergy: Where Ambitious Startups Mix ▶ mixergy.com/homepage

Entrepreneur magazine's Starting a Business ▶ www.entrepreneur.com/bizstartups

Open Forum: Powering Small Business Success ▶ www.openforum.com

Understand Accounting ▶ www.understand-accounting.net

▶ ▶ *Blogs by and for entrepreneurs*

Paul Graham ▶ www.paulgraham.com

Fred Wilson ▶ www.avc.com

Steve Blank ▶ www.steveblank.com

Mark Suster ▶ www.bothsidesofthetable.com

Sean Ellis ▶ www.startup-marketing.com

Ladies Who Launch ▶ www.ladieswholaunch.com

Brad Feld ▶ www.feld.com/wp

▶ ▶ *New media startup information*

Encyclopedia of the Future of News ▶ www.niemanlab.org/encyclo

Community Information Needs ▶ www.informationneeds.org

News Frontier Database ▶ www.cjr.org/the_news_frontier_database

Knight Community News Network ▶ www.kcnn.org

▶ ▶ *Ongoing coverage of digital media innovation*

Nieman Journalism Lab: Pushing to the Future of Journalism ▶ www. niemanlab.org

paidContent: The Economics of Digital Content ▶ paidcontent.org/

MediaGazer ▶ www.mediagazer.com

J-Lab: Igniting Ideas That Work ▶ www.j-lab.org/ideas

Poynter Online ▶ www.poynter.com

Knight Digital Media Center news blog ▶ http://www.knightdigital mediacenter.org/news_blog

Mediashift: Your Guide to the Digital Media Revolution ▶ www.pbs.org/ mediashift/

10,000 Words: Where Journalism and Technology Meet ▶ www.mediabistro. com/10000words

Mashable Media ▶ mashable.com/media

Journalism.co.uk ▶ www.journalism.co.uk

APPENDIX C

Glossary

Basic business vocabulary: The business world is fraught with buzzwords, acronyms and lingo that can make outsiders and newcomers feel as though they don't belong. Corporatespeak is no better, with euphemisms like "synergy" and "rightsizing" and "going forward." Much of that babble you can ignore, but some important terms with actual meaning can help you master the basics of business and communicate with other entrepreneurs, partners, investors and customers. Here is a short list of some of the most useful business terms to know:

Accrual-based accounting: A system of accounting that recognizes revenue when earned and expenses when incurred—not when received. This system is distinguished from the cash basis of accounting.

Angel investor: Someone who invests his or her own money in businesses. Investment levels are traditionally much smaller than those for venture capital investment.

Assets: Everything that a company owns, including hardware, software, licenses, patents, buildings, etc.

Barriers to entry: The factors that will prevent another company from duplicating the efforts of an existing company and stealing some or all of its business.

Beta: A work in progress and being developed, and not the final version. The beta product is undergoing testing and refinement.

Bootstrapping: Starting a company without investment and operating a company (and life) on the cheap, because there isn't any extra cash to go around.

Bottom line: Net profits, which are what's left over after all expenses are deducted from income.

Break-even point: The moment that a company can cover its expenses with revenues.

Business to Business (B2B): A business that sells goods or services to other businesses.

Business to Consumer (B2C): A business that sells goods or services to consumers.

Capital: Money invested in a business.

Cash basis for accounting: A system of accounting that recognizes revenue only when cash is actually received from customers or clients and expenses only when cash is paid to vendors. This system is distinguished from the accrual system.

Cash flow: Calculated by adding noncash charges (such as depreciation) to net income after taxes.

Corporation: An incorporated business and a separate legal entity from its owners.

Deal flow: The amount of proposals that potential funders (venture capitalists or angel investors) sift through.

Debt: Borrowed money that you or the business owes to a third party.

Deliverables: The actual work product that is expected to be completed.

Depreciation: The decrease in value of an asset over time.

Due Diligence: The investigation and vetting process used by investors to gather information on a prospective company before making an investment, or by an individual before signing a contract.

EBITDA: Earnings before Interest, Taxes, Depreciation and Amortization, which is a good metric to evaluate profitability but not cash flow.

Elevator pitch: A brief statement of a startup idea that is ideally no longer than about 30 seconds.

Equity: The difference between a firm's assets and its liabilities.

Exit: The end game, usually a sale of a company to another owner.

Fixed Cost: An expense that doesn't vary from month to month; for example, rent.

Generally Accepted Accounting Principles (GAAP): The most widely accepted rules of financial accounting.

Gross Profit: The difference between sales and cost of goods sold.

Income Statement: A basic financial statement that reflects revenue and expenses and attempts to measure economic performance in the most recent accounting period.

Iteration: Versions of an idea, product or company.

Liabilities: What a business owes to someone else, including the state and federal government, other businesses, or individuals.

Line of credit: An open source of funds up to a stated maximum that you can borrow as needed and pay back when possible with certain conditions.

Loss: Excess of expenses over revenues.

Market research: Finding out how big the market is for a potential business—how many potential customers there are, how much they spend, and what the competition is.

Milestones: Goals with time deadlines attached to gauge overall progress with specificity.

Monetize: Make money from something.

Operating costs: What it costs to run a business on a day-to-day basis.

Pivot: When a company, especially a startup, changes direction with its plan or strategy and pursues a new opportunity.

Product-market fit: Sometimes a great product doesn't work because it's not being sold to the right customers (market). For a business to succeed, this must reflect the right match.

Pro forma: A projected estimate, as in a pro forma income statement.

Profit: Excess of revenues minus expenses.

Profit Margin: The ratio of profit divided by revenue, displayed as a percentage.

Return on investment (ROI): A commonly used term that can refer to investment in money or time. If doing a particular task takes too much time to produce results, it doesn't have a good ROI.

Revenue. Cash received from customers or clients in exchange for goods and services provided.

Scale/scalability: The ability for a business to grow or replicate an isolated success (or product-market fit) in a way that will make money while expanding operations.

SCORE: Service Corps of Retired Executives; providers of free counseling advice for small businesses. See www.score.org.

Seed money: The cash you need to get started with your idea.

Skin in the game: Investment in an idea or company, usually by that company's founder. If a founder isn't willing to invest his or her own money, other investors may be leery.

Sole Proprietorship: A company with one owner.

Target market: The specific group of customers toward whom a company is aiming its products and services.

Traction: Opposed to simply "spinning your wheels," your business has traction when it has a growing number of users and customers.

User experience (UX): The experience a user has with your product, especially a digital service. There are specialists who study this type of experience to develop the most seamless, easy process for users to navigate a service and/or complete a transaction.

Value proposition: An assessment of the unique value that a company offers to users or customers and why anyone would visit a website or buy a product.

Variable Cost: Expenses that change in proportion to the activity of a business. For example, if a business has a commission-based advertising sales representative who has a great month, the business will owe that representative more money than the previous month.

Venture capital: Funding for companies that is managed by professionals who invest other people's money. Traditionally this type of investment is focused on large opportunities that will return millions to the venture capital firm if the startup is successful.

Index